*Best Business Practices
for
Global Competitiveness*

Best Business Practices for Global Competitiveness

Prof (Dr) Prashant Salwan

STERLING PUBLISHERS PRIVATE LIMITED

STERLING PUBLISHERS PRIVATE LIMITED
A-59, Okhla Industrial Area, Phase-II, New Delhi-110020.
Tel: 26387070, 26386209 Fax: 91-11-26383788
e-mail: sterlingpublishers@airtelbroadband.in
www.sterlingpublishers.com

Best Business Practices for Global Competitiveness

© 2007, *Prof (Dr) Prashant Salwan*

ISBN   978 81 207 3255 1   HB
        978 81 207 3464 7   PB

All rights are reserved. No part of this publication may be reproduced, stored in a retrieval system or transmitted, in any form or by any means, mechanical, photocopying, recording or otherwise, without prior written permission of the original publisher.

PRINTED IN INDIA

Printed and Published by Sterling Publishers Pvt. Ltd., New Delhi-110 020.

Contents

Acknowledgements — vi
Preface — vii

1. **Best Practice in Business** — 1
   Prashan Salwan

Section A
Information and Communication Technologie

2. **E-commerce – An Introduction to the Concept** — 19
   Sandhir Sharma and Gulshan Bansal
3. **Playing Leapfrog: Using Strengths in ICT to Energise the Manufacturing Sector in India** — 46
   Komolica Peres
4. **Achieving Best Practice in Business and Closing the Marketing Gap** — 62
   Prashan Salwan

Section B
Strategic Tools for Enhancing Performance

5. **A Strategic Tool for Enhancing Performance The Balanced Scorecard** — 97
   V.K. Gupta
6. **Government to Citizen Relationships Gyandoot— Tales and Travails—A Three-Year E-Governance Experience** — 119
   Sanjay Dubey
7. **Enterprise Resource Planning** — 135
   Anand Kr Tiwari

Section C
Outsourcing

8. **Outsourcing** — 167
   S.Venkat
9. **Operational Issues in Outsourcing** — 210
   S.Venkat

Annexures — 263

I Using the Technology (Theory) — 263
II E-Marketing Options—their Pros and Cons and Checklist for Implementation of an E-marketing Plan in Business

Glossary — 276
Index — 282
About the Contributors — 286

Acknowledgements

I would like to thank the following people for their assistance with my project: Dr Howard Machin, Academic Assessor, whose invaluable feedback and advice to 'focus' helped me to keep the text 'straight and narrow'; Dr Christine Challis, Director of the Gurukul Programme at LSE, whose suggestions and interest in the scholars helped us to formulate our own ideas in a coherent fashion; and Dr Arnauld Miguet, for his keen interest and guidance.

I would like to thank Brian Morgan, Department for Trade and Industry, Nicola Hughes, Project Co-Coordinator Winning Moves Ltd, Maria Stone, Project Manager Winning Moves Ltd, and Ms Margaret Ferre, Her Majesty's Stationery and Copyright Office.

I am extremely grateful to Lord Swaraj Paul and Baroness Thatcher of Kesteven Mrs Margaret Thatcher for their invaluable guidance.

I cannot forget the invaluable inputs given by professors at LSE and chief executives of various organisations, those who were very kind enough to share their experiences and guide me.

I would also like to thank my colleagues specially Prof Ms Komolika Peres, Prof. V.K. Gupta, Prof. S. Venkat Sandhir Sharma, Gautam Bansal and Dr Anand Kr Tiwari for their contributions.

Any views or opinions expressed in this study are of individual authors and do not necessarily reflect the views of the organisation they are associated with.

Dr Prashant Salwan

Preface

The pace of India's future progress will depend to a large extent on its ability to make available the latest and most useful knowledge to vast sections of the population and implement the latest ICT (Information Communication Technology) successfully in best management practices. Knowledge in the form of manufacturing technology will raise the competitiveness of the Indian manufactures to international standards of costs and quality.

Modern manufacturing industries depend as much for their success on the management of information relating to quality, cost and scheduling, as they do on the management of materials and production processes.

India is developing. Best practice can help business improve its performance. Many businesses are finding that they can make dramatic savings by changing the way they work with partners and suppliers. The key issues involved include: sharing information, joint planning and collaborative working. To improve the performance level of the business organisation one should focuss on: *(a)* getting the best from the employees and making them the most valuable asset. Many businesses are talking to their people and finding ways for them to contribute more at work. Most important here is to find and keep the right people. *(b)* Reviewing the internal processes which can deliver significant increases in efficiency and productivity. The key issues are measuring productivity and introducing new ways of working. *(c)* Realising the importance of the potential of technology to cut costs and increase sales and productivity. However, finding the right solution for your needs isn't always easy. The current big issues are: getting broadband, selling procedures over the Internet and guarding against viruses and hacking.

A business must identify its key competencies and utilise them to the full if it is to build a competitive advantage. Businesses that invest in the development of a marketing strategy and the development of their products and services are likely to grow more rapidly.

Successful businesses with an eye to growth and ongoing profitability view the development of new products and services as a business process that is absolutely critical. They use systematic approaches to identify promising ideas, allocate resources, monitor progress and conduct disciplined reviews at key stages.

This research is more important for India because, India's shift from material to knowledge-based resources opens up vast opportunities for the developing countries to accelerate the pace of development. India's rate of economic growth can be substantially increased if the country becomes a superpower in knowledge and if the potentials of information and information technology are fully understood and exploited. So far, the potentials have been narrowly focused on the export potentials of the IT sector. But far greater potential lies in the extension and application of IT to stimulate the development of other sectors of the domestic economy. Information is a revolutionary force in bridging the digital divide that currently separates the advantaged and the disadvantaged of our nation. Apart from generating new employment opportunities, the application of IT can vastly extend access to education, health care, markets, financial services, vocational skills, administrative services and other aspects of modern society, to many more people at far lower cost. It can dramatically reduce the cost of communications, improve access to technology and marketing capabilities for the rural poor, eliminate intermediary exploitation in the production and distribution chains, increase government accountability and stimulate democratic participation.

Hypothesis

a) Companies to be successful should incorporate best businesses practices like, vision and leadership, values and society, involving and developing staff, innovation and growth, learning from customers and improving quality.

b) Companies to be successful have to embrace the information and communication technologies which will help the companies in knowing their customers well, reaching out to them, as well as maximising their own potentials (production, logistics, marketing, etc.) and reducing the cost.

c) For closing the market gap, industries have to find the areas of improvement in their system. Benchmarking is a systematic approach to the recognition of good and best practice. It involves identification of goals, objectives and targets, the measurement of performance and the analysis of process—the understanding of how things are done. It is the comparison of similar or related processes between departments, functions, groups or organisations. It highlights areas of relative strength and helps managers focus their attention on those aspects of the business where they lag behind.

d) Outsourcing is a must for capitalising of demands and fighting competition.

Methodology

The economy of the UK experienced a turnaround after the Second World War. Initially, UK had been lagging behind Germany and France. She experienced market crash and low industrialisation. In the eighties due to Mrs M Thatcher's policies, UK's industries totally turned around which helped her economy to grow by leaps and bounds and soon overtake France and Germany in industrialisation. The major things, which were implemented, were best business policies and use of technologies for business and good government policies.

The sectoral composition of the GDP changes with economic development. The predominance of agriculture in the least developed economies is reduced by the increasing importance of manufacturing, and subsequently, services, as they move up the ladder of development. As this occurs, the rates of economic growth tends to increase. This transition is now occurring globally and is reflected in the explosive growth of the service sectors, especially in the fields of financial services, ICT, insurance, education and health.

India's service sectors has already become the dominant contributor to GDP, accounting for 46 per cent of the total, but its share is still far. Our notion of services may need to evolve further to recognise the importance of the emerging knowledge-intensive services. The use of ICT in Indian companies will change this.

In my project I will show what approaches have worked well for businesses in UK regarding implementation of ICT. How can Indian companies become more efficient, competitive and profitable irrespective of what the size of business is. In my project I will try to bring those best practice examples together to provide readers with a toolkit of practical advice.

I have studied many invaluable guides, case studies, factsheets and a range of self-assessment tools. I have in the book sought to draw inferences and incorporate suggestions based on—

(a) my interaction with various professors at the LSE, bureaucrats and business executives, officers at the Department of Trade and Industry and Winning moves —Benchmarking index group;

(b) from my reading on the subject; and

(c) contribution by industrial experts.

The aim has been to frame a hypothesis advocating no matter what the size or industry sector a company belongs to, successful companies have certain management characteristics in common and best practices in management and make business successful both domestically and internationally.

1
Best Practices in Business*

Prashant Salwan

In the past five years India has improved tremendously in attracting Foreign Direct Investment and emerging as a global player. *Financial Times* ('Investment Destinations', 14 October 2004) has ranked India as the third most attractive FDI destinations in 2004 below US and China. India jumped three steps from sixth position in 2003 to third in 2004. India as per a report (written by David Smith and cited in *Economic Outlook,* 12 October 2003) will overtake British economy in 2022 and Japan in 2031. As per Dan Fineman, Indian companies had higher returns on equity in 2003 than firms in China. China has grown very fast and Indian development model might never reproduce the multi year, double-digit GDP expansion that the Tiger countries and China registered in their peak years. Hypercharged investment fuelled by underpriced capital propelled those growth spurts. India's expansion can be limited by lower investment and saving rates. But India's model should prove more sustainable than the typical Asian strategy adopted by China. India is developing more efficient corporate, healthier banks, more robust service industries and a bigger consumer base. China has won the sprint. India is gearing for the marathon.

These figures and reports look very attractive but there is a big BUT in reaching these attractive and heavenly results. The service proportion of India's GDP has increased from 40.6 per cent in 1990 to 50.8 per cent in 2003, accounting for 62 per cent of the cumulative increase in the country's GDP; but the industry share of India's GDP has been essentially stagnant at 27.2 per cent of GDP. As a result, industrial activity has accounted for only 27 per cent of the cumulative increase in India's GDP for the last 13 years. India has to now concentrate on new practises and implementation of cost saving measures, maximising potential practises in the manufacturing sector (production, marketing, etc.) for more balanced growth. Even the growth achieved in the service sector cannot be sustained until or unless some fundamental changes in the business practises of the companies (service and manufacturing) are made.

I spoke to a number of people in different sectors of British businesses with the help of the department of trade and industry (DTI) and asked

---
* www.nmsu.edu/~iirm/articles/comenvir.html

them to identify which management practices make a company successful.

I found that many of the ideas are not new. They are all approaches to break down barriers in the way a business works, in order to allow it to move towards sustainable change. All the businesses involved agreed that their ideas were not complete solutions, they were the starting points for farther journeys.

Vision and Leadership

CASE STUDY — Box 1.1

The Aroma Company

Sector	: product demonstration technology
Location	: Oxfordshire
Website	: www.aromaco.co.uk

The Aroma Company showed that transforming a good idea into a winning product takes patience, a strong vision and excellent leadership. When Simon Harrop had an idea for a new product demonstrator, he was determined to see it through to profitability. His brainwave was that it is smell, rather than performance, that is the key factor for people buying products like washing powders, shampoos and deodorants. He saw that retailers would welcome a device that could reproduce the exact smell of a product and so reduce wastage of the product by customers tampering with the packaging. He produced the Aroma Box, which, though extremely effective, was deemed far too large for use in supermarkets and was not very user-friendly. Simon was faced with a choice to invest more time and money in getting the product to work or abandon the idea.

Convinced that he was on to something, Simon contacted his regional branch of Business Link to get advice on driving his vision forward. Business Link put him in touch with a product designer to help the company re-engineer the Aroma Box.

Taking a gamble, the Aroma Company, which at the time employed just three people, invested £50,000 in design, tooling and intellectual property rights protection. At the time this was about a third of the business' turnover.

In place of the unwieldy metal box came a mini bellows, small enough to clip on to a supermarket shelf. When the customer pressed it, a small whiff of fragrance was released. It could keep going for about eight weeks—the average length of in-store promotions.

The tiny, ingenious device caught on immediately. Initially used to promote air fresheners, it has since been applied to a wide range of products, filling the aisles of all the major UK supermarkets with the whiff of perfumes, shampoos, deodorants and even coffee.

The companies' turnover doubled in each of the next two years, staff numbers increased, and the company now has customers all over the world.

Source: DTI

Simon has some advice for small businesses who have a big idea but are running into difficulties: keep believing in it. If it's a good idea, the chances are that it's worth the extra investment of external design. But if you don't have spare cash to throw around, you will need a steady nerve.

- It improves staff morale. Employees like to feel good about the business they work for. If they do, they can become enormously powerful advocates for it.
- It matters to customers. A survey by MORI showed that three-quarters of the British population say that more information on the companies' social and ethical behaviour would influence their buying habits.

Social Responsibility

CASE STUDY — Box 1.2

BT

Sector : telecommunications
Size of firm : 105,000 employees

BT takes Corporate Social Responsibility (CSR) seriously, and its findings support the business case as well as the social benefits. Keen to show itself as a good corporate citizen, BT was an early adopter of CSR. It saw that it could give something back to the community and, at the same time, help dispel its image as a large, monolithic corporation.

One of its largest investments has been £8.5 million, committed to the BT Education Programme. The scheme, which is free and supports the national curriculum, will involve more than two million school children in drama presentations and communication skills workshops to bring the themes of good communication and citizenship to life. The programme's educational road shows have already visited 5,500 of UK's 28,000 schools touring 20 schools a day during term time. In addition, BT is backing a volunteer programme, running awards for teachers, and providing schools with educational support materials including videos, a CD-Rom, and a website.

BT sees a number of benefits from this social investment programme, which fits with its wider business objectives. The local BT element is especially important for regional public relations. The school visit have proved to be an excellent way to establish the company as a responsible member of the community in which it works.

Pinning down the commercial benefits of a social investment programme is always difficult. To help tackle this problem, BT has pioneered research into the impact of such factors on customer satisfaction levels, which are critical to its success as a business. The work concluded that BT's overall image and reputation is a major

> determinant of customer satisfaction and is considerably more important than other factors, such as how customers feel about the billing process or the cost of calls and rental charges relative to those of its competitors. As such, the CSR activities have proved to be an excellent investment as well as a valuable gift to schools.
>
> Judy Kuszewski and Kavita Prakash-Mani of Sustainability, the corporate responsibility and sustainable development business consultancy say: 'Companies that aim to take a CSR leadership position such as BT have a vital role in sharing good practice, tools and knowledge.'
>
> Source: DTI

Involving and Developing Staff

There are four aspects to involving and developing staff: motivation, development, communication and organisational change.

Motivation

Managers in the most successful companies told us that getting the best out of their staff is a priority. As one MD puts it, 'Motivated staff will be ten times more productive than unmotivated staff.' Another said, 'When a customer meets an employee he meets the whole organisation and often judges the whole on that basis.'

This highlights the two aims that form part of best practices in people management:
- making each employee feel that they are valued and have a degree of autonomy; and
- helping employees to identify themselves with customers.

Development

The best companies are passionate about developing their staff and unlocking their potentials. Some reported that as much as 10 per cent of employee's time was spent on it and others described it as the epicentre of empowerment and a competitive weapon.

The companies that put most emphasis on training and development are also the most rigorous about it. The best practice is to make sure that development is properly targeted, has a defined set of objectives, is measurable and is put in the context of improving the service that customers receive.

The companies also reported that the best results emerge when employees understand the value that training can have for them professionally. This doesn't mean, however, that training is only about formal training courses. The best organisations find a balance of formal and on-the-job training which is essential to raise skill levels.

Communication

Along with giving people the tools to do their jobs better, improved communications are a powerful way of helping employees feel valued at work. Successful businesses use a mix of routes, team briefings, newsletters, etc., and encourage feedback. The thinking is that the more you encourage communication, the more you can break down the 'them and us' culture.

Organisational Changes

In some businesses there are as few as three levels within the organisation: directors, managers and people. This isn't the result of cost cutting or stripping out middle management, but a deliberate effort to focus everyone in the business on what customers need, rather than on the demands of the bureaucracy.

As a result, the whole structure of many businesses has changed. For example, seniority and its rewards no longer comes with the length of service but as a result of experience and knowledge.

These organisational trends are opposite, which highlights the different factors that are transforming businesses.

Successful companies unlock the potentials of their people.

CASE STUDY — **Box 1.3**

Innovation and Growth

Fracino

Sector : manufacturing
Location : Birmingham
Website : www.fracino.co.uk

By getting designers, engineers and marketers working together, Fracino has been able to establish itself in a very competitive market.

When, in the 1990s, coffee drinking in many European and North American cities advanced from being an unremarkable everyday habit to the epitome of style, the Fracino team set out to produce a range of coffee machines. They aimed to supply the host of small businesses, which were suddenly competing with multinational chains.

Being a relatively small company, Fracino had no immediate hope of usurping the large volume of industrial roasting companies at one end of the scale or the low-end domestic mass producers at the other. So it targeted the gap between the two.

Company founder Frank Maxwell and his close-knit company developed a new method of fresh-roasting the beans in a glass chamber, which was visually appealing and produced a great aroma. Frank saw that the Roastilino machine could become a dramatic centrepiece for cafes that emphasised the experience as much as the drink.

To break into a competitive market, the company realised it needed a perfect blend of form and function. Maxwell decided that he wanted to create project teams of designers, engineers and marketers who could work together at all stages of the process to assure the

> quality of the final project. Now, a three or four-membered strong team sees each project from the original concept, through prototyping and testing, to component supply and assembly. This creates real dedication and focus and means that modifications can be made quickly and seamlessly.
>
> The company also involves a group of customers in the prototyping phase to make sure that the final product meets their needs.
>
> The result has been a range of products that have proved a great success at home and abroad. Fracino machines are being installed nationwide in one of the major UK coffee shops and the company has a comprehensive export programme to 12 countries. In addition, the Roastilino machine went on to win a Design Council Millennium Product Award and gave Fracino a reputation within the trade for innovation as well as quality.
>
> Angela Maxwell, daughter of Frank and an employee of Fracino, admits that the company struggled at first with exports. 'Exporting is seriously hard work. You will have to put up with many disappointments,' she says. However, the Millennium Product Award in 2000 proved a milestone. 'After receiving the award,' she observed, 'doors began to open.'
>
> The ways of working that Fracino adopted were not just geared for short-term success: they were intended to keep the company ahead of the game by generating a stream of exciting products. As Angela says, 'To stay competitive, the company has had to adopt a policy of continuous improvement.'
>
> Source: DTI

Successful businesses promote new ideas and new ways of working.

Innovation is no longer regarded as something intangible. The best businesses are measuring and targeting product innovation as they would for any other business process. One manufacturer, for example, has a goal of generating 80 per cent of its sales from products that are less than five years old.

Increasingly businesses are also interpreting innovation much more widely. It used to be narrowly associated with R&D, but now it is taken as a measure of the ability of all aspects of a company to improve the way they work. New ideas are encouraged and sought in every area—from production and administration through to customer service and after sales support.

As companies rationalise their own operations, they are also looking to their suppliers for further improvements. Many of the examples of best practice that we have seen have involved using new technologies to share information with suppliers to improve forecasting, cut stock holdings and cut administrative costs.

The other major trend we have seen has been a degree of caution about rapid expansion and new ventures. Having taken time to understand their customers and their markets, many businesses are instead opting for organic growth and strategic partnerships.

Successful Businesses Know Their Customers

A recurring theme with best practice businesses is not that they have all the answers, but that they recognise the need to keep learning.

Customers are one obvious source of ideas for new products and services but they can also be used to benchmark other aspects of performance against your competitors. Contact with suppliers, meanwhile, can provide process ideas as well as more direct product information.

Many businesses welcome visits to their premises, because conducting tours and responding to questions generate feedback and free advice. Similarly, visits to other businesses, even those in different sectors, can be a useful stimulus for lateral thinking.

While businesses have to be self-motivated, most regard customers as the people who keep them on their toes. Successful businesses see customers' raised expectations and demands for lower prices as an opportunity to drive them on and become more competitive. Many take it for granted that they have to know their customer and their customer's marketplace better than the customer themselves.

Learning from Customers

CASE STUDY — Box 1.4

Gecko Headgear

Sector	: extreme sports equipment manufacturing
Location	: Cornwall
Website	: www.geckoheadgear.co.uk

Gecko realised it could sell its lightweight headgear to many markets, but made sure the detail on each product was just right.

Jeff Sacree turned his small, struggling, surfboard business into one of Europe's leading specialist helmet manufacturers on the basis of a casual conversation. His business was extremely seasonal so he was looking to find a way of diversifying his products. Speaking to a lifeboat man, he found that RNLI needed a lighter, rustproof helmet for use on the seas. He had been working on a similar helmet for surfers and so was well placed to supply the RNLI.

With a big win like the RNLI under his belt, the question for Sacree was where to take the business next. Some potential markets sprang to mind immediately: specialist helmets could be usefully worn by river police, coastguard and customs officers and a recent model has been designed specifically for helicopter winchmen. But, as the craze for new, extreme sports blossomed throughout the 1990s, a much wider market suddenly presented itself. Skateboarders, snowboarders, mountain bikers and powerboat racers all needed protection.

Prototype headgear was produced, tested and modified for each discipline, and users were encouraged to respond with comments and suggested improvements. Gecko soon discovered that producing low-volume, handmade products was a distinct advantage when it comes to satisfying the niche markets of extreme sports. It involved less financial risk and allowed for the continual, minor improvements that customers wanted. 'Making everything by hand gives us the crucial advantage of flexibility, so we can add altimeters and video cameras, torches and two-way radio systems pretty well, anything a customer asks for,' says manager Dean Bunker.

Today, the Gecko trademark can be found in 15 European countries, stamped on between five and six thousand helmets a year. The basic models retail at £60–£100 a time, with heavily customised versions at two or three times that price.

The RNLI helmet won a Design Council Millennium Product Award and now the orders flow in all year round, removing the companies' dependence on the summer trade. Dean Bunker recalls an early image problem: at the outset, it was not regarded as cool for daredevil sportsmen to wear helmets.

Efforts were taken by the company to make young people feel good wearing them and that involved a bit of a culture change. It was overcome by sponsoring local powerboat and surfing champions to create positive brand associations. Jeff Sacree is pleased with the progress, but he does not get complacent. 'We keep looking at designs to see if we can improve them. We never stop exploring new avenues to create the ultimate product,' he says.

Source: DTI

Improving Quality

For most businesses this is about more than price cuts. One business said its strategy was to improve: quality, delivery and then price, in that order. Another business identified service as the key differentiator in an organisation's competitiveness.

Other businesses said simply that quality, low cost, performance and delivery time are no longer sufficient in themselves: they are the basics that any firm must offer if it is to survive in the market.

All the businesses agreed that innovative, customised products and services, supported by marketing and design, are the differentiators that allow companies to succeed. This was summed up simply by one senior executive: 'if the product is right, and you deliver what your customer wants, the world is your oyster'.

CASE STUDY   Box 1.5

Boa UK

Sector	:	kitchenware
Location	:	Croydon
Website	:	www.boahousewares.com

By listening to customers' needs, Boa UK realised that there was an untapped demand for a new type of kitchen knife. Brian Alexander invented the Constrictor, a gadget for removing stiff jar lids. In five years, he sold £20 million worth of Constrictors, which were made in a knife factory that he had bought for its manufacturing capabilities. When looking at how to build the business, he realised that the company had a lot of residual knowledge about the knife business that he could use to launch a new range.

Having lived abroad, Brian knew that high-end British-made products still attracted a premium. By talking to people in the kitchenware industry, he also established that there was a demand for quality lifestyle goods at a reasonable price. 'We looked at our competitors and realised nothing new had appeared on the market for quite a while,' says Brian. 'Most knives are shoddily made, with handles that are stuck on later. The quality of finish was generally very bad.'

Hiring award-winning designer Paul Priestman, the business invested £750,000 in equipment and design to create an innovative set of products which included a range of luxuriously packaged kitchen knives and knife blocks.

Boa housewares has managed to establish itself in its target markets. Around 80 per cent of its sales come from countries outside the UK predominantly the US, Japan, Germany and France. The company has a two-year target of £6 million in export revenues.

The continual process of refinement and testing won the business a series of design awards and an enthusiastic client base. Like the original product concept, this process of refinement comes out of its close knowledge of customer needs. For example, it found some customers, especially single women, feeling uncomfortable having a knife block because it might present a weapon to an intruder. Acting on this, Boa created a chopping board with an in-built knife drawer to store knives out of sight. The downside of getting it right is the time and money it costs. The Clamshell knife block, which is one of Boa's most popular products, was not arrived at overnight. Paul explains, 'The clamshell took months. We had to keep on telling Brian that we just were not there yet with the knife blocks.' In the end the idea came from a brainstorming session. It was a classic piece of teamwork. Boa was rewarded in its persistence by a Design Week Consumer Product of the Year award.

Brian is convinced that Boa will have to continue to innovate in order to outrun the competition. 'We have had to sacrifice a lot,' he says, 'but risk is fun.'

Source: DTI

Conclusion

Each year in *The Sunday Times* '100 Best Companies to Work For' survey, the best employers in the UK have the chance to showcase their best practice credentials, offering the secrets of their success to a wider public. The following is the gist of it.

Prerequisites of Successful Businesses

- Are led by visionaries, inspiring leaders who promote change. These people communicate a clear vision, and live by a strong set of values that they share with their staff.
- Have values that appeal to customers and staff. They focus on meeting customer needs operating in a way that lets staff take pride in their business and makes customers happy to buy from them.
- Unlock the potential of their people. The best businesses develop their employees, making them feel valued and encouraging them to contribute to the business.
- Promote new ideas and ways of working. They see that future success depends on constant improvement and innovation.
- Know their customers. They are always looking to learn from their customers and trying to anticipate and respond to their changing demands.
- Try to exceed their customers' expectations. They place great emphasis on continually improving the quality of the products and services they provide.

The one thing that all have in common is that they are about people—how they think, how they communicate, and how they work together.

Vision and Change

Vision and change begin at the top. It can be an individual, or it can be a team supporting the CEO that champions the continuous change process, but as one contributor observed, 'They do not manage change: they are change.'

The need to improve management and leadership is urgent. According to the International Institute of Management Development, the management efficiency of UK lags behind major countries. When DTI questioned, over a third of UK companies admitted to being dissatisfied with the quality of their managers.

From the top, the vision needs to be communicated and shared throughout the organisation. If you do not change your people, nothing will change, so you have to make sure everyone understands and supports what you are trying to achieve.

For many companies, best practice in change management involves putting customer needs at the heart of any change. This gives a clear reason for the changes and makes them much more comprehensible and acceptable to employees.

The best businesses also have staff who accept that continuous adaptation to market conditions and customer needs is vital. This means that a successful vision needs to promote not just a set of changes, but also the importance of change itself.

For example, if your business aims to create delighted customers as a way of building undisputed worldwide leadership and profitability, then your vision needs to explain how you are going to do it and how, in 15 years' time, you will still be doing it.

Leadership

Best practice organisations have enthusiastic leaders who:
- ensure the organisation has a vision, mission and strategy that are known and understood;
- oversee the setting of demanding but realistic targets;
- set an example in generating an open, communicative management style;
- champion a culture conducive to learning and continuous improvement; and
- distribute leadership responsibilities with necessary authority, training and resources.

People Development

Employees are enabled to develop and fulfil their potentials through best business practices.
- Make sure employees' contributions are recognised and adequately rewarded.
- Encourage equal opportunities regardless of age, gender, race or religion.
- Promote the acquisition and updating of new skills and knowledge at every level.
- Have effective internal communication systems to encourage the transfer of knowledge and information vertically and horizontally.
- Have effective employee consultation arrangements.
- Empower all employees by encouraging individual ownership and focus on customers.
- Maintain constructive relationships with trade unions (a 'partnership' approach).
- Provide as much employment security as possible.

Supply Chain Management

Successful business organisations manage their relationships with suppliers effectively and efficiently.
- Adopt appropriate supply chain management strategies across the total range of purchased products and/or services.

- Recognise the key role of suppliers in meeting strategic goals.
- Develop and manage suppliers to maximise capabilities and minimise risk.
- Manage relationships, including 'partnerships', with suppliers.
- Assist suppliers in developing their skills and competencies.

Customer Service

Best business practices involves listening to customers and exceeding their expectations.
- Know the drivers in their markets and understand the competition.
- Know and anticipate the needs of their customers.
- Maintain information systems to provide rapid provision of customer-relevant data.
- Cultivate active relationships with total customer satisfaction in mind.

Corporate Responsibility

Best practice organisations maintain a systematic approach to assessing and improving performance.
- Develop systems to measure performance in each of the key areas of the organisation's activities.
- Benchmark performance internally and externally, within and outside their sector.
- Learn from the practices adopted by others.
- Take appropriate and timely action on results.

Performance Measurement

Business organisations should perform as responsible members of the community and society.
- Promote health and safety and reduce nuisance or harm from the organisation's activities.
- Are involved in local communities, e.g., in education and training, the voluntary sector, sport and leisure.
- Contribute to the sustainable use of resources, e.g., in transport, utilities, packaging, recycling.

Innovation

Business competitiveness can be enhanced by exploiting new ways of doing things.
- Maximise use of technology to drive innovation.
- Continuously seek to improve management of resources.
- Encourage input from employees, customers and suppliers.
- Simplify internal systems and processes wherever possible.

Process Improvement

Best practice organisations constantly introduce new/improved products and services.
- Deliver continuous improvement in all customer-facing aspects.
- Customise products and services to increase added value for the customer.
- Constantly seek to improve time to market.
- Continuously seek to reduce customer costs.
- Encourage input from employees, customers and suppliers.

Hypothesis First

Companies to be successful should incorporate best business practises like vision and leadership, values and society, involving and developing staff, innovation and growth, learning from customers and improving quality players. This is a proved hypothesis.

Other things remaining the same, a few more points drafted by New Mexico State University for Planning in Competitive and Turbulent Environments which need to be taken care of are listed below.

Planning in Competitive Environments

The mindset:

(a) Hierarchical control.

Top management commitment will automatically generate acceptance of and successful implementation of strategic plans.

(b) Linear historical projection of trends.

Looking at a few selected historical performances and market criteria to extrapolate into the future on a linear timeline will produce incremental improvement in market share and position.

(c) Analysis is more important than synthesis.

Process, consolidate and aggregate hard data, based solely on technical and economic criteria using analytical techniques developed and managed by experts.

(d) Money controls performance.

People performance can be centrally controlled by a set of numbers tied to a compensation package based on competition between individual members of the enterprise, as well as units of the enterprise.

(e) The firm as a machine.

External complexity and uncertainty is managed by reducing the enterprise into strategic business units (parts), developing plans for each one, adding them up and ignoring the interactions across unit boundaries.

(f) People are cogs constrained by the machine.

Problem solving and improvement in technical processes are adequate to adapt the business to its environment.

People act as if...
(a) Stability is a given.

The enterprises environment (task and global) is stable and unchanging until it's hit by a discontinuity like a mealy bug, a Sony, a Toyota or a CNN.

(b) The old ways are the right ways.

Unspoken assumptions about how we can continue to be successful (embedded in unit boundaries, budgeting, rewards, information systems, etc.,) need not be explored.

(c) Problem solving is enough.

Success comes from reacting resourcefully to problems within predefined and unchangeable endpoints.

(d) Thought separate from action.

Responsibility for thinking and doing are divided over and over again as one steps from one level of the hierarchy to another.

(e) Cooperation can be mandated.

Political infighting and fiefdoms are part of human nature and must be dealt with by savvy managers. They can motivate people to act by telling them to be committed.

(f) One right way.

Reducing a leader's flexibility of response with financial controls/administrative procedures will establish a clear direction within which resources can be committed in a coordinated way.

Planning in Turbulent Environment

The mindset:
(a) Distributed control.

Commitment is earned through participatory strategic planning combined with responsibility for implementation of plans.

(b) Creative synthesis of trends and desired future.

We encapsulate the past and expected future in the present to design a desired future. Basic continuities are carried forward while environmental constraints are indirectly overcome.

(c) Analysis flows into synthesis.

The integration of analysis from multiple sources with direct perception arising from interaction with customers, associates, suppliers, etc., produces a synthesis or a holistic view of the environment.

(d) Determined people control their own performance.

Energy, commitment and initiative are captured when people's ideals are embedded in their plans for the future.

(e) The firm is a human community.

External complexity and uncertainty can be managed by building adaptive capacity into the organisation, its planning and all the people within the enterprise.

(f) People are flexible within an adaptive enterprise.

The ability to plan and respond quickly overcomes uncertainty and becomes an in-built capacity.

People act as if...

(a) Discontinuities are to be expected and searched for.

The environment (industry and global) can shift and change at any moment.

(b) Constant vigilance is necessary.

Assumptions of how to be successful in our industry and global environment must be continuously surfaced, updated and built into our internal systems to conform with the external reality.

(c) They are actively adaptive.

Success comes from sensing trends and initiating change by exploring all possibilities since the achievement of specific endpoints is uncertain.

(d) Devolution of authority.

Those responsible for different aspects of the business plan and have the necessary authority to implement those plans.

(e) Cooperation requires processes for managing conflict.

Sorting out what is agreed/not agreed and integrating work across groups makes us one community that will be able to cooperate to bring plans into action.

(f) Many paths to success.

People are purposeful. They can be responsibly creative to produce a desirable set of goals and be actively adaptive to achieve their endpoints with flexible behaviour.

Section A

Information and Communication Technologies

2
E-commerce – an Introduction to the Concept

Sandhir Sharma and Gautam Bansal

Change has become the normal feature of present business world. More precisely, if we interpret change as a transformation, we tend to look at those factors which induct the change. Majority of changes, currently in the global business environment, are technology-driven and thus points out *technology* as one of the prime reasons for such a massive transformation from traditional models of doing business to new and latest approaches of modern trade and commerce globally. It is technology only which has facilitated the use of information in various ways leading to a revolution in the business world. Information plus technology, i.e., IT has emerged as a giant factor responsible for changed business environment. Information Technology has become an unavoidable part of technology based revolutions since this is the only medium of globally managing, contemplating and using the information for business purpose.

E-commerce (EC) is an exemplary form of revolution in the business world in which buying and selling of goods is done on Internet further complementing the traditional way of handling products, markets and customers. This technology is moving so fast, that it is overtaken before it can even be validated. The emergence of the Internet as a vast public network with millions of people connected online has given rise to a new interactive marketplace for buying and selling.

Thus for some, EC simply means the capability to buy and sell goods and receive information and services online through computer networks. It is well suited to facilitate re-engineering of business processes occurring at many firms. The broad goals of EC are: reduced costs, lower product life cycle, faster customer response and improved service quality. E-commerce is concerned with systems and business processes that support creation of information sources, transfer of information over global network between individual companies and most important of all between computers.

E-commerce may refer as paperless exchange of business information using EDI (Electronic Data Interchange), Electronic Mail, Electronic Bulletin Boards, Electronic Funds Transfer and other network based technologies. India has yet to prepare and work in this field but the trend has already entered into the market. Customers are approaching products and companies through the Internet and have already started purchasing online. Not only individuals, but suppliers, manufacturers, consultants and outsourcing agents also have accepted the reformed version of their business and have already begun using technology for their trade and business. Information gathering, processing, manipulating and distributing is common to trade and commerce, no matter what commodity or service is being exchanged. Today, it is the velocity of information processing and dissemination which determines the speed of real commerce. Computers and networks, by virtue of their great speed are creating electronic marketing with the potential to be more efficient in finding and interacting with customers, communicating with trading partners and developing new products and markets.

E-commerce applications started in the early 1970s with such innovations as EFT (Electronic Fund Transfers). However, the extent of the applications was limited to large corporations, financial institutions, and a few daring small businesses. Then came EDI, which expanded from financial transaction to other transaction processing and enlarged the participating companies from financial institutions to manufacturers, retailers, services, and so on. In 1984, the EDI was standardised that led to CompuServe offers online in the early 1990s. With the commercialisation of the Internet in the early 1990s and its rapid growth to millions of potential customers, the term electronic commerce was coined, and EC applications expanded rapidly. With the development of Netscape in 1994, AMAZON.com and E-Bay.com, the two biggest names in EC, were launched in 1995. By the new millennium the retail spending on the Internet has crossed $20 billion, with the figure crossing $475 billion in 2002 an astronomical increase in EC activity by 2010.

E-commerce begins before personal computers were prevalent and has grown into a multibillion industry nowadays.

(a) It is estimated that 169 million people are online and this figure is likely to double even much more year by year.
(b) In 2000–1, 230 million shoppers spent an estimated US$28 million in the cyber market space.
(c) IDC estimates of online sales of consumers are set to increase more than twenty-fold by 2006.
(d) Areas expected to grow include financial services, entertainment, travel and groceries.
(e) The jackpot returns from EC depend a lot on how the business processes are being leveraged by the electronic transmission.
(f) In the next few years, the world of marketing in particular are to be entirely transformed by the yet-to-be realised potential of EC.

Definitions of E-commerce (EC)

E-commerce is an emerging concept that describes the process of buying and selling or exchanging of products, services and information via computer networks, including the Internet. *The narrow definition of EC is* doing business online or buying products and services through web store fronts. The products could include trading of any physical products such as tractors, cars, trucks, etc., while services could be that of distance education, online medical consultation with a hospital outside the country or arranging excursion.

It is buying and selling, marketing and servicing, and delivery and payment of products, service and information over the Internet, Intranets, extranets and other networks, between an inter-networked enterprise and its prospects, customers, suppliers and other business partners.

E-commerce can be considered as a:
(a) strategy;   (b) technology;   (c) system;
(d) separate business;   (e) sales approach; or   (f) mystery.

Electronic Commerce versus Electronic Business

Just as commerce is a subset although a very important one of business, EC is a subset of e-business. Business involved a whole set of transactions that must be completed before actually reaching the point where goods or services change hands for the agreed consideration. Current business models are honed to supporting the conventional or physical transaction, be it sales, purchase or administration. In the networked world, the customer is identified, contacted, interacted with, sold and served differently. The customer could be absolutely new, the geography totally different, and the competitor someone nobody knew before.

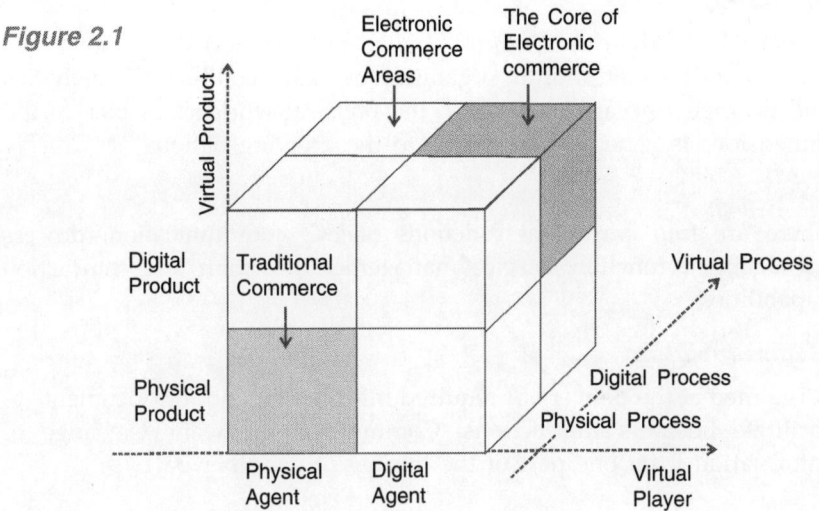

Figure 2.1

Source: Choi et al. (1997)

Dimensions of EC

Pure versus Partial EC

E-commerce can take many forms depending on the degree of digitisation of the product. Choi et. al, 1997 created a model that explains the possible configurations of the dimensions given in Figure 2.1.

A product can be physical or digital, an agent can be physical or digital and the process can be physical and digital. These create eight cubes, each of which has three dimensions. In traditional commerce all dimensions are physical (lower left cube), and in pure EC all dimensions are digital (upper right cube). All other cubes include a mix of digital and physical dimension. If there is at least one digital dimension we may consider the situation EC (but not a pure one), e.g., buying a book from Amazon is not pure because the book is delivered by FedEx. However buying software form Egghead is pure EC because the delivery, payment and agent are digital. E-commerce uses several technologies ranging from EDI to e-mail.

Broadly, there are three major dimensions.

Traditional Commerce

In traditional commerce all dimensions are physical, i.e., there are brick-and-mortar organisations and old-economy organisations (corporations); they perform all business off-line and sell physical products by means of physical agents.

Pure EC

In pure e-commerce all dimensions are digital, i.e., there are pure online (virtual) organisations, new-economy organisation and they sell products or services only online. It is a transformed model of traditional commerce with the help of digital and electronic devices.

Partial EC

In partial EC, there is a mix of digital and physical dimensions, i.e., There are click-and-mortar organisations, who conduct EC activities and do their primary business in the physical world. This part of the dimensions is generally applicable to the growing nations.

Functions of EC

There are four important functions of EC: communication, process management function, service management function and transaction capabilities.

Communication

It is aimed at the delivery of required information and/or documents to facilitate business transactions. Communication means exchange of information from one part of the business to another part.

Process Management Function

It covers the automation and improvement of business processes, e.g., networking two computers together so that they can share and transfer data rather than have a person to take data from one computer to another.

Service Management Function

Services are taken as the base of business nowadays. This function of EC covers the service management eventually leading to customer satisfaction and expanding the business functions and horizons.

Transaction Capabilities

It provides the ability to buy/sell on the Internet or some other online services. It increases the range of transactions among market elements. It also generates time and cost saving environment for any business model.

The Framework of EC

Many people think EC implies just having a website, but EC is much more than that. There are dozens of applications of EC such as home banking, shopping through online stores and malls, buying stocks, finding a job, conducting an auction and collaborating electronically on research and development projects. To execute these applications of e-commerce, we need necessary infrastructural base which is dependent on four major areas: people, public policy, technical standards and protocols, and organisation.

Classification of EC Applications

The applications of EC can be further divided into three categories:
(a) buying and selling goods and services, usually called e-markets;
(b) facilitating inter and intra organisation flow of information, communication and collaboration, referred as interorganisational systems; and
(c) providing customer services.

Electronic Markets

A market is a network of interactions and relationships where information, products, services and payments are exchanged. When the marketplace is electronic, the business centre is not a physical building but rather a network based location where business interactions occur.

Inter-organisational Information Systems and E-Markets

An IOS involves information flow among two or more organisations. The major objectives included efficient transaction processing, such as transmitting orders, bills, and payments using EDI or extranets. There is no scope of any type of negotiations; it is all execution whereas in e-markets, consumers negotiate, submit bids, agree on an order and finish the execution on or offline.

Providing Customer Services

Another important application of EC is providing customer services such as after sale, customer satisfaction survey, customer remarks collection, customer grievances, demand forecasts, Just in Time Manufacturing and providing solutions to customers.

Interdisciplinary Nature of EC

Electronic commerce, being a new field is just developing its theoretical or scientific foundations. It is clear that EC is based on several disciplines. Many issues of marketing offline are relevant to online EC—such as cost benefits of advertisements and strategies. Other issues are unique to EC ranging from online marketing strategy to interactive kiosks. Many of the issues listed in the infrastructure such as languages, multimedia and networks, fall into the discipline of computer sciences. The financial markets and banks are one of the major participants in EC. Also, financing arrangements are part of many online transactions. Issues such as using the Internet as a substitute for stock exchange and fraud in online stock transactions are a few of the many topics of the field. Theories of micro and macro economy, as well as the economic impacts of EC on firms, need to be considered in EC planning. The back office operations of electronic transactions are similar to other transactions in some respects, but different in other. Legal and ethical issues are extremely important in EC, especially in a global market. A large number of legislative bills are pending, and many ethical issues are interrelated with legal ones, such as privacy and intellectual property.

Advantages of EC

(a) Distance does not matter in carrying out trade; one can reach the world any time one wants. This helps companies to have a cheap and effective way of communication with suppliers on one side and customers on the other.

(b) Unlike a brick and mortar store, an online store works 24 hours a day, 7 days a week, 365 days a year and round the clock.

(c) Compared with retail outlet or new office, the cost of setting up an e-commerce website is very low.

(d) There is more flexibility to add and remove a product or products on a website than in catalogues or brochures.

(e) Being online, it potentially gives exposure to previously untapped market segments.

(f) Amount of errors get reduced because orders do not have to be re-keyed into order entry systems and efficiencies increase owing to the automation of the business process.

(g) Buying/selling of items from any place becomes easy.

(h) Services such as financial services, legal services, medical advice from appropriate portals can be availed.

(i) Anonymous friendly advice on items one may like to buy/rent is made available.

(j) Helps the business to reach out to a worldwide customer base at a very low cost.

(k) Inventory size reduced because of reduction in transaction time.

(l) Funds transfer is faster.

(m) Large number of potential business partners can be quickly found and contacted using appropriate search engines and e-mail correspondences.

(n) In some cases, middlemen such as retailers can be eliminated as manufacturers can reach out directly to customers and reduce costs and delays.

Disadvantages of EC

(a) Since the selling is online, customers are unable to touch and feel the enterprise. This is a psychological barrier; as consumers become more familiar with shopping online, this barrier is removed.

(b) Online stores don't exist for very long. Many companies don't know exactly how to set up a store, resulting in a large group of annoyed and dissatisfied customers who want to buy something but are not clear how they should and there is no one to guide like a shopkeeper.

(c) From the Indian context, internet access is not widely available at present.

(d) EDI standards have to be in place before B2B e-commerce can increase. Small businesses may find it difficult to conform to these standards.

(e) One of the major problems is security of transactions on the Net. Spies or hackers can steal and misuse credit card numbers if not careful.

(f) Portals have to be protected from virus attacks and other electronic vandalism and espionage by special security systems.

Status of E-Commerce

(a) Still 2.66 lakh Indian villages are to be connected to phones.

(b) Most of the villages don't even have electricity for charging the battery of their mobile phone.

(c) Globally, the average number of TV sets per 1000 people is 235; in India it is 64.

(d) In website presentation, access to voice, text and video are considered basic in affluent countries.

(e) Thirty per cent of Indians are still below poverty line and cannot even think of buying computers.

(f) South Asian homes constitute 23 per cent of the world population and have less than 1 per cent Internet users.

(g) Nearly 80 per cent of all websites are in English, although, the language is spoken by less than 10 per cent of the world population.

Business Modals

Business Modals are described as a set of business entities and the inter-relationship among them. The modals describe sources of revenue and potential benefits accruing to the involved business participants. In order to develop a successful business modal in any of the fields whether EC or manufacturing, services, etc., you have to make it sure that the modal should confine to why should the customers buy from you, i.e., value preposition; how will you earn from the business, i.e., revenue and profitability; what should be the size and type of market in which you are going to operate; what special advantage or unique proposition your firm or business is going to give to the customers and market; what type of organisational structural changes are required to carry your business plan, and finally, regarding the management team which is going to lead the business. All these above-mentioned factors, once monitored and implemented carefully, leads to successful implementation of the business modals.

E-commerce as a field is growing at a fast rate especially with the revolution in the field of IT, publishing, distribution, payments and security technologies. To cope up with the evolution, business modals have been evolving at a meteoric rate. Only less than a decade ago, online service providers such as American Online and CompuServe pioneered as elegant business modals for making money by providing contents. Despite the abundance of potential modals, it is possible to identify the major generic types of business modals that have been developed for the e-commerce arena and describe their key features. Here, a few business modals have been categorised on the basis of e-commerce sectors.

B2C Modal

Through Business to Consumer e-commerce, online business seeks to reach individual consumers. Consumers are increasingly going online to shop for and purchase products, arrange financing, shipments or take delivery of digital products such as software and get service after the sale. There are many modals which work on the base of B2C transactions such as portals like yahoo.com, MSN.com, and so on, which offer a package of services such as search, news, music and video downloads, chats and calendars, etc. Some of the portals are specialised in providing the services directly to the marketplace like iboats.com.

Yahoo and MSN are called horizontal portals as they define their marketplace to include all the users of the Internet whereas iboats.com is a vertical portal which is targeted towards a particular market segment and customers.

B2C e-commerce also includes online retail stores called E-Tailors. Like Amazon.com. as the name depicts these are stores on the Net in which the customer dials into the Internet, checks the different types of products and offerings, and places an order. This sector has been highly competitive as the total cost of entering into these markets is comparatively low. Some B2C e-business provides high value content to the consumers for the subscription fee. For example, *Wall Street Journal* and *Harvard Business Review* and many others charge customers for downloading the important information contents in addition to or in place of the subscription fee. Stock brokers and trade agents work online. e.g., e-trade.com, monster.com that help the customers in sales transactions by charging transaction fees and by increasing their productivity. There are many web based market creators that create markets for both buyers and sellers like e-bay.com, priceline.com. Some business supplements a successful web based ordering. These businesses are called catalogue merchants. e.g., avon.com, chefs, Omaha Steaks and Davids. There are many community sites that creates digital online environment and interact with like-minded people.

B2B—E-Commerce Modal

B2B is a modal in which the business focus is on selling to other businesses i.e., a company conducting its trading and other commercial activities through the net with its customer being another business itself. B2B modal involves three times more business as compared to B2C e-commerce, even though public attention is still focused on B2B. The major advantages of B2B modal are Direct Interaction with customer, focused sales promotion activities, high customer loyalty, saving in distribution cost and time, etc. B2B applications will offer assistance to business firms regarding products, customers, suppliers, product processes, transportation, inventory management, supply chain alliances, competitors, point of sale (POS), etc. The major modals utilised in B2B are listed below.

Aggregators

In this modal a company aggregates buyers to form a virtual buying entity and aggregates suppliers to constitute the virtual distributors/sellers. This modal helps in bringing buyers and sellers together to reduce the procurement costs for a specific industry, e.g., an electronic company that offers total home buying services, from search to financing through one site.

Trading Hubs

In this modal major stress is on integration of value prepositions through a managed process. Hubs host electronic markets and create value by reducing the cost of transactions between sellers and buyers. These hubs can operate either horizontally or vertically within one industry. For example, tradeout.com operates in horizontal integration and directag.com in vertical integration. Hubs host electronic markets and create value by reducing the costs of transactions between sellers and buyers. There are vertical hubs that serve vertical markets or specific industry such as energy, steel and plastics. On the contrary functional hubs specialise in horizontal markets across different industries. These hubs focus on business processes such as project management and maintenance, repair and operating procurement.

E-Distributors

These are the companies that supply products and services directly to individual business, e.g., Grainger.com: is the largest distributor of maintenance, repair and operation supplies.

Content

Content is the end product of this modal of B2B commerce. It facilitates trade and helps in generating revenue from subscribers and advertising. There are e-companies that sell information about contracts to bid market intelligence and analysis.

There are also many companies that rent internet based software applications to businesses like Salesforce.com, Corio.com. These companies are called as B2B service providers.

Auction and Dynamic Pricing Markets

These handle complex exchanges between buyers and sellers. Auctions are dynamic and are efficient mechanisms for mediating and brokering into the complex marketplaces like supply chain and procurement systems.

In fully automated B2B exchanges multiple buyers and sellers competitively bid on commodities and buy and sell products which are matched automatically like paperexchange.com.

The major B2B portals in India are agriwatch.com, apnatransport.com, bimaonline.com, castingworld.com, commodityindia.com, e-commerce.net, bijleeindia.com, etc. All these portals are major portals working in their specific areas to bring the companies and dealers together for trade.

C2C Modal

In this modal consumers sell directly to consumers via online classified ads and auctions or by selling personal services or expertise online. e.g. ebay.com (auctions) and tradeonline.com (Classified Ads). Before ebay, individual consumers used garage sales, flea markets and thrift shops to dispose of and acquire used merchandise. With the emergence of online auctions people need not venture out of their offices and houses in order to bid on the items of interest.

P2P Modal

Like C2C, P2P ventures link users and enable them to share files and computer resources without common server. The main focus is on helping individuals make information available for anyone else by connecting the user on the web, e.g., MP3.com: helps individuals share files and download songs.

EC Issues

There are a number of issues that have been identified that will be critical to the growth of EC and will require coordinated actions by both the industry and government. In our view, addressing these issues is integral to the creation of new commercial opportunities and an electronic environment, as each issue is related in some way to the increasing and sustaining levels of public trust and confidence in EC as a way of doing business. We have identified four major areas—commercial, security, infrastructure and socio-cultural—all of which are closely interconnected and reciprocal in nature. In all four areas, many of the issues are legal or have strong legal implications.

Commercial Issues

Commerce depends on confidence. For the electronic marketplace to flourish in both its customer and enterprise dimensions, both buyers and sellers must have at least some level of confidence in the outcome of EC as they have more traditional kinds of transactions. It must be possible for each participant in an electronic transaction to determine that both the transaction and the market environment in which it occurs are legitimate, in the sense that:

- the seller and buyer are who they claim to be;
- the seller has rights of sale over the item in question;
- the buyer has the resources to purchase the item;
- the transaction and payment mechanisms are available, legal and secure;
- the item sold corresponds to its description and is suitable for that purpose;
- the purchased item (be it a product or service) can and will be delivered to the buyer.

Furthermore, transacting parties also expect to gain economically from a market environment that is open and competitive, not artificially distorted so that it favours some market factors over others. All of these expectations give rise to some fundamental questions:

- where does an electronic transaction actually take place in terms of contractual obligations, assignment of liabilities and tax responsibilities?
- where are companies that trade electronically registered and regulated and are subject to which legal regimes?

- how are rights in tangible and intangible forms of property to be protected?
- what happens when a transaction goes wrong? who has the responsibility and liability?

Consumer Protection

Although currently most EC exists at the enterprise level, much of the information gathered by research groups stress the importance of the consumer interface in determining the future of EC. The intent is to harmonise the general environment in which electronic communications of all kinds take place. Thus, the electronic transaction environment is moving closer and closer to the individual. As different kinds of consumer transactions migrate to the electronic milieu, a number of issues become magnified that are fundamental to the creation of trust in EC as a way of doing business.

By definition, a product vendor using EC has no physical presence with respect to the consumer. In this respect, EC is different from the more established kinds of catalogue sales where the location and status of the trader can normally be determined and, more importantly, a physical record of the product description and the transaction details normally exist. All of this can be missing from an electronic transaction and, correspondingly, the possibilities for deception and fraud can increase. The non-territorial and intangible nature of EC calls into question the adequacy of existing law enforcement mechanisms that are still geared to tangible products and national legislations.

On the other hand, EC can also be used to document the transaction trailing great details and to process this information for product development and marketing purposes. This leads to questions about how to preserve the privacy of the consumer in an electronic environment (including the problem of aggressive direct solicitation). Vendors must also protect the confidentiality of information provided by the customer as part of a transaction. There are many legitimate purchases—medicines and professional services, for example, that consumers may prefer to keep confidential. Preserving consumer confidentiality involves the provision of mechanisms to prevent the use of transaction-generated information in ways that were not intended. It also involves ensuring that safeguards on the use of this information cannot be circumvented by the transportation of consumer databases between legal jurisdictions. At the moment, considerable discrepancies exist between the levels of data protection available in different countries.

A primary inhibitor to consumer use of EC facilities is the difficulty in locating the sources of products and establishing liabilities, should it be found that these products are not of the advertised quality or not fit for the intended use. This situation is exacerbated where intangible products are involved. To overcome these problems, legal, administrative and technological mechanisms are needed to certify the identity of traders and the validity of guarantees and product descriptions and to document electronically each stage in the transaction.

This could become a specially critical issue for new market entrants who have not yet established a commercial reputation in the non-electronic marketplace. One method, at least in the short to medium term, might be the use of endorsements. New product brands and vendors could enter the electronic marketplace under the 'umbrella' of a firm or brand name that has already established consumer trust in the marketplace. Credit card firms and platform companies could also perform the risk assessment, getting of third party and rating of new companies. Endorsements could be certified electronically by means of an encrypted accreditation code. Current litigation practices, however, could inhibit development of the endorsement system, particularly in the United States. Even when the purchasing part of the transaction is complete, consumers still have to be assured that they will receive the products they have purchased electronically in good order. At present, one of the weakest links in any consumer-oriented EC system involving tangible goods is the physical delivery infrastructure. Delivery can also be a problem for intangible products—entertainment and information services, for example, where the network backbone fails to provide access or to deliver adequate bandwidth. In general, most types of on demand delivery are expensive in most national markets and these costs tend to increase over time. Business efficiencies realised at the supplier's end through EC should result in more competitive prices to the consumer. These efficiencies can be easily wiped out by delivery costs, especially in countries where regulations keep these charges artificially high.

Ensuring Market Diversity and Competition

The members of the research groups are committed to the principle that the electronic marketplace should be open and competitive. Nevertheless, in preparing this Report, various actual and potential market barriers were noted that must be addressed if this principle is to be applied to the benefit of all buyers and sellers.

First, support for the principle of an open electronic market environment is not unambiguous. In migrating to this environment, incumbents want to preserve as much existing competitive advantage as they can. Moreover, incumbent companies may have an advantage in that they have already established consumer confidence in their trademarks and brandnames. As suggested in the previous section, this could be used to the advantage of new traders, but it is important that considerable emphasis is given to encourage consumer confidence as soon as possible so that new electronic market entrants are not seriously disadvantaged.

Second, although examples can be found of successful EC operations that were launched with minimal investment, especially in the purgeoning Internet milieu, most firms find that considerable investment is now required to implement successful EC applications. Often the major part of this investment is not direct capital costs, but the associated costs of implementing and maintaining new systems and acquiring new technological and organisational competencies. For small and medium-sized enterprises (SMEs), these costs can take up a proportionally larger share of available investment capital than for large firms.

Third, although the theory holds that information technology should act to increase the flows of information available to buyers and sellers, the experience of firms contacted by us was that EC leads to an increased awareness of the value of information as a resource and, consequently, to consolidation of partner networks and reluctance to increase the variety of partners or to change them. Some correspondents noted that in an electronic milieu, price is becoming a less important factor in choosing suppliers than confidence based on prior experience with a supplier and on existing levels of technological compatibility.

Finally, there is the possibility of retaliation by some retailers against companies that use EC to increase their volumes of direct sales to customers. The 'by-passed' retailers (particularly if they are large chains) could take countervailing action to limit exposure of these products in the stores, leading suppliers to form a consortia to break these retaliatory embargoes.

Security Issues

The term 'security' encompasses a very wide range of issues, but the main security concerns for EC are the protection of availability, maintenance of confidentiality and integration of information systems and the data that is stored and transmitted. First, the security of the networks themselves must be ensured. This involves quality of service provisions to ensure that network facilities for EC are robust and available as needed, and that unauthorised or malicious access to networks is minimised. Second, the security of commercial messages and network-based transactions must be ensured. This means ensuring that data and information is only disclosed to authorised persons, entities and process and that it is urate and complete, and has not been modified or altered in an unauthorised manner. Probably the central goal of any security scheme is to protect the integrity of transaction related information. Any kind of message can be intercepted, but intercepted electronic messages can be altered in ways that could be imperceptible to the intended receiver. Without safeguards, the potential for alteration can call into question the authenticity of electronic messages, i.e., is the content as read by the intended receiver the same as that provided by the original sender? It is also important that each transacting party can confirm the identity and status of the other. In an electronic environment, logos, brandnames and trademarks are easy to replicate and it can be easy for buyers and sellers to misrepresent their financial and legal status or even their physical locations.

How Secure is 'Secure'

E-commerce offers great opportunities for the business community and consumers, however, it also brings with it some significant risks. The explosive worldwide growth of open networks has raised a legitimate concern with respect to the adequacy of security measures for information and communications systems and the data which is transmitted and stored on those systems. The developing information infrastructure is a fertile environment for all kinds of computer-related crime, including fraud and privacy infringement, thus prompting demands for effective data security measures. Both technical and legal solutions are required in the electronic environment for the physical security of the paper-based world. It is important that solutions are trustworthy and that users and consumers have confidence in them.

Any security system can be broken and the worst intruders are often insiders. Probably the least effective way to instill public confidence in the security of networked transactions is to make blanket assertions that networks are completely secure. Rather, confidence building is dependent upon maintaining the public perception that the levels of security provided for each type of data exchange are reasonable and adequate, that breaches can be detected quickly, that corrective action can be taken and that the lines of responsibility between transacting and intermediary parties are clearly defined.

The expense involved in providing security must be weighed against the security expectations of transacting parties. No bank is immune from robbery, for example, but this does not dissuade depositors as long as they perceive the likelihood of sustaining severe personal losses due to robbery to be remote. Credit card companies generally work out the economics of increased security against an evaluation of what they can afford to absorb in fraud losses each year. For customers, the convenience of the credit card system may overshadow other considerations as long as the costs do not exceed a sustainable level. This defensive mechanism will help reducing security problems, and hence limiting the liabilities of individual customers.

Indeed, customer attitudes to security in general are varied and sometimes ambiguous. Individuals make purchases over the telephone using credit cards, with little knowledge about the security of these transactions and some seem already prepared to use credit cards on the Internet even though there was virtually no security at all for Internet transactions until very recently. A firm that expresses concerns about the security of 'online' transactions may completely overlook the negative security implications of transaction media like the telephone and fax machine, simply because these media are more familiar.

Much of the discussion about security revolves around the issue of 'cryptography' and especially the different attitudes of national governments as to the terms under which cryptography should be provided. Cryptography is an important component of secure information and communications systems and a variety of applications have been developed that incorporate cryptographic technologies to provide data security. Cryptography is an effective tool for ensuring both the confidentiality and the integrity of data and each of these uses offer certain benefits. However, the widespread use of cryptography raises other important issues and cryptography policy must balance a number of varied interests. In addition to its role in the operation of electronic commerce, cryptography has implications for the protection of privacy, intellectual property, business and financial information, as well as public safety and national security. Many believe that until government policies concerning cryptography are harmonised internationally, the growth prospects for EC will be damaged.

Cryptography is certainly a necessary part of any security system, but adequate security is not provided by the use of cryptography alone. The best cryptography in the world will not protect a network that is otherwise vulnerable because of design faults or careless procedures that leave critical interfaces exposed to intruders (this includes non-electronic interfaces as well as electronic ones). Ultimately, security is as much an organisational matter as it is a technological problem. Moreover, the relative priority and significance of security measures vary according to the information or the information system.

The Institutional Aspects of Security

The important task for developers of EC applications is to foster an environment in which public confidence in security arrangements for electronic transactions will grow. This is partly a matter of employing the best available security devices in networks that are keeping the designed security aspect in mind. It is also a matter of providing an institutional framework that can support various security functions. Institutional evolution will be required in three main areas.

(a) *Authentication and Non-repudiational Data Integrity:* There is a tremendous potential for fraud in the electronic world. Transactions take place at a distance without the benefit of physical clues that permit identification, making impersonation easy. The ability to make perfect copies and undetectable alterations of digitised data complicates the matter. Traditionally handwritten signatures serve to determine the authenticity of an original document. In the electronic world, the concept of an 'original' document is problematic, but a 'digital signature' using cryptography can verify data integrity and provide authentication and non-repudiation functions to certify the sender of a message. If a document itself has been altered in any way after it has been signed, the digital signature will so demonstrate it. Similarly, once a person signs a document with a cryptographic key, the digital signature provides proof that the document was signed by the purported author and the sender cannot deny having sent the document or claim that the information has been altered during transmission. The same technology can be applied to ensure the authenticity and integrity of documents achieved electronically. New regulations are needed concerning the registration and use of digital signatures and the liability of issuing authorities and proposals have already been made by the American Bar Association.

(b) *Certification:* The identity and many of the characteristics of transacting parties can be validated using certification procedures, usually by a third party that acts as a certification authority to provide information about the transacting parties.

Certification is necessary to ensure that transacting parties are not only who they say they are, but also that they will be able to provide the level of security necessary to complete the transaction safely. On the identity side, certification encompasses the problem of 'watermarking', ensuring that electronic 'representations' of identity, like logos and trademarks, are in fact genuine. At present, these devices can be forged with great ease in an electronic environment. On the security side, certification is necessary to ensure that any form of security protection that is claimed by a transacting party will actually be provided by that party, as in 'firewall' certification, etc. At this level, certification becomes an issue of trading standards and business ethics.

However, the certificate authority must be itself reliable, so the certifier may need to be certified. This issue could be addressed by both a hierarchy of certificate authorities and a system of cross-certified certificate authorities. Governments must assume responsibility for providing the legal framework for the registration of companies and this must be linked at some point to certification procedures. This is a function that could be undertaken effectively by private sector organisations. Indeed, in the United States, the Better Business Bureau and CommerceNet have plans to become involved in the certification of companies that trade electronically. The extent to which, at the international level, independent international management frameworks for certification may be required in addition to national arrangements is also open to question.

(c) *Data Protection:* The use of networks for commercial transactions increasingly generates vast quantities of data that can be easily and cheaply stored, analysed and reused and neither open networks nor many types of private networks, were designed with communications and storage confidentiality in mind. For EC to thrive in a commercial environment governed by the principles of open markets and free trade, participants in a market must be able to exchange commercial data freely across national boundaries, confident that there will be no unauthorised access to this information. In 1980, the OECD published guidelines which addressed the protection of privacy and transborder flows of personal data. While these guidelines have stood the test of time and are still applicable today, the implications for this issue have expanded in proportion to the explosive growth in digital computer processing and network technologies. Governments are challenged to balance the growing commercial requirement to exchange data of all kinds securely across national borders and to control and regulate data flows in relation to concerns such as privacy protection or security. Both the public and private sector need to address this issue by implementing appropriate technical and organisation measures to protect personal data against accidental loss, alteration, abuse and unauthorised movement between countries, disclosure or access, in particular where data is transmitted over a network.

Infrastructure Issues

Research groups collected a wide range of observations on the infrastructure problems associated with the development of EC. It is clear that many wide variations persist in the technical capabilities and administrative conditions of national telecommunication systems and that the current electronic networking environment is full of anomalies. It was noted, for example, that essential communications for airline safety and maintenance (service bulletins and air worthiness directives) are sent out on Telex as this is still the only infrastructure with any real claim to being available anywhere in the world. It was noted also that much of the data exchange in the insurance industry is still accomplished by the physical transport of tapes, not because data communication facilities do not exist, but because physical transport is often cheaper and quicker than telecommunications.

Given the front-runner status of the Internet as the first networking environment capable of achieving a widespread presence in virtually all areas of EC, an immediate goal is the development of a managed Internet backbone—a secure, widely accessible, fully interconnected high speed international network that will guarantee the availability of bandwidth sufficient for the requirements of EC. A recent survey suggested that currently less than five per cent of US corporate network managers are using Internet as the backbone of their wide area networks and nearly three-quarters of managers surveyed reported no plans to migrate to Internet in the near future. This response is partly due to the fact that firms have already made significant technology investments and must maximise their returns on these investments. Nevertheless, it is also due to the many residual technological and administrative constraints that still inhibit the growth of network services markets.

Network Capacity

Even in the most advanced countries, growth in available bandwidth is generally much too slow to promote EC as a universal market access medium. The bandwidth problem is even worse in a 'mobile data' environment, potentially a high growth area for EC. Estimates provided by Deutsche Telekom indicate that data communication makes up less than five per cent of digital cellular traffic. Growth is inhibited by the scarcity of available radio frequencies and by lack of international harmonisation in the current technical and administrative regimes. The bandwidth problem in both fixed and mobile networks is exacerbated by tariff structures that are not cost-or usage-based. It is important to establish more realistic pricing regimes, especially considering that, in the long term, rapid growth in traffic volumes will mean that telecommunication costs for EC are likely never to decline in total terms. Ultimately, it is expected that the increase in data flows will continue to outrun the decline in data transfer costs.

Network Access

Most Internet applications run on telephone lines in the public network, but the persistence of restrictive national regulatory structures remains a major inhibitor to the provision of Internet services in many markets. Furthermore, in most countries, public telecommunication operators are still not oriented to the networking needs of EC. Operators prefer to offer value-added services rather than backbone management as such. This has encouraged the exploration of alternative media for Internet access, particularly satellite and cable television systems. In the United States, there is more diversity in approaches. While the main telecommunication companies offer new ATM-based infrastructures, the Home initiative plans to develop a nationwide managed Internet backbone by utilising the facilities of many local cable television companies. This system is intended to provide a facility for secure commercial transactions on the Internet. With the growth of cable systems, particularly in Europe, the concept could eventually extend beyond the United States. In most markets, in any case, use of cable networks for EC will require substantial investments in order to re-engineer these facilities to provide two-way capabilities. A recent OECD study has shown that there is a relationship between the degree of openness in the telecommunication markets in OECD countries and the penetration and pricing of Internet access. In 1995, leased line Internet access in countries with no infrastructure competition was 44 per cent higher than in countries allowing infrastructure competition. Likewise, dial-up access charges were three times as expensive in makes with no competition.

Network Development

The Internet was designed for resilience, but not for security, ease of use or even reliability. This must change, but change may not come easily. In general, Internet Service Providers (ISP) do not invest at levels that are necessary to support EC. Employing 'quick fixes' in pursuit of immediate returns will not result in an increase in the overall quality or reliability of the Internet. Internet-based solutions to business networking problems are being developed by a variety of software houses, systems integrators and even content providers. Applications and software developers are continually demonstrating that the performance envelope of the existing Internet environment can be expanded considerably. In many cases, however, this merely exacerbates the backbone management problem. It is likely that the impetus for managed network development internationally will emerge not from the public Internet, but from the proliferation of private Internets. Some ISPs may move into the intranet and extranet environments.

Standards

Electronic Commerce intersects the domains of telecommunications, broadcasting and computing. Each domain has different institutional structures for the development of technical standards for the interconnection and interpretability of network technologies. In many cases, these structures are reinforced by separate regulatory regimes.

Furthermore, each of these domains has different attitudes towards standardisation; the computer sector being far more amenable to a mixture of proprietary and non-proprietary standards. Institutions are still focused on standards requirements for 'Electronic Data Processing' (EDP) and EDI and have yet to engage fully with the standardisation requirements of EC as defined and described in this book.

Although some progress is being made on the harmonisation of standards for core services like EDI, these standards are still inadequate even after many years of development. Many other EC service environments are similarly bedevilled by a plethora of partially compatible or incompatible standards. Many now expect that EDI, as a paradigm, may give way to a variety of Internet-based approaches to data transfer, thus heralding the end of standards frameworks like EDIFACT and X.12. Eventually, however, a more extended range of standards may be required for EC standardised electronic contract formats, for example, or standardised protocols for the exchange of technical and product specifications.

Although many of the firms contributing to this study identified the need for more and better standards for EC, it is clear that some types of business are more amenable than others to the standardisation of different EC elements. In manufacturing industries, for example, internationally standardised formats for commodity descriptions would expedite commercial transactions considerably. In the insurance industry, on the other hand, customers choose products more on evaluations of insurer quality than on 'trade descriptions' of products or even price. For products that are not commodities, national or international standards may be so difficult to negotiate that emerging de facto standards will have to be accepted.

Social and Cultural Issues

Commercial relationships are shaped to a considerable extent by social conditions and cultural attitudes. Diffusion of the benefits and opportunities of EC could be limited by factors such as language, social attitudes and conditions of access to the ICT infrastructure. It is already a fact, for example, that most of the commercial and non-commercial services on the Internet are oriented to English language and that Internet access is heavily concentrated in a handful of highly developed economies. Also noted were concerns about the effects of EC on social behaviour and in particular, the problem of network content that raises moral, political and social objections in different cultural settings.

The research group was highly sympathetic to these concerns, not least because responsiveness to social and cultural conditions is recognised as an important factor in building commercial relationships of all kinds. Nevertheless, it is quickly becoming impossible for firms, countries and individuals to avoid the impacts of EC, irrespective of the degree to which they participate in it directly. The issue of information 'haves' and 'have nots' is a crucial one for EC and it applies to individuals as well as countries and regions, especially in the newly industrialising and developing world.

The characteristics and implications of EC will inevitably produce social and cultural pressures. At this point, however, there is great uncertainty about the form these pressures will take and how serious they will be in terms of maintaining social stability. There is urgent need on an international basis to monitor the social and cultural changes that are occurring in response to the proliferation of electronic services of all kinds, including EC.

E-CRM—an Introduction

Customer Relationship Management (CRM) can be considered as one of the largest grouping of IT Concepts as on date. It has the concept of shifting the ownership of the customer up to the enterprise level and away from individual departments. These departments have the responsibility for customer interactions, but the enterprise has the responsibility for the customer. In order to achieve CRM the enterprise brings automation to each customer touch point in the areas of sales automation, the Internet, point of sale and call centres. In broad terms, CRM includes:

(a) interaction with existing consumers, dealers, distributors, detailers, wholesalers, agents and all associates;
(b) handling grievances;
(c) after sale services;
(d) converting prospective customers into potential customers;
(e) front desk services/facilitation services;
(f) customer retention;
(g) campaigning and marketing;
(h) analysis of the customer behaviour;
(i) channel management; and
(j) work flow management.

The so-called typical customer no longer exists, and companies have been learning this lesson the hard way. Until very recently, business was more concerned about the 'whats' than about the 'whos'. In other words, companies were focused on selling as many products and services as possible, without regard to who was buying them.

Nowadays, the competition is just a mouse-click away. Embattled companies are slouching towards the realisation that without customers, products don't sell and revenues don't materialise. They have been forced to become smarter about selling, and this means becoming smarter about who is buying. Indeed a good definition of CRM is

'The infrastructure that enables the delineation of and increase in customer value, and the correct means by which to motivate valuable customers to remain loyal—indeed, to buy again.'

Customer Relationship Management (CRM)

Customer is the king and modern day businesses fully endorse that view. Corporates have long understood the value of customer relationship management, that is, the discipline of identifying, attracting and retaining the most valuable customers to sustain profitable growth. In a regulated environment, where the aims were universal access and the ability to serve all customers equally well, the industry naturally has targeted its resources and attention on building efficient infrastructure and systems, rather than on understanding and forging relationships with various customer segments. This has given birth to a new concept called Customer Relationship Management (CRM).

Most senior communications executives know intuitively that managing customer relationship is very important. The fundamental dilemma is determining which customer relationship management capabilities have the greatest financial impact. Because of an inability to quantify a capability's financial impact, executives often make investment decisions on intuition alone. Sometimes due to this a wrong decision is made and the opportunity to make money is lost. Customer Relationship Management is a panacea to most of the above dilemmas.

What is CRM?

Customer Relationship Management is a management approach or model that puts the customer at the core of a company's processes and practices. It leverages the cutting-edge technology, integrated strategic planning, up close and personal marketing techniques and organisational development tools to build internal and external relationships that increase profit margins and productivity within a company.

Customer Relationship Management helps companies improve the profitability of their interactions with customers, while at the same time, makes the interactions appear friendlier through individualisation. The essence of CRM is to treat individual customers individually and knowing that the customer is crucial. It thus extends the concept of selling from a discrete act performed by a salesperson to a continual process involving every person in the company. It is the art/science of gathering and using information about your customers to build customer loyalty and increase customer value. To succeed with CRM, companies need to match products and campaigns to prospects and customers, in other words, to intelligently manage the customer life cycle.

To sum up, CRM is a business strategy, process, culture and technology to enable organisations to optimise revenue and increase the shareholder's value through a better understanding of the needs of the customers.

Why CRM?

Businesses face the problem of customer churn, and fresh marketing efforts which succeed in attracting new customers, have not been able to prevent it. Businesses have learned the hard way that it is more efficient to retain customers than to merely attract new customers. Furthermore, loyalty is desired primarily in a specific category of the client base. Studies show another manifestation of the old 80/20 rule: most organisations find that roughly 20 per cent of their client base generates 80 per cent of the profits. It just goes on to show that old loyal customers are most profitable. It is now critical that businesses identify the salient characteristics of this group, retain these highly desirable customers, and find ways to increase the size of this category.

The idea behind customer relationship management is to have a single enterprise view of the customer for the purpose of cultivating these high-quality relationships that lead to improved loyalty and profits. This means being able to identify all the services/products the customer had brought from the organisation and thus being able to identify the buying behaviour/pattern of the customer. This would result in the company being able to give to the customer the same kind of approved experience where the customer had been delighted with the service/product. The distinguishing feature of modern CRM is the emphasis on an *enterprise* view of the customer, not simply a departmental view.

CRM Essentials

Customer Relationship Management programmes involve three basic business processes: marketing automation sales force automation, and customer service. Each of these three areas is based on many specific CRM capabilities. Marketing, for example, includes capabilities such as 'measuring marketing effectiveness', and 'executing effective marketing plans'. Sales includes 'developing and executing an effective channel strategy'. and 'measuring sales effectiveness'. Service includes 'understanding customer profitability and cost to serve', and 'developing differentiated/tiered customer service.

Business Benefits of CRM

In addition to the cultivation of loyal customers who exhibit the profitability profile businesses seek, CRM brings other benefits to the enterprise. An improved and detailed understanding of customers, their needs and expectations, and how the company interacts with them is emerging as a critical success factor of both supply chain management (SCM) and electronic commerce (e-commerce). Successful CRM initiative will provide a better ability to model and classify various customer market segments, leading to improved business-to-consumer (B2C) e-commerce performance.

Business Challenges of CRM

Although CRM initiatives enjoy high return on investment (ROI) compared with other IT initiatives such as SCM or enterprise resource planning (ERP), there is also a high purported failure rate (55 to 75 per cent). This failure rate applies specifically to the sales force automation (SFA) dimension of CRM; call centre, marketing automation and data warehousing application projects typically fare better. In such cases, the failure rate is often due to a failure to account for cultural issues associated with the sales organisation. Poor executive sponsorship is another significant contributor.

Thus it can be said that the main challenges to CRM are: appropriate end user-driven methodology, lack of appropriate executive sponsorship, lack of cultural preparation, application design approach, over-automation, poor accounting for extensibility, poor support for mobile synchronisation and lack of appropriate network infrastructure.

Businesses cannot afford to fail when implementing CRM. Delaying the initiative until the window of opportunity is lost or implementing a system that does not meet the organisation's objectives or is not accepted by users can be disastrous for the entire enterprise. Many businesses are looking for vendors that can help them meet these challenges and ensure that a successful CRM initiative is delivered in a timely manner.

Relationship marketing is becoming the core marketing activity for business operations in fiercely competitive environment. On an average, business houses spend six times more to acquire customers than they do to keep them. Therefore, many firms are now paying more attention to their relationships with existing customers to retain them and increase their share of customers' purchases. Worldwide service organisations have been pioneers in developing customer retention strategies. Banks have relationship managers for selected customers, airlines have frequent flyer programmes to reward loyal customers, credit cards offer redeemable bonus points for increased card usage, telecom service operators provide customised service to their heavy users, and life insurance companies have personalised services for their regular customers.

From CRM to E-CRM

In an era of rapidly changing technology and increasing reliance on the web, lasting customer relationships are critical to thrive in the marketplace. Reorganising a company has become a competitive mandate, not an option. E-CRM is just the right way to go about it. The need for E-CRM is dictated primarily by the new global electronic economy.

Industry analysts predict that CRM will be the hottest selling business applications of the ongoing century. This prediction is based on the growing need for company's influence of the Internet as a vehicle for purchasing goods and services is only likely to accelerate that need- transiting from normal CRM to E-CRM. Innovative one-to-one marketing strategies are required to identify and retain the most valuable customers, E-CRM enables companies to understand customer needs and buying habits better to leverage the new/better product or service offering to the customer. Basic market drivers are cost and competition and the reality that it is less costly to retain a customer than acquiring a new one.

Few years ago, CRM was used only for mediating an enterprise's relationship with its customers. Today it is an integral part of IT strategy for many business organisations have started restructuring their operational systems with ERP packages. Most of the CRM developments are taking place in the e-commerce domain with B2B and B2C. Hence we may say

$$E\text{-CRM} = E\text{-commerce} + CRM$$

In a nutshell, it is clear that the advent of MNCs have created a lot of technology and CRM based pressures on Indian companies, making them realise that E-CRM is no longer an option, but a necessity for survival, in competitive environment.

Need for E-CRM

It can be broadly divided into three parts:
1. Business Point of View
   (a) Reaching the customer in a lesser time;
   (b) building customer information database;
   (c) speeding up the processes;
   (d) being cost-effective;
   (e) reaching the mass; and
   (f) sharing and generating knowledge.
2. Customer Point of View
   (a) Easy accessibility;
   (b) wide choice;
   (c) displaying empathy;
   (d) providing reassurance;
   (e) increasing reliability;
   (f) adding a personal touch, and
   (g) increasing customer loyalty by reducing the cost per unit.

3. Market Point of View
   (a) Improving returns on investment;
   (b) large players and big markets;
   (c) healthy competition;
   (d) industrial growth;
   (e) capital generation;
   (f) identifying and exploring new market opportunities; and
   (g) tuned marketing.

The need for CRM has been there always because there cannot be a business without customers and customers of value only be acquired and retained through relationships. But E-CRM has added many new opportunities and challenges to his axiom. The 'e' create an 'anytime, anywhere, through, any medium of communications' paradigm that is one challenge. The next challenge is the increasing realisation that E-CRM is a process of high velocity and real time. Hence it succeeds only when it is a part of an overall business process. Supply Chain Management and other business processes must be integrated seamlessly into the customer facing processes. Thus E-CRM is an enterprises's comprehensive relationship management strategy.

E-CRM Architecture

E-CRM architecture would comprise (a) sales force automation, (b) e-mail management system, (c) interactive voice response, (d) knowledge management, (e) call centres, and (f) instant online querying through chat.

E-CRM is customer centric and is not just technology. Customer Relationship Management is a philosophy that put the customer at the design point, it is getting intimate with the customer. It can be considered more as a strategy than as a process. Customer Relationship Management is to be designed to understand and anticipate the needs of the existing and new anticipated customer base a company has.

E-CRM Scenario—Indian Perspective

It is still at childhood stage at present, but is expected to have a huge growth in the next three to four years. Several companies are jumping into the bandwagon. There are at present approximately 35,000 people in India representing various E-CRM companies. It is expected to reach at least two million representatives of E-CRM in India by 2010, accounting for a business of almost $25 billion. The domestic market size at present is estimated to be around $45–50 millions with an anticipated growth rate of 35 per cent to 40 per cent. Several Indian companies have implemented various components of the CRM service umbrella for some time now. India is now regarded as the location of choice for remotely delivered CRM with its abundance of skilled English-speaking graduates at a very nominal cost at which the needed skills are available. This had led to several companies entering the E-CRM service space. Key players of E-CRM in India are: Talisma Corporation, Customer Asset.com, 24/7 customer.com, Bank office.com, iSeva Inc. Tata steel and HCL Info systems.

Other than this there are three major trends in the industry which will create an explosion of E-CRM services—

(a) explosion of broadband telecommunication networks and services;

(b) penetration of mobile data devices; and

(c) customer care using offshore labour and web based technologies.

Future of EC

There is a consensus regarding the future of EC—it is bright. Differences exist as to the anticipated growth rate and the identification of industry segments that will grow the fastest. The future of EC is based on the following trends and observations:

- *Increase in the usage of Internet*—technological availability and accessibility.
- *More opportunities for buyers*—more number of products and services.
- *Incentives on purchasing*—buyer's advantage.
- *Security and trustworthy transactions*—improved transactions.
- *Efficient information handling*—generation of info houses.
- *Innovative organisations*—technology based organisations.
- *Payment systems*—emergence of e-cash cards.

Many people conclude that the impact of EC on our lives will be as much as, and possibly more than, that of the Industrial Revolution. No other phenomenon since the Industrial Revolution has been classified in this category.

3
Playing Leapfrog: Using Strengths in ICT to Energise the Manufacturing Sector in India

Komolica Peres

This chapter looks at the use of ICT in increasing the competitiveness of Indian manufacturers. This begs the question: what is an Indian manufacturer? is it only those businesses fully owned by Indian business houses? or those which are joint ventures with MNCs? where might the line be drawn?

Without going into the finer points of corporate ownership and for the purposes of the following discussion, it is best to keep in mind that an Indian manufacturer is one who manufactures and markets his/her goods in India. These businesses conduct their affairs in the Indian ethos and face similar challenges in the Indian marketplace.

Of late, a prodigious amount of newsprint and digital space has been taken up with 'The Great China–India Comparison' debate. It is practically impossible to open a business magazine or website without seeing some aspects of this debate. In its scope it ranges from opinions on differences in forms of governance to genetic traits of the inhabitants of these two countries.

However, one undeniable fact, and one that a lot of the debate centres on is this: China's growth has come about through a huge growth in its manufacturing sector whereas concurrently India's growth has been led by its service sector.

This in turn gives rise to another interesting question: does this mean that Indian manufacturing is indeed in a state of decline and therefore all our policy making and budgetary support should therefore go to improve the service sector?

Those for the motion say that indeed it makes very little sense to keep hoping for a manufacturing resurgence in the face of the spectacular success of the service sector. Roach, for example, points out that not only is the manufacturing sector hampered by a lack of infrastructure, a low national saving rate and anemic inflows of foreign direct investment, there is also a mistaken assumption of the job-creating potential of the sector. He cites the example of companies like Tata Motors who have enhanced the productivity of their manufacturing operations to significantly reduce the labour component of their end-product. Hence increased investment in manufacturing, he advocates, will not go far enough to create the number of jobs that are needed to shift some of the 66 per cent of population engaged in agriculture into alternative sectors.

The opposing point of view holds that in the final analysis, the numbers of jobs in the service sector are open only to 10–12 per cent of the population of a country of about a billion people who are able to communicate in English. Admittedly, the visible part of India's progress deals with the success of its English-speaking, literate urban population in professions that involve some familiarity with technology. But to conclude that a majority of India's population is employable in such a manner is an error.

Compelling arguments aside, the purpose of this chapter is not to choose for or against either view. India's manufacturing sector, as it stands provides significant employment and productivity to the country and can, in all practicality, hardly be written off. However, rather than taking a view on services versus manufacturing, this chapter proposes an alternative perspective: using our skills in services—both implicit and explicit—as a leverage, is it possible for an Indian manufacturer to develop world-class capabilities in running its business?

The Indian Market: a Hard Battleground

A developing country can be a hard battleground for a manufacturer. The incomes are low and the consumers are a demanding lot. The exchange rates are unfriendly for importing advanced technology and equipment. A number of times, these constraints come in the way of a manufacturer reaching global scales of operation.

However, there is an alternate point of view that states that developing economies—with their attendant constraints—are the cauldrons for brewing up innovations in products and processes that could be key to an organization's success in the twenty-first century. John Seely Brown and John Hagel are of the opinion that multinational organisations need to stop viewing developing markets in an 'imperialistic' fashion, that is, as a market to sell products developed for consumers in the home country. In fact, multinational companies—a case in point here being the automotive companies—have often got their fingers burned in trying to introduce older or outdated models in the Indian market and hoping for quick incremental sales. Instead they need to move towards a radical new approach to developing products and processes tailored for the specific country which it is trying to address. The rewards for doing this, they state, are the adoption of new business practices which may well save the day for the company in a global market.

Examples of such practices are India's very own Ranbaxy which used an unique patent regime to manufacture protected drugs at extremely low cost. Ranbaxy differentiated itself from a hundred other domestic pharmaceutical firms who were essentially doing the same thing, by investing in sophisticated research capabilities and state-of-the-art factories where a new drug could be synthesised and productionised at high speed. After India signed on with the WTO regime, Ranbaxy realised that the same strengths could be utilised to manufacture drugs going off-patent in developed countries. The pursuance of this strategy, along with strategic acquisitions in the US market, has made it one of the world's top ten generics manufacturers.

Drawing parallels with another sector in another country, HSBC's current success is owed in large measure to its innovative strategies in dealing with smaller deposits of its clients in Hong Kong which made it learn to operate with a much lower cost-to-income ratio than other global banks. This operating discipline, coupled with its trade finance capabilities that go back to the bank's origins, helped fuel its expansion into markets in the Western hemisphere and become one of the largest financial institutions in the world.

Ratan Tata's ambitious plan for the Rupees-One-Lakh car is another example of how companies seek to innovate when faced with challenging conditions in the domestic market. As of this point in time, it remains to be seen whether these particular ambitions gain fruition.

Manufacturing Excellence: Contribution of the ICT Sector

No doubt manufacturing excellence can be gained by initiatives in many directions. In this chapter we concentrate on how the specific skills in which we have gained in ICT can be used to develop world-class capabilities in Indian manufacturers.

The arena of ICT development for India is once again a much discussed topic. It stands as a sterling example of how rational policies matched with an entrepreneurial private sector can achieve quantum leaps in growth, employment and productivity. Economists like Diana Farrell points out the possibilities of achieving similar gains in other sectors by a mix of policy and direction-setting. In fact, she observes that India's automobile sector is already an example of how the correct direction has set the stage for growth in the range of 15–20 per cent per annum.

However, going beyond policy prescriptions, the services success story has possibly had a larger impact on the Indian psyche and attitude. As Gurcharan Das points out in his book, *India Unbound*, Indians have 'decolonised' their minds. This infusion of a can-do attitude is surely the seed capital for the development of entrepreneurship.

What then are the strengths developed in the ICT—implicit and explicit—sector that can be translated into real skills for manufacturing?

Ease in Technology Usage

Since the establishment of the Indian Institutes of Technology in the 1950s following the recommendations of the Sarkar Committee, India has steadily invested in and harvested the benefits of trained technical manpower. This has directly benefited the manufacturing sector in terms of skills in product and process technology. The availability of skilled technical manpower also gave ICT development in the country a momentum which has been kept going by the annual availability of 400,000 graduate engineers.

The service sector success story has generated a large degree of comfort with technological tools for Indian businesses. From a point of time even a decade ago where all calls for computerisation brought forth strident protests from labour unions, it is now at a stage where most Indian manufacturing companies have a technology policy in place and are confident of having the requisite skills available to implement the solution they need. Even in the public domain, central and state governments are increasingly under pressure to define a technology policy and adopt technology initiatives—even in the heartland of rural India.

Thinking on a Global Scale

'The Indian Multinational' seems to be the new business entity on the block. Bolstered by our success in the services arena, Indian organisations are redrafting their business strategies in the context of the global market. The examples for this abound from the success of Asian Paints and the Tata group in acquiring companies abroad to the aforementioned success of Ranbaxy in gaining a foothold in the US market. The success stories span industry sectors including companies as diverse as Moser-Baer, Bharat Forge, Sundaram Clayton and Hero Honda.

This is not to say that all of these companies have moved operations overseas or have acquired operations abroad. But these organisations are 'global' in more fundamental ways. They serve global customers—most of them serve customers in dispersed geographies. They operate globally—their operations are organised to serve their customers across the planet. And perhaps most significantly, they benchmark globally, they compare themselves to international standards of operation, whether in cost (Tata Steel), or size (Bharat Forge) or quality (Sundaram Clayton).

In reality, we still have a way to go, for example, it will take Tata Consultancy Services another six–seven years to get into Fortune 500 with the present minimum qualifications and current growth rates. But Indian manufacturers have woken up to the fact that the world is knocking on their door and they need to develop the tools to beat the global corporations at their own game.

A Habit of Innovation

Practically every venture the service sector considers is an innovation over existing business practices. Whether it is call centre and business process outsourcing or medical transcription, the offshoring of the business implies a new approach to doing things. The momentum of innovation has moved from large-scale ventures sponsored by corporates like General Electric to smaller, more entrepreneurial ventures by small and medium-sized businesses—a case in point being the recent trend for online tuition services being offered out of India to schoolgoing children in the United States.

Innovation in one sector can foster innovation in related sectors. At the height of the dotcom craze, a number of Indian companies started thinking about ways in which e-business could be harnessed to make fundamental changes in the ways they ran their businesses. Spurred in part by the small but significant number of employees choosing to leave the industry to set up their own dotcom businesses, some established players even encouraged their employees to come forward with viable business plans for using ICT or, more specifically, Internet-based technologies to change the existing business model.

Of course, subsequently, the dotcom bubble burst in a spectacular manner—however, the injection of fresh ideas into the old ways of doing business had a ripple effect in spreading innovation into various aspects of the way these organisations ran their businesses.

As we will see in subsequent discussions, the culture of thinking differently impacts the manufacturing sector profoundly —using our strengths in ICT, Indian manufacturers are experimenting with their business models to see what works best. All of the arrows they shoot into the air may not find their mark but even if only a certain percentage does, it could give Indian manufacturers a valuable edge in the global marketplace.

ICT in the Manufacturing Value Chain

Together the gains from ICT form a virtuous cycle of being able to access technological tools, being able to benchmark ourselves at a global level and to be able to think 'outside the box' on matters that ultimately constitute business survival.

In order to narrow this phenomenon down to its detailed application, this chapter takes the approach of deconstructing the value chain elements of an organisation and looking at how ICT has enhanced the operations at each of these stages. Primarily these relate to:
- research and development;
- sourcing and procurement;
- manufacturing;
- logistics and distribution; and
- sales and customer management.

ICT in Enabling Research and Development

Innovation and development form the starting point of mapping an organisation's value chain. Till a couple of decades ago, the debate around India was one of the great brain drain—in essence, how India's best brains were increasingly being lured to foreign shores to provide intellectual horsepower to the Western economies, notably the US.

From there to the current situation is a sea change. What started out as outsourcing for processing of low end transactions has gradually become offshoring of higher end research work that can be done at a fraction of the cost in India. Technological integration with project teams around the world is possible with advanced team management software and communication facilities.

Texas Instruments was one of the first multinationals to tap India in 1985, after which came companies like GE, Motorola, Intel and Philips, followed by IBM and Cisco. Even smaller MNCs like Techbooks and Google are now making a beeline for India. These set-ups are fast becoming centres of innovation, and attaining a far greater importance in the larger scheme of things. For example, IBM set up India Research Labs in 1998, and today more than 70 researchers are working on projects ranging from bioinformatics to media mining, from eCoupons to grid computing and speech recognition for Indian languages. A lot of the technology developed in IRL is crucial to IBM products globally.

The Intel research and development centre in Bangalore has started a Wi-Fi mobility design centre that's working on chipsets with 2006 time frames. Clearly, this is not about merely shifting low-end jobs, but about producing cutting-edge workout of India. At Motorola's research and development facility in Bangalore, a 1200-strong workforce works on 3G phones, Bluetooth technology and CDMA infrastructure development projects. The number of researchers has been on the upswing, as are investment numbers.

What has been the contribution of ICT to this? In a nutshell, ICT has made possible the phenomenon of globally dispersed research teams working in tandem to realise a common objective. The realisation that locating research teams in India could give companies quality research at a fraction of the cost went hand in hand with the development of computing and communication technology that could integrate the workings of a dispersed research team.

What does this mean for domestic manufacturers? The pragmatists are quick to point out that much of the research work that is being done in India is the sort that is funded and utilised by large multinational organisations in global initiatives. Our homegrown organisations are unlikely to fork out resources for such nature of work; so in terms of skills there is a mismatch.

This may be true. However, this chapter argues that the concentration and development of research skills will have a spillover into other areas. Indian manufacturers already have established skills in process, product and capital engineering. In the case of the automotive industry, suppliers developed by global automakers have consistently developed lower cost products for them—the McKinsey Quarterly cites the example of one such supplier who designed a new steering system in six months for an automaker who had been trying for four years to develop the same thing in other low cost countries.

Recognition of skills in these areas have led to setting up of initiatives like the GM Engineering and development centres being set up by General Motors in India in partnership with the Tata Group of companies. The influx of serious capital in developing India's research talent can only help to create a knowledge base that helps the domestic manufacturers as well.

The auto components industry is a particularly good example of how this works. This sector more than any other, has been proactive in implementing world-class quality standards in its manufacturing processes—a testament to the fact that a number of the prestigious Deming prize winners come from this sector of industry. Serving a clientele which consists of some the world's largest automobile companies, the auto components manufacturers were forced to take a closer look at developing design and development capabilities—this was one of the ways they could differentiate themselves from other second tier or first tier manufacturers. For example, Deming prize-winner Sona Koyo's foray into design and development started off with the establishment of a small independent engineering outfit to cater to the requests of international customers. In three years it has moved from doing basic IT work to much more complex reverse engineering solutions for clients. This is true for a number of other players in the auto components industry. Bharat Forge has invested in design and development capabilities and in setting up the largest single location forging plant in the world to speeden up the marketing process—from a global standard of 6 – 12 months to just 3 – 4 weeks.

As a natural consequence of the momentum being generated in the design and development space and the concurrent availability of higher-end research skills, it is but a matter of time before Indian manufacturer's begin to leverage higher-end research and development talent in earnest.

ICT in Enabling Sourcing and Procurement

Procurement is the key value chain activity that relates to the sourcing of raw materials for an organisation's factories and subsequent distribution. In India, the procurement activities have always been hampered by poor integration of the supply chain, which is an outcome of business practices as well as owing to the technological backbone being used.

In business-to-business procurement, for instance, the enabling ICT technology for integrated supplier management has been available for quite a while. Indian corporates are familiar with practices like Just-In-Time inventory management which preaches the benefits of tighter supplier integration in achieving significant inventory reduction and enhancement of efficiency. However, only a small number of Indian manufacturers report an extensive adoption of practices like Just-In-Time inventory management or extensive sharing of real time inventory data with their suppliers. The emphasis seems to lie rather more heavily on tracking supplier performance and measuring the real cost of supply. This would seem to suggest that Indian industry is still some distance away from achieving a significant degree of operational integration with their suppliers, irrespective of available technology.

However, an area of procurement where ICT is likely to have a more lasting impact is in the area of sourcing of raw materials in foodstuffs. Here the procurement operations are hampered by the lack of information, the poor transportation and storage facilities, absence of scientific inspection and grading standards and the sheer geographical size of rural India. Processed foods companies perforce have to operate through mandi agents, thereby paying a high margin for goods of uneven quality.

One of the landmark initiatives in this direction is the much-lauded e-Choupal model, launched by ITC to enhance its soya procurement operations in rural India. The e-Choupal model, which bypasses the traditional mandi-based buying and selling, is conceptualised as a gateway to give the farmer better pricing information so he can take a more optimal selling decision, enable transparency in the measuring, grading and weighing of the product and provide other services which a village trader normally provides to the farmer, e.g., selling seeds, fertilizers, and providing crop/weather information.

The core idea behind the initiative is essentially a network of information centres (e-Choupals) consisting of a computer with an Internet connection located in each farming community. The *sanchalak* or coordinator has the prime responsibility of running and maintaining the e-Choupal outlet in the village. The second key agent in the system is the local commission agent or *samyojak* who provides the logistics support at the procurement hub.

The farmer can check the previous day's mandi closing price on e-Choupal. This price is inputted by the commission agents at the mandi and is typically a Fair to Average Quality price. If interested in selling, the farmer presents a sample of his crop to the *sanchalak*, who inspects it and gives a conditional quote to the farmer.

The farmer can then transport his crop to the nearest ITC procurement hub, where, after further quality tests and weighing of the produce, he may collect his payment in full, as well as the reimbursement for his transportation costs from village to mandi.

Farmers benefit from access to information on market prices and other related information, faster processing time, prompt payment and accurate weighing of produce. At the same time, ITC benefits from net procurement costs that are lower as compared to operating through mandi agents and it has more direct control over the quality of what it buys.

The e-Choupal is also used to order seed, fertiliser, and other products such as consumer goods from ITC or its partners, at prices lower than those available from village traders. Increasingly, the e-Choupal is being used by other consumer goods and services companies to sell their products — a case in point in the selling of rural insurance by ICICI through the portal. ITC has plans to continue the proliferation of e-Choupals, such that a farmer need travel no more than five kilometres to reach one.

No doubt the e-Choupal initiative is a watershed in the use of ICT to procure (and sell) agricultural goods. But it is by no means the only initiative trying to use ICT to forge better links with rural India. A case in point is the development of the Akashganga solution to automate the milk collection process at the dairy cooperatives that form the backbone of the successful Milk Cooperative movement in India.

The Akashganga solution, developed by Shree Kamdhenu Electronics, consists of an integrated milk collection and processing system consisting of an electronic weighing system, a milk analyzer, a personal computer and accounting and management software. A faster and more accurate milk collection process ensures that the milk can be collected and quickly sent on to the cooperative union for processing, thereby reducing wastage of milk considerably; the transparency of milk quality analysis increases the trust the participating farmers have in the process and finally, an added incentive is the prompt payment for collected milk. Local cooperatives can be run more efficiently with fewer employees but with more enhanced reporting and planning records.

Currently, Akashganga has upwards of 600 installations, the bulk of them in the states of Gujarat and Maharashtra. The company is also in the process of developing an integrated milk supply chain management software, which aims to integrate the milk societies, milk unions and milk federations on a single technological platform.

As these initiatives show, the pace of procurement from rural India is likely to be picked up by the specific deployment of ICT technology. It may be argued that not only will this technology enhance the procurement functions, but will also improve the system when it comes to selling products and services to the rural customer. We will take a renewed look at this in the sales and customer management section.

ICT in Enabling Manufacturing

Arun Shourie, in his term in the ministry of disinvestment, compiled a list of Indian manufacturers who have reached excellent scale of operations—possibly to silence those who felt that Indian manufacturing had lost out to the globalising world or to the factories of China or both. There were a number of surprises on the list for almost everyone but what was possibly even more surprising was how the list seemed to cut across industry sectors, ranging from fields as diverse as steel to electronics to high-precision technology. It would seem, on first principles, that irrespective of the macroeconomics, India does possess a number of outstanding manufacturers whose manufacturing operations can justifiably be called world-class.

When one looks at the value chain of Indian manufacturers, the thing that strikes the observer the most is how, for some time, most of the investment in technology and advanced equipment has been used to enhance manufacturing capability. Faced with an external world consisting of unreliable transportation, insufficient infrastructure capacity and undeveloped vendor/reseller capability, the manufacturers did the only thing they could to ensure quality in operations—turned their manufacturing into 'islands of excellence' with as much independent operations as was possible.

Assessments of supply chain maturity for Indian manufacturers bear this out; typically a significant number of companies report extensive adoption of advanced practices in manufacturing, in particular those stressing on preventive maintenance, focused factory production systems, quality control and quick changeover. There is great focus on improving metrics like manufacturing cycle time with practices like JIT, constraint based planning and focused factory production systems having the maximum impact. At the same time, manufacturers report actively exploring options for contract manufacturing and outsourcing to reduce costs and enhance productivity.

The investment in manufacturing excellence is borne out by the high numbers of Deming prize-winners being nominated from India. The Deming prize is the highest award for manufacturing excellence and the growing numbers of Indian winners point to the overall maturation of manufacturing processes.

The overall manufacturing maturity has to go apace with investment in ICT tools. Each of these manufacturers have invested or are investing in tools that enable them to reach higher standards of manufacturing excellence. For example, Enterprise Resource Planning software have become de rigeur for most manufacturers to assist in planning for manufacture. The factory shop floors are enabled by various categories of manufacturing execution systems and there has been a trend by specific manufacturers (Asian Paints, GNPL, Marico) to implement advanced planning and scheduling software for more advanced capabilities.

Interest still remains high, however, in use of ICT for optimisation of specific manufacturing dimensions. These set of problems represent industry-specific optimisation issues (waste minimisation, order queuing, routing optimisation) which needs to marry operational research techniques with technology know-how. Possibly this is one area where more ground-up ICT development will take place in the future.

For a large number of medium-to-small sized manufacturing enterprises, however, the prohibitive costs of licensed high-end software act as a deterrent for adoption of advanced IT packages. Also, the need for custom-built packages that address more completely the needs of the specific industry vertical are required since the small and Medium businesses (SMBs) cannot afford to spend large amounts on implementation, customisation and support.

A number of global and local players are looking to cash in on this market and provide enterprise software that can be used by medium-sized enterprises. However indigenous skills in custom software development keep warring with the complete ERP (Enterprise Resource Planning) package vendors for a share of the SMB pie — of the 35 per cent or so SMB organisations involved in enterprise implementation, only about a third have chosen packaged ERP solutions (Gartner, 'Moving up the Value Chain, *Business World,* February 2003).

Quantum jumps in manufacturing productivity in future will not owe as much to ICT as to canny business strategy and the ability to identify a manufacturing opportunity. In specific niches like manufacturing constraint optimisation or SMB enterprise resource planning, ICT can still make a difference but its overall impact will not be as large when compared to some of the other value chain activities.

ICT in Enabling Logistics and Distribution

Logistics and distribution has typically been one of the primary areas affected by India's lack of enabling supply chain infrastructure. Transit time variability is extremely high in India, leading to often significant delays in shipment. This in turn results in buffers of inventory being held all the way along the chain to provide against the uncertainties of transport.

The ICT technologies in this part of the value chain, therefore, go to enhance visibility and tracking and generating early warnings of supply chain failures. Investments in ICT in this segment have largely been done by the Third Party Logistics service providers since they, almost as a majority, handle the shipments for Indian organisations across the country.

A large part of ICT usage for these vendors till date has been in developing customer front-ends which the customer can use to track the delivery of a package. This can range from individual customers tracking their packages on the Internet to large corporations tracking their consignments across the country in order to make timely deliveries to their customers. Before the Internet era, many logistic vendors had to provide the requisite hardware for customers to connect to their systems. After the Internet revolution, vendors launched their own websites. It became possible for many customers to integrate their logistics information with supply chains, incorporating stock-in-transit information into their production cycles.

Technology is also used by logistic vendors internally to plan their deliveries in a more efficient manner. This may range from use of technology to sort packages or shipments or for obtaining real-time information which can lead to more efficient vehicle utilisation and routing. For instance, FedEx has a fleet of about 700 aircrafts. Technology provides them with real-time information about weather conditions and airport closures helping them plan package delivery better.

Some of the particular problems encountered by logistic vendors have led them to develop their own technology solution in-house or in collaboration with software vendors. There is a general perception that the complex business requirements and the required flexibility are better managed by a dedicated team of developers rather than rely on packaged software. Blue Dart, for instance, has a quick response team, which studies the business requirements of its customers and develops appropriate solutions. Logistics Company TNT Corp. (TNT), again, has an in-house development team based out of Atherston in the UK to develop location-specific solutions for its own offices. The IT department of FedEx has a partnership with Mphasis in India where a team of professionals work on a number of IT projects. It has also supplied handheld pocket PCs to all couriers to help them advice customers on service availability and country-specific documentation.

Additionally, recent approaches to the use of ICT in logistics management have focused on more specific problems in tracking goods consignments across the country. Almost every manufacturer has faced the problem of vehicle tracking across India—a truck leaving a factory in Bangalore may or may not show up in three–four days in north India. In any case, all the information comes to the company later, there is absolutely no information en route.

An estimated 2.5–3 million trucks criss-cross the country every day, carrying a wide basket of products. Trucks in India log 300 km a day against 800 km in developed countries, which means that two–three days of country's production is locked up in idle time. Even a small order of increase in the productivity of the trucks would garner significant savings for the nation as a whole.

Vehicle tracking solutions aim to solve this problem. First generation products of data logging were a start although this had limitations as data would be logged on the device in a truck and could be downloaded only after the vehicle reached its destination.

Second generation products in the form of infra-red towers also were not workable as huge investments were required to set up the towers along the highways to track the vehicles. The third-generation product involved GPS/GSM models with fixed software—this was found to be an expensive option. Current ranges of products have tried to match the GPS/GSM models but adapted to be a cheaper and more flexible solution with two-way interaction between the truck owner and the driver all through the journey. There are plans to upgrade these solutions through the use of telematics or voice communication and remote control of temperature in the vehicles, which is important for trucks carrying refrigerated products. A number of vendors are working on solutions in this market and this area will possibly see more innovation on the product front in the future.

Clearly for logistic vendors (third party logistics service providers like courier services and distribution companies), investment in ICT is a way of staying ahead in the game—as Indian companies expand their businesses across the country and the continents, their dependence on logistic vendors is bound to increase. Technology will be a key enabler for logistic vendors to differentiate themselves from their competitors.

ICT in Sales and Customer Management

Till few years ago, significant usage of ICT in Sales and Customer Management was restricted to service enterprises like banks in their targeting of the urban middle-class consumer. Using internally developed or off-the-shelf packaged customer management software, banks and other service organisations set up their call centres to interact with their consumers and subsequently, build up customer databanks which would be used in a number of sales functions from prospecting to collections.

For manufacturing enterprises, most of which have multi-tiered distribution networks to reach the final consumer, traditional usage of Customer Relationship Management (CRM) software is limited by the nature of the business model. However, the area of significant gain in this instance has been the use of ICT to manage the sales and distribution network itself.

A slew of ICT initiatives by Indian manufacturers have centred on solutions to manage distribution intermediaries like dealers and distributors as well as to provide adequate ICT support to the sales force to do their job more efficiently.

Fast Moving Consumer Goods (FMCG) companies like Hindustan Lever Ltd (HLL) have implemented distributor management software to track sales and product movements across the country. Hindustan Lever's RSNet solution, which connects the enterprise to its 3500-odd stockists, aims to support Hindustan Lever's growth by ensuring product availability and outlet-wise sales tracking throughout the country. Currently, the system covers about 80 per cent of its revenue base with varying degrees of connectivity.

On the other hand, automobile companies have implemented dealer management systems to cope with sales and inventory of automobiles as well as the host of post-sales activities that relate to the sale of a single automobile. This may relate to warranty administration, defect tracking, spare parts management, etc. Very often, a tighter control over these will mean a healthier chunk of profits for the auto maker.

If successfully implemented, the DMS can have a positive effect on almost anything from sales forecasting, inventory management to cash management and order fulfilment. Implementation of dealer management systems however, have been hampered by a number of issues. One of these is the whole question of connectivity from dispersed dealerships across India. This will, however, progressively get resolved and is currently not a major factor for most of the major dealers of a typical manufacturing-distribution company. Other issues like the dealers' perception of the imposition of the manufacturer's agenda and the sharing of the system costs require more careful navigation —a successful negotiation on these issues can mean the difference between a successful or a failed system implementation.

The other area of interest in terms of ICT usage is the use of technology to enhance the efficiency of the sales force. The salesperson on the move in the market needs to be in touch with the factory or the warehouse to monitor product availability and financial status. The ICT solutions in this area have ranged from using SMS technology linked to the ERP to push information to the salesperson's mobile phone (Dabur) to the use of PDAs with customised applications that capture relevant information on stocks, sales, financial information and outlet management (ITC, HLL). While the hand-held devices do not aim to completely replace products like the laptop computer, products like the Simputer (developed in the Indian Institute of Science, Bangalore) aim to provide basic laptop-type functionality at a fraction of the cost, along with linguistic support that could be invaluable in a country like India.

The dealer management and sales force automation solutions extends the connectivity one step further in the distribution chain but it is a far cry from reaching the final consumer. In truth, the connectivity to the final consumer is a tricky question when one talks about the rural Indian heartland. The cost of extending contact with customers over a vast and dispersed country is often prohibitive and presents difficult logistical challenges.

One of the examples of ICT usage in this area that stands out is not a manufacturer's initiative, but it probably deserves mention as it deals with the same challenge and innovative response that has characterised some of the other examples discussed previously.

The ASAN Automated Teller Machine (ATM), which has been specially designed for rural India by NCR Corporation, has been implemented in some sample locations by ICICI Bank. The ATM, which has been designed partly based on inputs from the Industrial Design Centre at IIT, Mumbai, incorporates an Intelligent Power Management (NIPM) system which ensures that the ATM completes the ongoing transaction in case of power failure, useful for areas witnessing power outages.

The special adaptability of the ATM to rural India as well as its low cost of installation and operation, has made it one of the planks of ICICI's strategy for rural India. ICICI has now launched the Kisan Loan Card which enables farmers to obtain loans and withdraw cash through the ASAN ATMs.

Here, as in other examples above, innovative use of ICT technology has provided a cost-effective route for a company to provide accessibility to its customers and deliver a higher quality of service.

In Conclusion...

The examples illustrated earlier represent a vanguard of change. Individually, they represent instances of specific problem solving by Indian manufacturers. However, taken together, they point to a specific trend of skills and learnings moving from the 'knowledge' sectors to the more traditional manufacturing sectors, resulting in solutions crafted more innovatively and better tailored to meet India's needs.

However, some of these initiatives may be isolated, may be still under development, and may be limited to high-visibility sectors like FMCG or automotive only. Certainly, ICT cannot be a panacea for all the ills that dog the manufacturing sector's footstep; it cannot provide a solution for the erratic power and gridlocked infrastructure.

However, there seems to be an increasing recognition of what ICT can give the manufacturing sector—a chance to think about its business differently. Using the expertise built up by years of technical education and comfort with advanced software, Indian manufacturers are in a very strong position to innovate and develop new solutions for themselves that can jump-start their competitiveness in the global market.

The initiatives highlighted in the earlier section are but an illustration of the changes happening in the sectors. Regardless of the relative impact of these, it points to a willingness to experiment with ICT in manufacturing that bodes well for India's future. It remains to the shrewd manufacturer-marketer to take advantage of this and forge ahead.

References

Annamalai, Kuttayan and Sachin Raowhat. 2003. 'What Works: ITC's E-Choupal and Profitable Rural Transformation', Web-Based Information and Procurement Tools for Indian Farmers, August.

Balasubramanian, Ramnath and Ashutosh Padhi. 2005. 'The Next Wave in US Offshoring', *The Mckinsey Quarterly*, no. 1.

Brown, John Seely and John III Hagel. 2005. Innovation Blowback: Disruptive Management Practices from Asia, *The Mckinsey Quarterly*, no. 1.

Chandra, Pankaj and Trilochan Sastry. Competitiveness of Indian Manufacturing: Findings of the 2001 National Manufacturing Survey, Working Paper no. 2002-09-04, Indian Institute of Management, Ahmedabad.

Cohen, Nevin. 2001. Grameen Telecom's Village Phones: A Digital Dividend Study by the World Resources Institute, June.

Farrell, Diana, and Adil S. Zainulbhai. 2004. 'A Richer Future for India', The *Mckinsey Quarterly*, Special Edition: 'What Global Executives Think'.

Goswami, Arun, Gantakolla, More, Mookherjee, (CII) and Dollar, Mengistae, Hallward-Driemier, Iarossi (World Bank); Competitiveness of Indian Manufacturing: Results from a Firm-Level Survey, January 2002.

Grover, S.P.S. 2004. 'Tailoring ERP for Micro-Verticals', *Express Computer*, June.

Gulyani, Sumila. 1999. 'Innovating with Infrastructure: How India's Largest Carmaker Copes with Poor Electricity Supply', *World Development*, vol. 27, no. 10, pp. 1749–68.

Huyett, William I. and Patrick S. Viguerie. 2005. 'Extreme Competition', The *Mckinsey Quarterly*, no.1.

Joseph, K.J. and Patarapong Intarakumnerd. 'GPTs and Innovation Systems in Developing Countries: a Comparative Analysis of ICT Experiences in India and Thailand'.

Krause, Daniel R. and Robert B. Handfield. 'Developing a World-Class Supply Base', Center for Advanced Purchasing Studies, Michigan State University.

Luthra, Shashank, Ramesh Mangaleswaran and Ashutosh Padhi. 2005. 'When to Make India a Manufacturing Base', *The Mckinsey Quarterly*, Special Edition: 'Fulfilling India's Promise'.

'Moving up the Value Chain'. 2003. *Business World*, February.

Prahalad, C.K. and Allen Hammond. 'What Works: Serving the Poor, Profitably—a Private Sector Strategy for Global Digital Opportunity', The Markle Foundation, World Resources Institute.

Roach, Stephen S. 2004. 'India's Policy Paradox', *Business World*, November.

Sharma, Ajay and Akhilesh Yadav. 2003. 'Akashganga's It Tools For The Indian Dairy Industry: Using It To Increase Efficiency In Rural Dairy Cooperatives', *What Works*, August.

Shourie, Arun. 'Before the Whining Drowns It Out, Listen to the New India', arunshourie.voiceofdharma.com

____. 'When the Sky is the Limit', arunshourie.voiceofdharma.com

Sinha, Jayant. 2005. 'Global Champions from Emerging Markets', Mckinsey Quarterly, *no. 2.*

Tipson, Frederick S. and Claudia Frittelli. 2003. 'Global Digital Opportunities: National Strategies of "ICT for Development"', Markle Foundation, December.

4

Achieving Best Practice in Business and Closing the Marketing Gap

Prashant Salwan

Achieving Best Practice in Business

An Introduction to E-business

Over the last few years, companies of all sizes and types have made great strides in adopting technology. Internet access and e-mail are now an everyday part of our working lives, while extranets and mobile communications are beginning to transform the way we work internally, and with our customers and suppliers.

The challenges facing businesses now are how to help their staff get the most out of existing technology and how to prioritise further investment, balancing the benefits of integration with the costs and potential risks of dramatic change.

I will try to show that any business can work more efficiently by using technology. My report will cover the benefits of using technology in all areas of business.

The Business Mix

Design and Product Development

Electronic communications can help you dramatically speed up the design process by enabling clients, suppliers and employees to work together better.

Design and production is all about close collaboration and teamwork. It is an ongoing process of continuous refinement, approval stages and tight deadlines. New ways of sharing information and working together can simplify this process.

Cut time, not corners.

Share every aspect of the development process—documents, images, designs, project plans and technical data—amongst a project team, regardless of where its members are based. E-mail lets you send documents anywhere in the world instantly. Many common software packages have document management and version control facilities that track changes and approvals, and let several people work on the same file at the same time.

Meetings with Travel

Some things are best dealt with face-to-face. However, the cost and time involved in gathering together people from different locations can be prohibitive. Video and data conferencing offers a way round this, putting people in touch by video link.

File Sharing

An extranet is effectively a website with restricted access. If you already have a website, then at low cost you can build an extranet to share files, like high resolution photos, Computer Aided Design/Computer Aided Manufacturing (CAD/CAM) files or presentations, which are too large to e-mail to clients. Using proper security measures, an extranet is suitable for even the most sensitive and confidential information.

Sharing Information

Sharing manufacturing information can speed up the production process without harming quality control. For example, using a Virtual Private Network (VPN) to share your production plans with suppliers lets them adjust their stock levels and processes accordingly. This can result in shorter lead times and make just-in-time deliveries possible.

Let us study the case of Phoenix Precision. Phoenix Precision, which manufactures sheet metal enclosures for electronic companies, has used technology to streamline its whole design and production process. Computers are networked and staff use e-mail for sending and receiving quotations, photographs and drawings. An integrated module-based software system handles stock control, invoicing, estimating, costing and purchasing, with scope to add e-commerce modules.

'Our niche is small to medium-sized OEMs (Original Equipment Manufacturers) who might put out a million pounds worth of sheet metal per year and we might get a third of that business,' explains George Grainger, Managing Director. 'The 3D drawings which are mailed by the respective departments, customers and are fed to a CAD/CAM system to produce a prototype and engineers progress further and incorporate changes as desired by the project through the e-mailed exchange of drawings.' 'More than 60 per cent of our jobs come in on e-mail and the percentage increases every year,' says George.

A dedicated ISDN line is set aside for videoconferencing and Phoenix's website provides customers with a comprehensive service portfolio.

'The engineering package saves us so much time,' says George. 'We take a 3D model drawing directly into our system. It's getting to a stage where a customer doesn't send us dimensions with their drawing. They are so confident that if their draft is correct, our tooling will automatically tool that part to the right dimension. We achieve the same turnover with three engineers that we used to achieve with four. The production process would be impossible without our CAD/CAM, e-mail and integrated management system.' E-mailed drawings can be turned into parts by the next day.

Phoenix has invested around £70,000 on technology over the years to tackle the varied technology needs of its supply chain partners. 'Originally the aim was to organise ourselves as a company internally, but we made sure we put in a scalable system which could move outwards into supply chain management.'

Future projects include collecting shop floor data and introducing barcoding to track and record jobs efficiently, enabling the website to handle transactions, and installing a new broadband telephone system.

Operations

> **CASE STUDY**   **Box 4.1**
>
> ### Chance and Hunt
>
> Chance & Hunt has embraced technology right across its business producing new service offerings and an extensive degree of supply chain integration.
>
> The company, which markets and distributes chemicals, is using a telemetry system to manage its clients' inventories. This system constantly monitors client inventories checking stock levels against optimum levels. Should stocks fall below this level, the system delivers alerts to the client budget holders and relevant sales staff, before channelling orders back to Chance & Hunt's internal systems.
>
> Chance & Hunt's recent investment in technology includes the infrastructure to provide remote network access, online credit card purchasing and an integrated ordering system that checks stock and links to the warehouse, which has reduced processing time and has speedened up dispatch.
>
> Last year the company saw profits grow by 5 per cent. This was higher than the industry average, something that Chance & Hunt attributes to its technology infrastructure. This has resulted in more efficient order processing, more sales leads, improved customer service and satisfaction, and reduced administrative burden allowing reassignment of staff to sales work.
>
> Chance & Hunt also uses a Customer Relationship Management (CRM) system. This provides valuable information about customers' buying patterns and enables customer profiling, contact management and campaign management. It also invested in a Virtual Private Network (VPN), which gives staff working remotely dial-up access to in-house systems.
>
> With an eye on the future, Chance & Hunt has run a series of EDI (Electronic Data Interchange) trials, linking its systems with those of key suppliers. The company is sure that, in the long term, supply chain integration will be an important source of competitive advantage.
>
> Chance & Hunt doesn't see technology investment in isolation, but believes it will deliver growth, cut costs, improve service, help win

> new business and build its brand. Dr Peter Fields, the Managing Director, explains: 'E-business is embedded in the business plan and strategy. E-business is a fundamental enabler of the total business which helps to grow sales and cut costs.
>
> Source: DTI

If you are looking to create a more flexible workforce, use information more intelligently or manage your processes better, technology can help you create a leaner, more focused operation.

Storage and Retrieval

Computers have brought massive storage benefits—a single CD-Rom can hold 300,000 pages of text, and a database can draw together information from across the business. However, the absence of a single, physical location for information can cause problems with duplication of work, the inability to find the right file or the use of out-of-date documents.

Investing in document management software or an intranet can remedy these problems. They allow staff to store documents in one location where several people can work on them at the same time. Alternatively, a simple cost-effective way to improve access to electronic information is by creating a filing and archiving procedure, setting out where staff must store files and how they should title them.

Relational Databases

If your business has many different sets of data or regularly changes price or product information, you could take one step further and invest in a relational database. This ensures that if you make a change in the pricing section of the database, that change is also made automatically in the accounts, invoicing, stock and other price-related areas too. It makes it quicker and easier to update information, and your business can make better use of more accurate data.

Internal Communication

An intranet is a network whose use is restricted to the staff of the same company. Its main purpose is to share information and computing resources among employees. Depending on your needs and budget an intranet can be used simply to store contact details, corporate news and company forms, or as a complicated workflow management programme.

Workflow

Companies with complex internal procedures or important quality control processes could invest in workflow management software to link and control the different stages and documents. This would ensure that correct processes are followed, and allow management control and review.

Flexible Working

E-mail and Internet access means your staff can now work much more flexibly. With the right security arrangements, they can work on-site, on the move or from home. The increasing availability and popularity of mobile communications, such as Personal Digital Assistant (PDAs) and Wap phones, also means it is much easier to work away from the office without losing touch. Not only can this flexibility improve productivity, it can be an excellent way of attracting and retaining skilled staff, many of whom see the opportunity to work from home as a valuable benefit.

Purchasing

The Internet can widen your search for any product to a global level and help you make significant savings.

Effective purchasing means sourcing supplies at the best price — delivered on time, in the right amounts and to the right specification. Technology does not just give you access to a wider range of suppliers; it can change the way you buy and cut costs and paperwork.

Sourcing Supplies

Millions of businesses around the world now have websites. Everyone from the smallest niche suppliers to huge corporations promote their wares online. This gives you a simple way of investigating products and comparing prices to find the best deal.

Purchasing Alternatives

Increasingly, online marketplaces that aggregate supply or demand are springing up. This means small purchasers can cut costs with group discounts, while small producers can band together to pitch for larger contracts.

Some larger companies are also investing in online auctions to simplify their procurement process. This allows them to manage the whole bidding process electronically and negotiate discounts from suppliers.

Streamlining Transactions

Working electronically with your key suppliers can help cut time from the way you work and increase your efficiency, for example, by exchanging orders and invoices for automatic processing.

Transmitting data electronically including payment data, ensures tight, efficient control of the purchasing process and faster payment. Electronic Data Interchange (EDI) can streamline transactions, allowing faster and simpler processing with less paperwork and fewer mistakes. Electronic Point of Sale (EPOS) is also a useful way of getting products from your warehouse to your point of sale quickly. It is most useful for companies with many regular sales, or who have suppliers and customers that need fast, accurate product information.

CASE STUDY   Box 4.2
Clarkes Stationers

Clarkes, has really grasped technology to improve the way its supply chain works. As a result, the company's turnover has increased by 25 per cent and it has managed to crack the lucrative business market. Clarkes' website is an impressive e-commerce sales tool: 'We try to get all our business customers to order online. They can log on with a user name and password and get budgeting reports, customer history details, tailor-made pricing structures and bespoke products,' explains Clarkes' Sales Director Kiren Patel. When it comes to ordering from its own suppliers, Clarkes does that electronically too. The company is part of a buying consortium and all members have special software to connect into the purchasing system direct from their computers. Kiren continues: 'Online ordering is established for general stationery and computer consumables and contracts are arranged by our buying group—all communications in these areas are done via the web.' Launched in January 2002, the office intranet improves communication between staff members and sales representatives in the field, as well as cutting down on phone bills. Kiren has seen a change for the better in Clarkes' relationship with both customers and suppliers thanks to around £55,000 of technology investment over three years. 'Suppliers have opened up and offered us special deals for trying out their electronic ordering systems. And with customers it's the 'feel good' factor—we're now able to look after them better and give them a more personal service. We're all about having partnership relationships with our long-term customers and suppliers.' One big customer has put 20 per cent more business through Clarkes since it started ordering online. The website has also pulled in new customers, as Kiren explains: 'We've just picked up our largest customer to date because they saw the website and they called us in to tender. They knew we existed but hadn't realised our B2B (Business to Business) capabilities until they'd seen the site.'

Source: DTI

Using technology to get your message across to existing and new customers has never been easier, but this also means new ways of working. Technology is not a solution in itself but a way of enabling you to market your business more effectively and more widely. E-mail, websites and other new technologies are giving businesses better and more flexible ways to market their goods and services to customers.

E- marketing

What is E-marketing?

E-marketing means using digital technologies to help sell your goods or services. These technologies, like e-mail and websites, are a valuable complement to traditional marketing methods whatever be the size of the company or business model.

Customers Spend £1 billion a Month Online

Businesses spend £23 billion a year on goods and services.

The basics of marketing remain the same—creating a strategy to deliver the right messages to the right people. What has changed is the number of options you have. Simply put, e- marketing gives you lots of new ways to reach your customers, many of them cheaper and more effective than traditional channels.

British consumers now spend over £1 billion a month online—6 per cent of all UK retail sales. And half of all UK firms buy goods and services online, spending £23 billion in the process a year. In India the figure is approximately 2 per cent of the total amount spent on business. After introduction of Internet B2B management (business to business management), this figure will further increase.

Obviously, these figures do not tell the whole story. Not all sales made online are the result of e-marketing and not every business has benefited equally. What is certain though, is that many businesses are producing great results with e-marketing and its flexible and cost-effective nature makes it particularly suitable for small and medium-sized businesses.

The Benefits

It is no exaggeration to describe e-marketing as a revolution for the marketing industry. For the first time, it gives the businesses of any size access to the mass market at an affordable price and, unlike TV or print advertising, it allows truly personalised marketing. Specific benefits of e-marketing include: global reach, lower cost, trackable and measurable results, 24-hours marketing, shorter lead times, a level playing field, personalisation, one-to-one marketing, more interesting campaigns, better conversion rate, etc.

Global Reach

If you build a website you can reach anyone, anywhere in the world provided they have Internet access. This allows you to tap new markets and compete globally with only a small investment. This can be particularly useful for niche providers, companies whose products can be posted easily, or businesses that are looking to expand geographically but cannot afford to invest in new offices or businesses.

Lower Cost

A properly planned and effectively targeted e-marketing campaign can reach the right customers at a much lower cost than traditional marketing methods. You can build a website for as little as a few hundred pounds or send e-mail for a fraction of a penny.

Trackable and Measurable Results

Marketing by e-mail or banner advertising makes it easier to establish how effective your campaign has been. If someone clicks on a banner advert, or a link in an e-mail or on a website, you can see how they arrived at your website. This detailed information about customers' responses to your advertising allows you to assess the effectiveness of different campaigns.

Twenty-Four-Hours Marketing

With a website your customers can find out about your products even if your office is closed.

Shorter Lead Times

If you have a website or an e-mail template, you can react to events much more quickly giving your marketing a much more contemporary feel. If one of your products is in the news or something important happens in your industry, you can capitalise on it without having to print or post anything.

A Level Playing Field

With a well-designed website, you can show yourself to be as professional and credible as your larger competitors.

Personalisation

If your customer database is linked to your website, then whenever someone visits the site, you can greet them with targeted offers. The more they buy from you, the more you can refine your customer profile and market effectively to them. A great example of this is the Amazon website which suggests products based on your and other people's previous purchases.

One-to-One Marketing

E-marketing lets you reach people who want to know about your products and services instantly. You do not have to wait until they come home from work and switch on the TV or open their mail. People have a different, more personal relationship with most new technologies. For example, many people take mobile phones and PDAs wherever they go, and a surprising number feel lost without their e-mail. Combine this with the personalised aspect of e-marketing, and you can create very powerful and targeted campaigns.

More Interesting Campaigns

E-marketing lets you create interactive campaigns using music, graphics and videos. You could send your customers a game or a quiz whatever you think will interest them. One of the great successes of e-marketing has been film companies letting people download trailers for forthcoming movies. Other small companies have picked up this idea. A radio controlled car company sends customers designs or photos of new products in development while clothing companies send out sneak previews of the new seasons range.

Better Conversion Rate

If you have got a website, then your customers are only ever a few clicks away from completing a purchase. Unlike other media, which require people to get up and make a phone call, post a letter or go to a shop, e-marketing is seamless. The change from reading an e-mail to buying on a website is negligible. No special effort is required, meaning that your call to action can be much more direct.

Using its website, Mansfield Motors now trades globally, with customers as far a field as Borneo and Mongolia.

Effective Websites

Most UK companies have websites, though not all are getting the best from them. When people surf the net they tend to jump from page to page, skim reading to find the information they want. If you want them to linger, you need to review your site regularly to check that visitors can find what they want in the format they want it. Not everyone wants to read masses of material, so you could make information available in Portable Data Format (PDF) for them to download and print. Often simple oversights, like the lack of a telephone number or pages that don't work, can be enough to send users away. It is worth monitoring your competitors' sites to see what they offer and if you need to improve your site.

Targeting Prospects

Visitors to your website can give you a tremendous amount of valuable information. By offering prizes, discounts or premium content you could get them to fill out questionnaires or surveys. However, this kind of research should be a fair exchange—people will find it off-putting if you bombard them with questions or ask for too much information. If you intend to use personal information for marketing purposes, make sure you have a clear privacy policy.

New Marketing Channels

E-mail and SMS (short messaging service, otherwise known as text messaging) offer exciting new ways to reach customers. The increasing sophistication of mobile communications means that you could also consider MMS (multimedia messaging), which allows you to send images or video or music, alongside a text message. Unlike advertising or direct mail, these are very personal media. You can time when people receive the messages and, in the case of e-mail, monitor with whom they share this information. Most interestingly for businesses, bulk use of e-mail can reduce the cost of each message to only a few pence. The flipside of e-mail and SMS is the danger of overuse—irrelevant or constant marketing can provoke a strong negative reaction.

If you intend to run an e-mail campaign, you also need to have the facilities in place to handle the response. While you can encourage people to phone you or visit your website, many may want to reply by e-mail.

If you experience a surge in responses, using an automated e-mail reply will help you manage them without disappointing your customers.

CASE STUDY   **Box 4.3**

Antec International

Antec International has transformed itself from a supplier of disinfectants to a total bio security provider with specific experience in emergency disease control. Its website has been crucial in achieving this expansion. Antec's website is a vital resource for customers and allows Antec to respond quickly to the needs of its supply chain partners. The site provides information about all the products Antec distributes, and the pages are available in ten languages, including Japanese and Mandarin Chinese. Mark Blackwell, Antec's Marketing and International Sales Director explains: 'All enquiries from the site are automatically added to our database. The system logs which country the e-mail is from and sends an e-mail to the nearest distributor.' The site includes PowerPoint presentations, video clips and the Product Calculator, which suggests appropriate products for customers according to the user's country and bio security procedures. Antec's account customers have taken the online ordering and invoicing route. There are also secure areas specifically designed for partner distributors.

As a marketing tool, the site is invaluable. Mark says: 'The cost of delivering the same amount of information to the same people by other means would be enormous. The cost of a one-page ad in Pig International is $4,000 and that buys us a lot of web pages.' The site has improved Antec's communication with its distributors and changed the company's business model. 'Our distributors are now partners and engage in full two-way information exchange. Since we implemented the new model we've increased our export of healthy animal products by 80 per cent.' Antec has also cut the cost of distributing information to its 80 business partners around the world. 'We've developed our intranet to give instant access to product information. We used to spend three days photocopying press clippings and handouts to post to them. Now we just send out a weekly e-mail update.' Mark is bullish about the benefits of technology: 'Knowledge equates to power and if you don't invest in knowledge you will lose power and you'll lose your competitive edge.'

Source: DTI

Sales

On the Internet, your company website could enable customers to browse detailed descriptions of your products and prices, check delivery times and place orders. With appropriate security measures, you should also be able to accept payments online.

A Global Shop Window

Not all products and services lend themselves to e-commerce, but you can certainly use your website to stimulate interest in your business and help prospective customers through the buying cycle. This could include offering product specifications, detailed lists of frequently asked questions or video demonstrations of your products.

Making Sales

There are few more important ambassadors for a business than its sales team. As the public face of your company, it is essential you provide them with the resources to present your business in the best light.

Using mobile communications, you can keep them in constant touch with the company. With a PDA or laptop with internet connection, sales staff can access information on the move. At a simple level, this can mean keeping up-to-date with any important developments in the business by e-mail. At a more advanced level, giving staff access to the company's systems could give them the tools to clinch more deals on the spot—they could check stock availability, prices and delivery times, send orders back to head office and generate invoices.

Smoothening the Path

The Electronic Point of Scale (EPOS) system helps you to process your most popular products from warehouse to point of sale in the shortest time. An EPOS system can be a costly investment, depending on the type of system you need for your business, but it can bring a lot of benefits, such as handling payments quickly, updating inventory lists and providing instant stock information. It can help you focus on more profitable lines, improve your demand forecasting and minimise inventory.

Make it Easier to Pay

If you are planning to use your website as a new route to market, and allow customers to order and pay online for your goods or services, you will need to consider setting up an online payment system. There are lots of different ways of doing this, and the costs will vary accordingly.

> **CASE STUDY** **Box 4.4**
>
> ### Farmrite Animal Health
>
> As a result of integrating technology into its business, Farmrite, an agricultural supplies company, has seen its sales increase by 40 per cent in two years. Farmrite has used its e-commerce-enabled website as a powerful selling tool. It is able to offer its customers 5,000 stock items. 'We simply couldn't run this number of stock lines without the appropriate technologies,' comments Managing Director Philip Crawford. 'We computerised our stock system from the start. We originally used a Psion handheld and designed a database for that to manage the stock. This has now grown and we use a Sage accounting product integrated with a few custom written utilities. We estimate that, without these systems, we would be carrying an extra £70,000 of surplus stocks.' E-enabling the stock lines has also removed the need for a massive printed catalogue and all the associated costs. According to Philip, the website has also enabled the company to extend the range of its business from outside of its immediate commercial area. 'Our website has enabled us to attract new customers from beyond the immediate geographical region of our base—the proportion of our customers from outside our area has risen to 15 per cent from 2 per cent. 'In addition to the website, we also use technology throughout our other business systems. The point of sale, stock and accounts systems are fully integrated and there is a custom designed database system for stock control.' Technology has given Farmrite a valuable commercial edge over its competitors by offering customers greater choice. 'We can give our customers the benefit of a 24-hour service, they can ask questions and investigate stock availability as well as track deliveries, and at a time that suits them. We also offer a specialist service to farmers where we can produce the statutory tags for their livestock here on the premises. This procedure is carried out using lasers and specialised computer systems.' Farmrite's decision to use technology to e-enable its business has driven it to become one of the leading farm suppliers in the country, able to offer its products nationally from a single base.
>
> Source: DTI

Customer Service

Electronic communication has changed the nature of the customer relationship, bringing new opportunities and new challenges.

In an increasingly competitive world, new technology could give you the edge with your customers. By offering customers the chance to determine their own information needs, you could increase their satisfaction and cut your costs.

Customer in Charge

Answering phone calls is an expensive and time-consuming activity. Sometimes, it's not even necessary—a well-structured website, with good e-mail support, could provide product details, prices, delivery times, stock availability, contact details, FAQs and account information. Whatever you offer, it's important to manage customers' expectations. If you give e-mail support, explain how long it will take to reply. If you offer online ordering, make it clear whether the item is in stock and how long delivery will take.

After-Sales Service

E-mail is an excellent, low cost way of monitoring customer satisfaction. If you send some of your customers a questionnaire, possibly with an incentive to complete it, you can get valuable feedback on what you are doing right and how to improve the service you offer.

Information Your Staff Need

Of course, sometimes customers will want to speak to someone. Here, Computer Telephony Integration (CTI), which links up your computers and telephones to handle all voice, fax and data traffic, can resolve queries quickly and increase customer satisfaction by giving the staff instant access to customer details and history on screen when they take a call.

Computer Telephony Integration is particularly useful for customers who call regularly, or if your staff spends a lot of time on the phone dealing with incoming calls or outbound telemarketing.

Customer Relationship Management

A more ambitious undertaking is CRM (Customer Relationship Management). This seeks to use technology to build up a picture of each customer's habits and motivations so that you can tailor your service to meet their needs and target your marketing.

Although the philosophy behind CRM is useful for most companies, it may not be necessary to invest in costly CRM applications.

International Business

Geographical boundaries are disappearing as the Internet makes your business accessible anywhere in the world. While many small suppliers of niche products are thriving by selling over the Internet, service companies are finding they can promote themselves, source products and tap into new markets abroad.

Reducing the Costs

Using EDI (Electronic Data Interchange) with your suppliers and customers can streamline shipping, dispatch and money transfer, and minimise the documentation, charges, risks and delays of currency exchange.

Rapid Customer Contact

Register your site with some search engines, and you could start to pull in customers from all over the world. Of course, if they are in different time zones, you need to think about how you are going to handle enquiries and orders in out of office hours. One simple step is to set up an automated e-mail reply service that sends an acknowledgement e-mail stating when they can expect to hear from you.

Pick a reasonable response period—say, within 24 hours—and stick to it. For an extra outlay, you could invest in an automated e-commerce package letting your customers order and pay by credit card online.

Talking to Your Customers

The Internet gives you access to a potentially huge customer base, but for many customers, English won't be their first language. One simple step you can take to make things easier for customers abroad is to make sure your website is written in plain, clear English without colloquial phrases.

If it's worthwhile from a business perspective, you could even employ a specialist company to create foreign language versions of your site.

Complying with the Law

If you intend to use your website to operate abroad, you need to be aware of potential additional costs and constraints, for example, export restrictions, business regulations and data protection guidelines in other countries. Because legislation dealing specifically with e-commerce is still evolving, it is worth monitoring developments on an ongoing basis.

CASE STUDY — Box 4.5

M/s Europa Bio Products

When Europa bio products launched its website, the turnover was £1 million a year and there were just six staff members. Today, thanks to the efficiencies information technology has brought, there's still a workforce of six, but turnover has increased by 50 per cent. Europa, which distributes high-value biochemical products, has been using information and communications technology to reposition its business from bulk supply to the supply of small quantities to a large number of individual researchers. The company's website is set up for online ordering and also carries extensive technical information about the products.

It hasn't only increased its turnover, Managing Director Mike Bannister says it's been 'bombarded with companies from Asia, especially Taiwan and China, who want to find a distributor in Europe. We now have a distribution agreement with a company in Korea, something that came from them posting to our website.'

> The website carries the entire product range with minimum quantities and prices. Online ordering is handled by the ISP (Internet Service Provider) on a secure server and sent to Europa by e-mail. Customers can pay by credit card and, when product and stock databases are integrated, stock checking and order confirmation will be automated too.
>
> Europa has worked with a software consultant to develop a customer database that links customer orders and purchase orders to manufacturers, and handles stock control and invoicing. With bio products, technical information can be more important than price. Europa makes sure that prospective customers can get all the information they need online, including links to technical data on Europa's suppliers' sites. 'At one time telephone calls were driving me mad,' admits Mike. Now, using the website to carry product details and data sheets has saved the time that used to be spent dealing with telephone enquiries. And the company hasn't needed a printed catalogue for five years.
>
> The company has used IT to make itself more competitive in supplying directly to researchers. Electronic working had made it possible to process a large number of small account customers more efficiently. As a result, Europa can compete well against the major catalogue companies and still make a profit margin of 30 per cent.
>
> Source: DTI

The Benefits of Exporting

Many companies are exporting successfully from the UK to all over the world. Following are the case studies of different businesses, which have successfully exported using ICT.

E-commerce has enabled DGC Distribution Limited, a Durham-based music retailer, to fortify international ties.

The objectives of DGC Distribution is to import and distribute musical instruments and accessories, based in Spennymoor, County Durham. Under the successful brand name Guvnor, the business designs and manufactures its own range of musical instruments and accessories to customers in the UK, Ireland, Europe and the USA.

British exporters of all sizes are finding and developing new markets, competing globally and growing their businesses. Examples of products and companies included in this leaflet do not in any way imply endorsement or recommendation by DTI. Bear in mind that the prices quoted are indicative at the time it was published.

> **CASE STUDY**   **Box 4.6**
>
> ### DGC Distribution Ltd
>
> Its aim was to use e-commerce to avoid overhead costs and to strengthen existing business relationships in China.
>
> *Solution*
>
> DGC set up www.guvnor.com to allow international trade customers to search the product database, review special offers and place orders online. It developed a software system, which was fully configured to meet the requirements of the company, the customer base and the industry as a whole. This included a unique aggregated shopping cart system and a set of offline tools, which enabled customers list their own products on the site.
>
> *Results*
>
> DGC has seen an increase of 30 per cent in their annual sales figures and has projected a further net revenue increase of 40 per cent for next year. The use of the Internet and intranet have also reaped benefits, enabling the company to source overseas suppliers from the import lines and to communicate inexpensively with their manufacturing operations in China. The intranet has given the staff more responsibility in managing customer accounts, which has increased job satisfaction and employee retention rates. Simon Cohen, managing director of DGC Distribution said: 'Our success is a great vindication of what small businesses can achieve through e-commerce. We are a small company with only six employees, but through determination and a true focus on our objectives, we have succeeded in creating major opportunities for growth.'

> **CASE STUDY**   **Box 4.7**
>
> ### Frumba Ltd
>
> Thanks to a carefully considered expansion plan, Frumba has boosted sales of its healthy snack bars across Europe.
>
> *Objectives*
>
> Established four years ago, Buckinghamshire's healthy snack company Frumba Ltd has a solid UK base selling its snack bars, which contain over 20 natural energy-boosting ingredients, in health clubs across the UK. With an increasingly health conscious European population, Frumba was keen to explore the potential for its Frum'boost bars. So the company signed up to UK Trade & Investment's Passport to Export Programme in summer 2003 in order to find foreign distributors.

> ### Solution
>
> Together, Frumba and UK Trade & Investment developed an action plan and set out some goals. Once objectives had been set and potential markets agreed, they looked at possible distributors. As part of the Passport to Export Programme, potential European markets for Frumba's products were assessed and contact was made with embassies. UK Trade & Investment then provided translation services, flyers publicising Frumba's products and market research reports on Holland, Sweden and France.
>
> 'Without UK Trade & Investment we faced a long search with unreturned calls and blind alleys,' said Doug Struthers, founder of Frumba Ltd. 'Our international trade adviser was able to provide a fantastic list of contacts of potential distributors and customers, who we then met on follow-up visits.'
>
> ### Results
>
> Frumba Ltd is now exporting its new range of real fruit snack bars to Holland, Sweden and France, with possible further contracts with distributors in Norway and Denmark. The company expects exports to a total of several million pounds, accounting for 50 per cent of its total business within two years. Frumba is delighted with the results. 'Our plan now is to consolidate progress in these markets before moving further a field.'
>
> For e-marketing options their pros and cons and checklist for implementation of an e-marketing plan in business, see Annexure II.

Understanding Your Customers

How to give your customers what they want? Why does it matter?

The purpose of understanding customers better is simple: to make your business more profitable by being able to offer your customers what they want, when they want it.

Broadly, you do this by:

- finding out about your customers' purchasing habits, opinions and preferences;
- profiling individuals and groups to market more effectively and increase sales; and
- changing the way you operate internally to improve customer service and marketing.

Most banks operate the same systems; offer similar products and change closely aligned interest rates. They are in competition, but not in a way that leads to a significant differentiation between them. Customers are loyal through inertia rather than affection. They stay as customers because they believe bonus are all the same and change is not worth the effort, not because they are pleased with the service they currently receive.

Mr Fric Daniels, Chief Executive Officer of Lloyds TSB in the UK says that he would like to change this and he knows building customers and customer satisfaction is a long slow job. 'You build customer satisfaction one person at a time', he says, but he also knows that if he succeeds it will deliver a significant competitive edge.

Technology will drive this. What we are beginning to see is the harping of computer power to more regions the processing of transactions and the maintaining of records. Tomorrow's computers create profiles of customers and their preferences. Their activity is recorded in ways that anticipated emerging consumer's needs. The aim is to be ready to offer to the consumers the financial services relevant to their evolving lifestyle age and income, just at the point where they are likely to need them.

Technology and knowledge backed system will soon drive the relationship of the bank with the individual because they will tell the bank when the customers is likely to be receptive. The banks will be coming to the customer with an offer of help before the customer even realises he or she has a need.

As economic conditions change, as interest rate rises, as the exchange rate falls, it can isolate those customers who might find these changes troublesome and move to deal with any emergencies before they become dangerous.

Better technology means a more moderate response when conditions change, a response tailor-made to individual needs. This leads to much less waste, much less available bank rigging and a much better loan performance from the banks.

CASE STUDY   Box 4.8

The Everyman Theatre

The Everyman Theatre in Cheltenham stages around 400 shows a year to which it sells 200,000 tickets. It has 30 employees. Like all businesses, the theatre needs to work hard to attract business and sell tickets. Its success relies not only on choosing shows and events that are attractive to its audiences, but also on effective marketing and a high level of customer service.

Like many regional theatres, a high percentage of the Everyman's ticket sales are to a group of regular theatregoers who can be relied upon to return year after year. As Philip Bernays, Chief Executive of the Theatre, says: 'We have always been very keen to develop long-term relationships with our customers and increase their use of the Theatre.' The problem was how to identify the business's most valuable customers and increase the frequency of their visits. The Everyman already had a range of IT systems in place, but the marketing potential of their customer data was being lost because it was not all stored in one place or stored in a convenient way.

> Eventually, the Theatre's directors decided to tackle the problem by investing in ways of identifying and targeting specific customers, and by developing the ability to manage marketing campaigns with clear goals and objectives.
>
> The brief was to create a system that would 'enable them to form individualised relationships with customers, with the aim of improving customer satisfaction and maximising profits'.
>
> How they did it?
>
> 'But I already know my customers inside out...' Just how well do you know your customers? If your business has a small number of big clients locked into long-term relationships, it could mean that you already provide excellent customer service. However, even with years of accumulated knowledge, there's always room for improvement. Customer needs change over time, and technology is making it easier to find out more about customers and make sure that everyone in an organisation can exploit this information.
>
> Source: Deloitte Research, 2002

Think about Your Business and Ask Yourself How Good Is Customer Service?

Does staff always have the right information when they speak to customers? Are customers kept waiting or put on hold? Are there complaints and how are they dealt with? Are there acceptable response times for fax and e-mail enquiries? Are customers satisfied? Is your customer retention rate good? Are customers loyal? Do you get many customer referrals? How good are sales? Are you happy with your revenue per customer? Are you happy with your customer acquisition costs? Are your marketing campaigns as successful as they could be? How good is communication? Does your support service have good links with the rest of the business? Do sales teams work closely with the rest of the business to spot opportunities and pinpoint weaknesses? Is everything you know about customers and prospects accessible to all your people?

If the answer to a number of these questions is no, then you should consider how you can make your business more responsive to customer needs.

The Everyman Theatre introduced a range of technical and process changes, including a comprehensive customer relationship management (CRM) system, to help improve its understanding of its customers. The benefits it experienced include:

- improved trading relationships—with customers, theatre companies, and other service providers such as printers and accountants;
- reduced costs and greater efficiency—through better targeting of marketing efforts, which reduced the cost per sale; streamlined administration; and automation of the booking process;

- improved competitiveness—through more effective marketing, better communication with theatre production companies, and a reputation for professionalism and advanced use of IT;
- more sales—the net result of all these improvements has been a tangible increase in sales. Revenue has more than doubled in the last five years.

Benefits of Good Customer Service

Understanding your customers can bring benefits for businesses of all sizes in all sectors. Potential benefits can include:

Increased Sales

- You can encourage existing customers to spend more by targeting them with appropriate offers and by spotting cross-selling opportunities.
- More effective customer acquisition, i.e., the more you know about your customers, the easier it is to identify new prospects and increase your customer base.

Improved Efficiency

- If you have transaction, customer and billing details available centrally, it reduces error and speeds up transactions.
- If errors do occur they can be resolved more quickly and more satisfactorily.
- The more you know about customer demand, the more accurately you can predict buying patterns and stock requirements. Recent research shows that companies which connect their client management functions to their supply chain applications are 81 per cent more profitable than those that do not.
- Increased customer satisfaction.
- Better access to customer information means that you can deal with customers faster and more appropriately.
- Tailored product offerings and personalised treatment will show customers that you value their business.

The Process

The Everyman Theatre (referred earlier) found that there are six stages in obtaining accurate, timely information about your customers and using it wisely across your business:
- collecting information;
- storing information;
- accessing information;
- analysing customer behaviour;
- marketing more effectively; and

- enhancing the customer experience.

Looking at the experience of Everyman and the other companies referred in the case studies, it is clear that creating a customer-focused business is a continual process. The most successful businesses monitor and refine their processes, consult with customers and test new product offerings extensively to make sure they're always delivering what their customers want.

International Benchmarking Study

The sector analysis has identified significant variations in the level of technology adoption and deployment across sectors. In general, financial services businesses have the highest levels of adoption and connectivity, while businesses in the primary and construction sectors typically have the lowest.

- Ninety-six per cent of UK financial services businesses have a website, versus 80 per cent of UK construction businesses and 74 per cent of UK primary businesses.
- In the other 10 nations surveyed, an average of 88 per cent of financial services businesses have a website, versus 60 per cent and 68 per cent for construction and primary businesses respectively.

Many of the variations in the ICT profile between sectors can be attributed to the inherent differences in general business processes. For example, manufacturing businesses are more likely to benefit from systems that are integrated with suppliers than most service businesses.

Levels of e-commerce also vary significantly from sector to sector.

- The average proportion of total purchases online (by businesses that order online) is highest among retail businesses (36 per cent in the UK and 38 per cent on average in 10 other nations) and lowest amongst construction businesses (17 per cent for UK businesses and 21 per cent for the 10 other nations).
- Similarly, the average proportion of sales made online (by businesses which enable customers to order online) varies in the UK between 28 per cent (transport and communication) and 10 per cent (primary) of businesses.
- In other nations, the proportion varies from 30 per cent in financial services businesses to 13 per cent in government.

Sector variations in the levels of e-commerce reflect differences in product characteristics and the composition of the supply chain. Orders placed by retail businesses are typically well suited to online procurement. The retail business are of high volume, and the products are standardised as per quality but different as per size and shape. Retail also experiences high percentage of repeat orders from a core supplier base.

Hypothesis

As can be seen from the above examples, for companies to be successful, they have to embrace the information and communication technologies which will help them know their customers well, reach out to them, as well as maximise their potentials (production, logistics, marketing, etc.), reducing cost at the same time.

Closing the Marketing Gap

Benchmarking is the continuous process of measuring producers, services and practices against strong competitors or recognised industry leaders. It is an ongoing activity that is intended to improve performance and can be applied to all facets of operation. Benchmarking requires a measurement mechanism so that the performance 'gap' can be identified. It focuses on comparing best practices among dissimilar enterprises. For details see: www.columbus-chamber.org/workforce/glossary.htm

Definition of Benchmarking in Net

A structured approach will be identifying the best practices from industry and government, and comparing and adapting them to the organisation's operations. Such an approach is aimed at identifying more efficient and effective processes for achieving intended results, and suggesting ambitious goals for programme output, product/service quality and process improvement. Benchmarking hence suggests performance comparison of organisational business processes against an internal or external standard of recognised leaders. Most often the comparison is made against a similar process in another organisation considered 'world class' (see www.ch.doe.gov/programs/iap/glossary.html).

An improvement process, in which a company measures its performance against that of best in class companies, determines how those companies achieved their performance levels and uses the information to improve its own performance. The subjects that can be benchmarked include strategies, operations, processes and procedures. (see www.asq.org/info/glossary/b.html).

We can say that Benchmarking is a systematic approach to the recognition of good and best practice. It involves identification of goals, objectives and targets, the measurement of performance and the analysis of process—the understanding of how things are done. It is the comparison of similar or related processes between departments, functions, groups or organisations.

The primary driver for conducting benchmarking is obtaining focused performance improvement—either through cost reduction or by a significant improvement in the level of delivered service. Also, by undertaking a benchmarking study, your organisation will gain a greater understanding of its processes and behaviours.

Benchmarking Steps

The benefits of conducting a benchmarking exercise are:
- creating a better understanding of the current position;
- increasing awareness of changing customer needs;
- encouraging innovation;
- developing realistic, stretching goals; and
- establishing realistic action plans.

There are four basic types of benchmarking:

- **Internal**—a comparison of internal operations and processes.
- **Competitive**—specific competitor to competitor comparisons for a product or function.
- **Functional**—comparisons of similar functions within the same broad industry, or to industry leaders.
- **Generic**—comparisons of business processes or functions that are very similar, irrelevant of the industry.

Figure 4.1

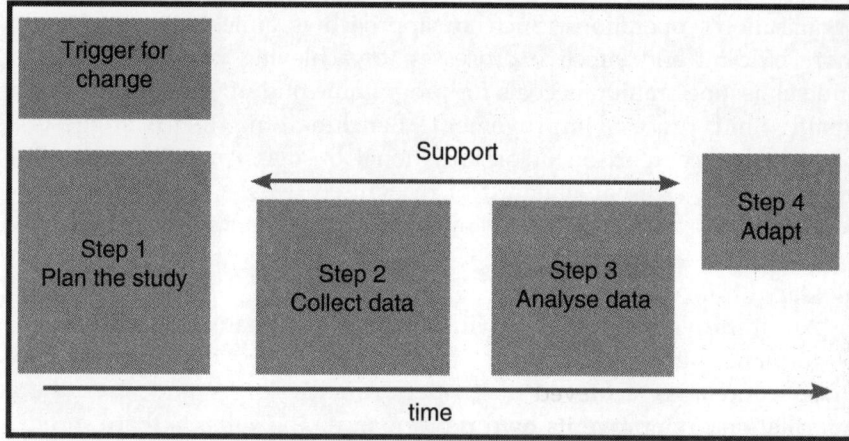

The Benchmarking steps have been listed below (also see figure 4.1)

Step 1—Plan the Study
- Establish benchmarking roles and responsibilities.
- Identify the process to benchmark.
- Document the current process.
- Define the measures for data collection.

Step 2—Collect the Data
- Record current performance levels.
- Find benchmarking partners.
- Conduct the primary investigation.
- Make a site visit.

Step 3—Analyse the Data
- Normalise the performance data.
- Construct a comparison matrix to compare your current performance data with your partners' data.
- Identify outstanding practices.
- Isolate process enablers.

Step 4—Adapt Enablers to Implement Improvements
- Set stretching targets.
- 'Visualise' an alternative process.
- Consider the barriers to change.
- Plan to implement the changes.

To determine if your business, unit or organisation is ready for benchmarking, complete the following questionnaire, based on American Productivity and Quality Center (APQC) material.

	Most	Some	Few	None
Processes have been documented with measure to understand performance.	☐	☐	☐	☐
Employees understand the processes that are related to their own work.	☐	☐	☐	☐
Direct customer interactions, feedback or studies about customers influence decisions about products/services.	☐	☐	☐	☐
Problems are solved by teams.	☐	☐	☐	☐
Employees demonstrate, by words and actions that they understand the mission, vision and values.	☐	☐	☐	☐
Senior executives sponsor and actively support quality improvement projects.	☐	☐	☐	☐
The organisation demonstrates, by words and actions, that continuous improvement is part of the culture.	☐	☐	☐	☐
Commitment to change is articulated in the strategic plans.	☐	☐	☐	☐
Add the columns:	☐	☐	☐	☐
Multiply by the factor:	× 6 =	× 4 =	× 2 =	zero
	☐	☐	☐	☐
Grand total:				

In the United Kingdom Benchmarking is done by Winning Moves Ltd. The Benchmark Index service is one of the most important tools currently available to British business to measure its performance.

Benchmarks Index highlights areas of relative strength and helps managers focus their attention on those aspects of the business where they lag behind.

Achieving sustained sales growth in a rapidly shrinking sector it is not the best of times to be involved in manufacturing especially when you specialise in the supply of automotive components.

In recession best of the best companies fail. We have examples from industry when the economy is in recession yet those companies have shown phenomenal growth due to implementation of best benchmarking activities. One of the companies is Plastic Engineering which has managed to achieve constant and impressive growth despite the recession in the sector.

For a manufacturing company, Plastic Engineering is in a rather unusual position from a marketing perspective. As a second tier supplier, it has no products to sell. Even the products it makes for others are not end products; it usually makes components for components. And sex appeal in the plastic injection molding industry is in short supply! So the marketing the company undertakes is almost exclusively of the company itself.

The company first used the Benchmark Index Marketing and Product/Service Development module as part of a comprehensive Benchmarking exercise in 1998. Managing Director Mike Hart explains: 'When you become MD, you spend a lot of time thinking about which way to go. Benchmarking was an obvious part of this process, quite simply because it highlights the bits you're not good at.' 'To be honest, I was surprised and disappointed by some of the results. Whereas we scored more highly than we anticipated for customer satisfaction, we were doing a lot worse in some other respects than I'd thought.' But when Plastic Engineering used the Benchmark Index again last year, Hart was pleased to confirm what he'd already hoped for—there had been a lot of improvement in the areas, which most needed it. This was particularly the case for the marketing module.

'Marketing took a little more thought than some of the other modules. You couldn't just fill in some numbers,' explains Hart. The exercise back in 1998 was worth it because while management was aware that marketing strategy was not all it could be, it became apparent that there wasn't really a marketing strategy to speak of in place at all. 'We had little idea how to market ourselves, we sell no products. We hadn't quite got our heads around how to market the company itself.' Since then, Plastic Engineering has adopted a far more coherent plan for strategic alliances. Agreements with customers and other companies have allowed it to develop relationships with existing and new customers respectively. The strategy has obviously worked—growth that consistently stands at around 8 per cent per annum in an industry that has been in recession since 1999 is a remarkable achievement; particularly when the workforce has grown despite impressive gains in efficiency that has seen the stock turn drop from 30 to less than 20 days since 1997–8, and that allows the switch to a new product line take place in a matter of hours. 'Delivery times are just so important to customers,' says Hart. 'If you can't be this flexible, you are not even allowed to play the game. These days' cars are pretty much made to order, two cars coming off the production line are scarcely the same. Flexibility is vital. That is where we have now succeeded in our marketing,' he says. 'Even moving office to a new, attractive location has helped. We've changed perceptions so that we're no longer regarded as a back street player; people know that we can deliver. We knew how to deliver before; we just couldn't deliver the message. I can say without doubt that if it hadn't been for the Benchmark Index exercise, we wouldn't be where we are now. We did it to ascertain our weaknesses, and we've improved on them.' Hart concludes, 'We're about to use the Benchmark Index again, and I look forward to the results.'

Strategic Planning

Unless a business knows where it's going to, it will not get very far. Strategic planning is essential to allow a business to carefully consider the markets and customers that it serves and assess what changes are likely to occur. A business must identify its key competencies and utilise them to the full if it is to build a competitive advantage. These competences can take the form of skills, knowledge or processes.

If strategic analysis reveals areas of weakness that cannot be addressed from within the company, an alliance with one or more complementary businesses can be considered. Marketing could be a key element of such alliances, since the perceived strengths of any party in the alliance could be conferred onto others, thereby helping to address the weaknesses. But the evidence suggests this approach should be regarded with caution. Businesses that invest in the development of strategy for marketing and the development of their products and services are likely to grow more rapidly and achieve higher sales than those that give a lower priority to strategic planning. They also tend to have a bigger turnover and to achieve higher margins. A similar pattern is apparent for companies that formulate financial and non-financial goals as part of their strategic planning process and communicate them widely amongst their staff. This allows every level of the organisation to work towards clear goals and objectives. Businesses that follow such an approach grow more quickly than those which are less clear in their target setting. But unlike strategic planning, strategic alliances appear to have little impact upon business growth. Analysis of Benchmark Index data reveals that participating in joint new product development projects and combining competences in areas such as purchasing and after-sales contributes nothing to business growth—but nevertheless profitability tends to be higher.

Businesses that invest in the development of a marketing strategy and the development of their products and services are likely to grow more rapidly.

Developing New Products and Services

Internal processes are key to successful development. Successful businesses with an eye to growth and ongoing profitability view the development of new products and services as a business process that is absolutely critical. They use systematic approaches to identify promising ideas, allocate resources, monitor progress and conduct disciplined reviews at key stages.

Research suggests that they are also more prepared to accept mistakes and benefit from new developments that 'didn't quite make it'. Committing resources to research and development is less important than using appropriate business processes. Those companies that have no formal R&D budget or occasionally include it as a special item in their budget tend to grow slowly. By contrast, those businesses that view R&D as an integral part of their planning and budgeting grow somewhat faster. Companies that grow slowly have a similarly negative attitude to new ideas. Even if they pretend to welcome creativity and innovation, they have no clearly defined process for identifying new areas of opportunity. The fast growing businesses are far more likely to have well developed processes and structures for capturing and cultivating new ideas, and some even invest resources to carry out systematic market scans to identify the most promising creative concepts.

The few new business ideas under development within slow growing companies proceed in an ad hoc, unstructured manner, while those within fast growth businesses treat new product development as a systematic and organised business activity. They often work closely on these programmes with suppliers, customers, universities or research organisations. The creation and development of new ideas for innovative products and services should not be the responsibility of a self-contained research and development team. New concepts are unlikely to succeed unless they take account of all elements of the company's activities.

It is important, therefore, that all areas and departments are involved in the development process.

Cross-functional teams will provide valuable insights and harmonise the efforts being invested, as well as ensuring that production issues are addressed during the design process. The benefits of this shared effort are clear. When businesses run cross-functional teams and communicate their findings and progress across the whole organisation, the process is more effective. Companies that carry out research and development in this way are not only fast growing, but enjoy above-average sales growth and are more profitable too. Taking production issues into account at an early stage is extremely important. Firms that fail to address key questions about the production cost and operational efficiency of new products and services seldom rank amongst the most profitable or fastest growing. Those that establish clear links between production process considerations and the other elements of research and development grow faster and are more profitable. Though it is clearly important to involve personnel from all parts of a business in the development of new products and services, it is equally important to ensure that the process is rapid. The process should be managed by a 'champion' who is keenly aware of the significance of a short time to market. The new product champion must also be given sufficient resources to support the process and ensure adequate support to implement it quickly. The benefits are clear. Businesses that adopt this approach are more profitable and much faster growing. However, it would be taking it much too far to give carte blanche and unlimited resources to a product development champion. The fastest growing companies measure their product development teams against established goals and measures. They systematically record and analyse cost and sales data against forecasts and keep the whole development process under rigorous and ongoing review.

Lower Costs and Higher Sales

Benchmarking brings a new focus on efficiency and marketing. Manchester-based Vita Liquid Polymers produces both liquid polymer PVC and latex compounds for a wide variety of manufacturing industries. PVC compound, for example, is sold to makers of wall coverings, automotive filters and moulded articles such as boat fenders.

With 60 employees, the turnover has been fairly consistent at around £15 million over the last 10 years. The apparent stability belies a changing marketplace. A downturn in some of the industries buying latex means PVC now accounts for 60 per cent of sales, a reversal of the 40 per cent of what it took five years ago. Traditionally, Vita had been largely concentrating on maintaining or increasing orders for existing products, many of which have been custom built to the requirements of a specific customer. Customer retention rate last year was an impressive 97 per cent, but Vita recognised that it couldn't carry all of its eggs in one basket. Relying on several big clients leaves a company in a vulnerable position. With the UK market becoming saturated and global competition on the increase, Vita realised the need to increase the sales of its existing product portfolio, rather than reacting to customer enquiries. Many of these are for 'custom' products and therefore require a significant investment in research and development.

The sales effort had been concentrated mainly in the UK, with European sales handled by agents, who are not selling the Vita product portfolio exclusively. Realising that the agent network alone would not maximise Vita's impact on foreign markets, greater support is now being given in terms of joint visits abroad, formalised market research and product literature in several European languages. A restructuring of the sales department, giving managers sales territories based on product rather than geographic areas, has boosted market knowledge and improved relationships with sales agents. Benchmark Index analysis prompted decisions to improve production efficiency, which led to a reduction in staff numbers and an increase in output. Vita has also employed a full-time marketer, who rebranded the existing product lines to give them a stronger market identity. Communications strategy was also improved, with more informative product literature and a redesigned, more customer friendly website.

As well as exploring new markets, the company is also rationalising the product portfolio: the company currently has 400 products compared to 300 customers. 'We've already done an analysis on which customers are profitable for us, and we anticipate that the number of products we have will fall away naturally as we start to develop new, more widely marketable products', says Managing Director Jim Murphy. Vita has also negotiated a new distribution deal with German company Polymer Latex Ltd, which manufactures and sells synthetic latex as opposed to latex compounds. This has allowed Vita to reach new potential clients and generate an extra £1/2 million annual sales. Jim Murphy explains: 'The Benchmark Index has been of great value, and we shall certainly continue to participate.' The marketing module is of key interest, especially with the creation of a new marketing function within the company.

Market Analysis

Understanding your competitors is key to survival and success markets change quickly. The competition is always changing. Companies that fail to react to this volatility can quickly find themselves struggling to compete. It is essential to have a keen external perspective. Businesses must have procedures in place to continuously assess the competitive environment and formulate strategic plans to address the changes in customer behaviour.

Businesses that invest time and effort into gathering information on competitors' activities grow more rapidly and achieve higher sales than those that do not. This monitoring takes into account the market share, price data and financial information about their rivals. With competitive analysis procedures in place, it is possible to build a clear understanding of a firm's competitive advantage and address the areas of weakness – which helps to ensure the business grows more quickly than others in its sector. Market analysis plays a key role in decisions about promotional activities and pricing policy. If a business has a clear understanding of demand patterns, costs, competitors' prices and the perceived value of each of its products, then it is far better equipped to set and modify its prices. These pricing mechanisms can help the company to ensure its customers perceive superior value, which in turn helps sales to grow more rapidly. Understanding what one's competitors are up to builds greater confidence to invest in all areas of marketing activity.

Timely and accurate feedback from customers regarding all elements of the marketing programme is essential if a business is going to take account of the rapidly changing business environment. But gathering information is not enough. It must be disseminated amongst managers, considered carefully and acted upon.

Simply reacting to changes in customer needs might be enough to keep abreast of change. But if a business is going to improve in terms of profitability or growth, it must keep one step ahead by anticipating the changes before they occur. Companies with well-established procedures to collect and review information about their customers and product sales tend to grow more quickly. Customer-focused companies are also proactive in carrying out customer satisfaction surveys and monitoring customer complaints. Results from these activities have a considerable impact on strategic planning for the business.

Markets change quickly. The competition is always changing. Companies that fail to react to this volatility can quickly find themselves struggling to compete.

Businesses that invest time and effort into gathering information on competitors' activities grow more rapidly than those that do not. Gathering information is not enough. It must be disseminated amongst managers, considered carefully and acted upon.

Building a Brand

Promotional activity plays a central role in long-term brand building.

The brand of a product, a service or a business is more than just a name. It is a statement to the company's customers, shareholders, employees and trade partners. Not only must the statement be clear, it must also incorporate something distinctive that marks out the sustainable competitive advantages of the company or the product.

Effective branding can be a valuable source of strategic competitive advantage, but it needs to be properly managed. Brand management requires regular and systematic measurement of the business or product compared to rivals in the marketplace. Decisions to invest in 'brand building' should not be driven by short-term opportunism. Such investments should only be taken if the expenditure will help to ensure a longer-term contribution to sales and profitability.

Bigger and faster growing companies pay more attention to branding strategy. They view marketing expenditure as an investment, and invest time and effort into establishing a long-term strategy for their marketing. Branding is viewed as a source of strategic competitive advantage, so branding issues are regularly discussed, the value of its brands is widely recognised within the company, and there is less reluctance to spend money on marketing and promotions.

Building a brand requires promotional activity. In many companies decisions about the best forms of promotions are made on a subjective basis by senior managers. Bigger and faster growing companies take decisions about the promotional mix on a much more scientific basis. They formally assess the relative importance of the various promotional tools, track the success of promotional activity and operate a carefully integrated marketing and communications strategy.

Decisions to invest in 'brand building' should not be driven by short-term opportunism.

The brand of a product, a service or a business is more than just a name. It is a statement to the company's customers, shareholders, employees and trade partners. Bigger and faster growing companies view marketing expenditure as an investment, and invest time and effort into establishing a long-term strategy for their marketing. Market activity, accurate data about customers and markets ensures effectiveness. Gathering and using information about the market can take a wide variety of forms. With accurate data about competitors and the specific market sector in which it competes, the company can plan its activities with greater confidence. The information is most valuable if the process is rigorous and systematic. Arguably the most precious of all is data about customers. Unless a business can accurately assess customer expectations and measure how well their products or services are satisfying those expectations, it is unable to identify the areas of weakness that it must rectify. Companies that invest time and effort in market research and forecasting tend to be bigger and considerably more profitable than those who do not. Detailed research enables a company to divide up its market into segments and spot those areas that are growing at the fastest rate. Forecasting in this way allows a business to concentrate upon the business sectors that offer the greatest opportunities, and encourages faster growth, as the Benchmark Index data clearly reveals. A full and complete understanding of the performance of the different market segments is key to developing its marketing programme to suit their different needs. It may be necessary to adjust specific elements of the marketing mix, such as price, packaging, sales channels or promotional activity to suit the needs of the market segment. The businesses that refine their marketing programmes most effectively grow substantially faster and achieve greater sales than their rivals.

The faster growing companies are also better at training their personnel to understand the needs and wishes of their customers. Their training programmes are on-going activities to reflect the changes in market needs, and employees are kept well informed about other developments amongst the business' competitors.

With accurate data about competitors and the specific market sector in which it competes, the company can plan its activities with greater confidence.

Detailed research enables a company to divide up its market into segments and spot those areas that are growing at the fastest rate.

A full and complete understanding of the performance of the different market segments is key to developing its marketing programme to suit their different needs.

Hypothesis

As can be seen from these examples, for closing the market gap, industries have to find the areas of improvement in their system. Benchmarking is a systematic approach to the recognition of good and best practice. It involves identification of goals, objectives and targets, the measurement of performance and the analysis of process; the understanding of how things are done. It is the comparison of similar or related processes between departments, functions groups or organisations. It highlights areas of relative strength and helps managers focus their attention on those aspects of the business where they lag behind.

Section B

Strategic Tools for Enhancing Performance

5
A Strategic Tool for Enhancing Performance— the Balanced Scorecard

V. K. Gupta

Introduction

Prompted by the economic reforms initiated in the aftermath of the 1991 crisis, winds of change have blown in every segment of the economy. The Indian financial sector has undergone a period of considerable change since 1990s. The growing complexity of financial markets and activities has led to a series of mergers and acquisitions in the banking industry and the emergence of financial conglomerates. ICICI has drawn a strategy of becoming a universal bank in this context of a macro economic environment. The assessment of the universal banking strategy as adopted by ICICI to become ICICI Bank and as a pioneering universal bank in Indian context has to be evaluated in an appropriate multidimensional approach. This chapter presents the strategy of ICICI as a focused banking company amalgamating with ICICI Bank and its performance evaluation in the innovative model of Balanced Scorecard (BSC) approach as evolved by Kaplan and Norton (1992). The BSC as a tool helps the organisation's focus, improves communication, sets organisational objectives and provides feedback on the strategy adopted. The scheme of the chapter is to describe the BSC framework and then to illustrate it with the strategy and approach of ICICI from the perspectives of BSC and discusses the emerging benefits of adopting the BSC approach. Incidentally, the chapter also incorporates an evaluation of the bank's coping with the changing times of the banking industry.

The Balanced Scorecard (BSC)

The Balanced Scorecard is an approach to performance measurement that combines traditional financial measures with non-financial measures to provide managers with richer and more relevant information about the activities they are managing.

The BSC provides a framework for effective performance management and addresses the potential failures of strategy execution. More than 20 years ago, Tom Peters and Robert Waterman had introduced the McKinsey 7-S model of excellence to address the issue of effective strategy execution. The model posits that organisations are successful when they achieve an integrated harmony among three 'hard' Ss—strategy, structure and systems, and four 'soft' Ss—skills, staff, style and super ordinate goals (now referred to as 'shared values'). The McKinsey 7-S framework is as follows:

Strategy

The positioning and actions taken by an enterprise in response to or in anticipation of changes in the external environment, and intended to achieve competitive advantage.

Structure

The way in which tasks and people are specialised and divided, and authority is distributed; how activities and reporting relationships are grouped; and the mechanisms by which the activities in the organisation are coordinated.

Systems

The formal and informal procedures used to manage the organisation, including management control systems; performance measurement and reward systems; planning, budgeting, and resource allocation systems; and management information systems.

Staff

The people, their backgrounds and their competencies, how the organisation recruits, selects, trains, socialises, promotes and manages the careers of employees.

Skills

The distinctive competencies of the organisation: what it does best along such dimensions as people, management practices, processes, systems, technology and customer relationships.

Style/Culture

The leadership style of managers: how they spend their time, what they focus attention on, what questions they ask of employees, how they make decisions. Also the organisational culture: the dominant values and beliefs, the norms, and the conscious and unconscious symbolic acts taken by leaders (job titles, dress codes, informal meetings with employees, and executive 'perks' such as dining rooms and corporate jets.)

Shared Values

The core or fundamental set of values that are widely shared in the organisation and serve as the guiding principles of what is important; vision, mission and value statements that provide a broad sense of purpose for all employees.

However, according to Kaplan, the BSC goes a step further to integrate all the seven Ss for effective strategy execution. By defining the specific, measurable behaviours desired in leaders, the BSC forces previously implicit choices to become explicit, actionable and accountable.

Two common and important characteristics of BSC designs are the clustering of similar types of measures into groups (often called perspectives), and a focus on limiting the number of measures reported to improve clarity and utility. First introduced in 1990s, the BSC concept has become widely known, and various forms of it have been widely adopted around the world.

Balanced Scorecard: Where to Go and How to Get There?
- Team effort involving future users.
- Based on jointly held strategic vision.
- Identification of key strategic activities and outcomes.
- Express management team's theory about which activities drive which outcomes.

Balanced Scorecard builds on the following key management concepts:
(a) *Causality:* Identify the actions required to deliver key outcomes.
(b) *Learning:* Using feedback to identify ways of improving performance.
(c) *Teamwork:* Using consensus to ensure everyone is clear on what needs to be done.
(d) *Communication:* Providing clear and unambiguous information on goals, roles and performance

The structure of the Balanced Scorecard (see Figure 5.1) is as shown below:

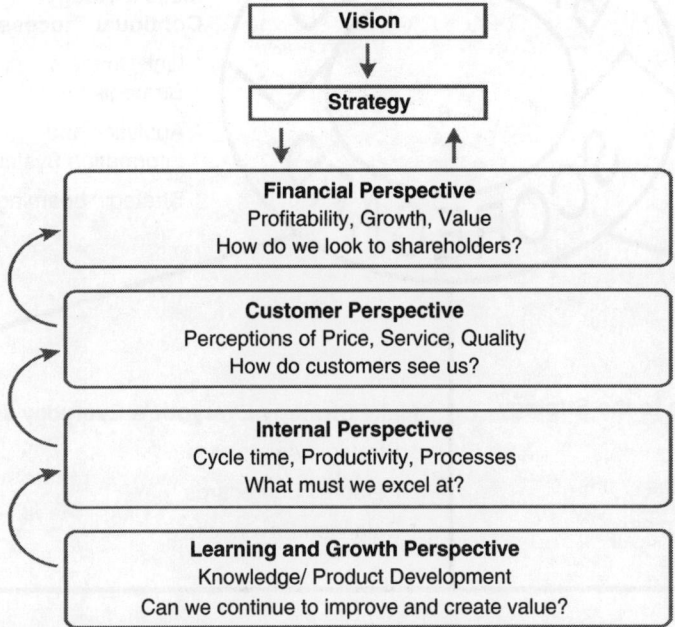

Figure 5.1: The Balanced Scorecard Perspectives

The shift from an industrial economy to a knowledge-based economy has led to a renewed importance of strategy, which further propelled the use of BSCs. The BSC uses the language of measurement to define more clearly the meaning of strategic concepts like quality, customer satisfaction and growth. Companies that successfully implement scorecards do so by reinventing every part of their management system to focus on strategy. This is unlike the traditional approach, where the performance management systems are linked to the financial frameworks like budgets or non-financial frameworks like total quality. These successful organisations created a performance management system that put strategy at the centre. The successful implementation of the BSC is based on the following principles of a strategy-focused organisation (see Figure 5.2).

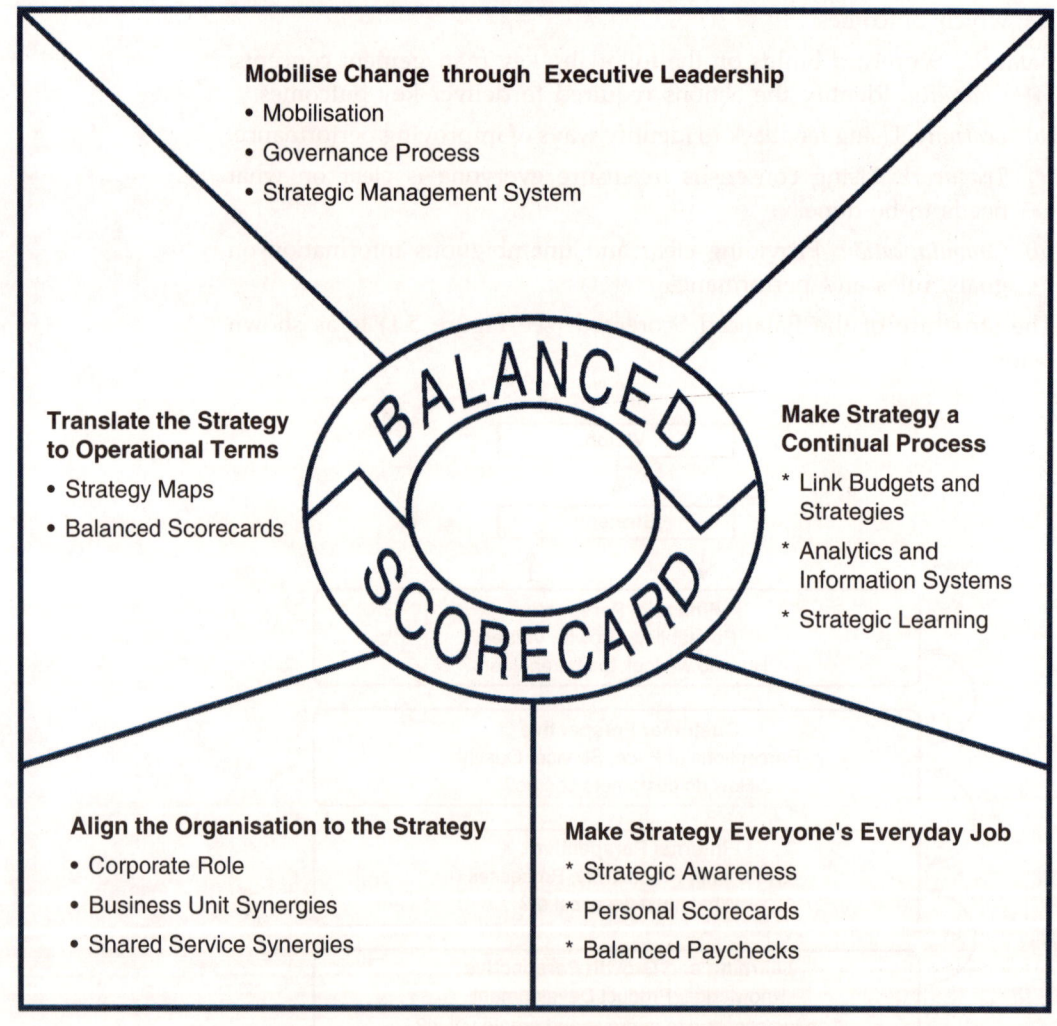

Figure 5.2: The Principles of a Strategy-Focused Organisation

Principle # 1: Build an Executive Leadership Team to Mobilise Change

The transformational change must begin at the top with three discrete actions by the leaders.

Establish a Sense of Urgency

Sometimes the need for a change maybe felt at the top level, but may not be apparent to the rest of the organisation. People are comfortable with the traditional ways of working. Hence to bring about a change successfully in the organisation, it is important to make the need obvious to all.

Create the Leadership Team

The dynamics of the executive leadership usually determines whether the scorecard succeeds or not. It should be a well-balanced, strategically focused, cross-functional and integrated team.

Develop the Vision and Strategy

The framework of the BSC provides a structured way for the team to work together to guide the development of a new shared vision and strategy.

Principle # 2: Translate the Strategy into Operational Terms

Putting strategy at the centre means that it should be clearly described, so that it can be understood and acted upon. For this purpose the BSC requires the formulation of a strategy map, which defines the 'architecture' of the strategy. The description begins with the definition and linking of all the perspectives of a BSC.

Principle # 3: Link and Align the Organisation around Its Strategy

Business units are often combined to form larger organisations based on the belief that greater synergy can be achieved across the units. The assumption is that, if the business units can be coordinated, the whole will be of greater value than the sum of the parts. The BSC can and should be used to define the strategic linkages that integrate performance of separate but related organisations. The corporate scorecard should provide a high level template that defines common goals and themes to be adopted by all business units. The linkages between business units should be made explicit so that they can be actively managed.

Principle # 4: Make Strategy Everyone's Job

The Business Scorecard takes care that everyone in the organisation understands that the strategy is aligned to it and is capable of executing it. For this purpose it is required that there is:

- communication and education to create awareness;
- personal alignment, which can be achieved through personal goal setting process, which may be cross-functional, long-term and strategic; and

incentive compensation. Most successful BSC users conclude, that to modify behaviour as required by the strategy and as defined in the scorecard, change must be reinforced through incentive compensation. When the Scorecard is linked to incentive compensation then the level of interest in the implementation of the scorecard visibly increases.

Principle # 5: Link Strategy and Budgeting

Most strategic initiatives do not have a direct impact on budgeting primarily because a strategic investment is a cluster of activities, not a simple line item. For this reason, most organisations must redefine their planning and budgeting process to reflect these structural features. The strategy can be divided into themes. Initiatives (along with their costs) required to achieve the above-identified themes can be listed out. The management of these strategic themes and initiatives can provide a vehicle to link long-term strategies with short-term investments.

Principle # 6: Make Strategy a Continuous Process

A strategy is a hypothesis about what the future will look like and how to get there. Hence a BSC can monitor the organisational performance against the short-term targets for the scorecard's financial and non-financial measures. The strategy implementation process can, therefore, be continuously monitored and reviewed.

Developed by Kaplan and Norton (1992) the BSC System facilitates translation of strategic objectives into a set of performance indicators at the sub unit level. The Business Scorecard is a mechanism for linking long-term objectives with short-term operational performance at the sub unit level. It is a powerful strategic measurement system and is extremely relevant for management control systems. It ensures goal congruence between subunits and the organisation as a whole. The performance measures in the BSC system achieve an optimum balance between:

- financial and non-financial measures;
- short-term and long-term measures;
- outcome and driver measures (leading and lagging); and
- past and present performance.

Figure 5.3 shows how a company had changed to strategic management system from management control system using the BSC.

Balanced Scorecard Is a Double-Loop Feedback

In traditional industrial activity, 'quality control' and 'zero defects' were the watchwords. In order to shield the customer from receiving poor quality products, aggressive efforts were focused on inspection and testing at the end of the production line. The problem with this approach—as pointed out by Deming—is that the true causes of defects could never be identified, and there would always be inefficiencies due to the rejection of defects. What Deming saw was that variation is

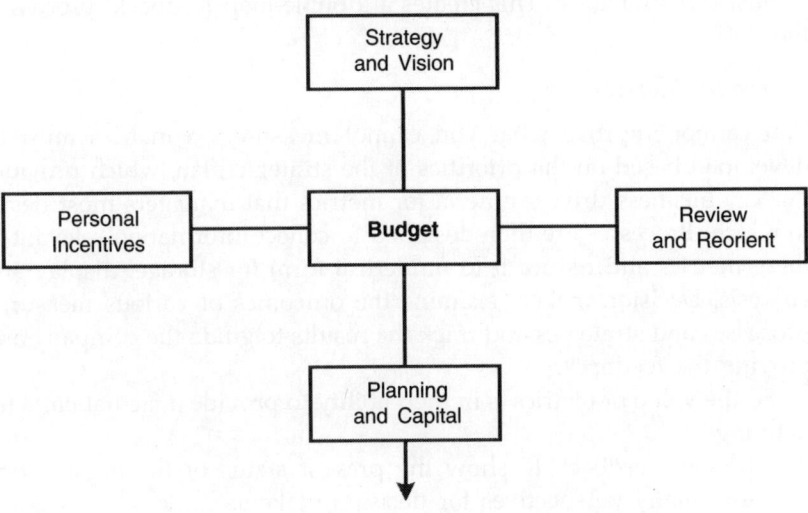

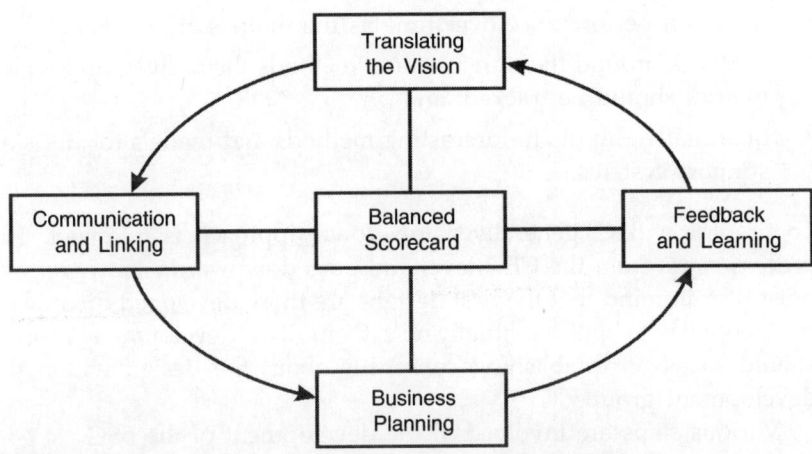

Figure 5.3: Transition from a Management Control System to a Strategic Management System Using the Balanced Scorecard

created at every step in a production process, and the causes of variation need to be identified and fixed. If this can be done, then there is a way to reduce the defects and improve product quality indefinitely. To establish such a process, Deming emphasised that all business processes should be part of a system with feedback loops. The feedback data should be examined by managers to determine the causes of variation, what are the processes with significant problems, and then they can focus attention on fixing that subset of processes.

The BSC incorporates feedback around internal business process *outputs*, as in TQM, but also adds a feedback loop around the *outcomes* of business strategies. This creates a 'double-loop feedback' process in the BSC.

Outcome Metrics

You cannot improve what you cannot measure. So metrics must be developed based on the priorities of the strategic plan, which provides the key business drivers criteria for metrics that managers most desire to watch. Processes are then designed to collect information relevant to these metrics and reduce it to numerical form for storage, display and analysis. Decision makers examine the outcomes of various measured processes and strategies and track the results to guide the company and provide the feedback.

So the value of metrics is in their ability to provide a factual basis for defining:
- strategic feedback to show the present status of the organisation from many perspectives for decision makers;
- diagnostic feedback into various processes to guide improvements on a continuous basis;
- trends in performance over time as the metrics are tracked;
- feedback around the measurement methods themselves, and which metrics should be tracked; and
- quantitative inputs to forecasting methods and models for decision support systems.

Creating a Balanced Scorecard for Strategic Control

To prepare a BSC, generally a top–down approach is followed. The process starts from the CEO level and goes downwards. However, we must bear in mind that the best designs are those developed directly by the people who will eventually use them. The development process should focus on establishing consensus about the design within the development group.

Various steps are involved in the development of the BSC.

(a) Create a Vision Statement

One should start with the articulation of and agreement to a strategic vision statement—a fairly detailed description of where the company, business unit or department is expected to be two to five years later, provided current plans are successfully implemented.

(b) Create and Link Strategic Objectives

One needs a set of objectives that describe the core elements of the management team's plans to achieve the vision outlined in step 1. Focus on the limited number of objectives and consider the 'causality' between the objectives (e.g., X causes Y). Thinking about the objectives and causality will enable the management team to focus on the measurable actions needed to deliver their strategic vision.

(c) Further Describe Strategic Objectives

Before the design team forgets, get them to write down clear statements that describe each chosen objective, and how they think it might be measured. It will help subsequent communication of the BSC design and also that the team will not forget the fine detail of their thinking since it is promptly recorded.

(d) Identify Relevant Measures

Measure selection is normally influenced by the need to obtain information quickly and cheaply and to use sources that update fairly frequently. For each objective one should aim for one or two measures that will track organisational progress towards the objective over time.

(e) Create Implementation Plans

Having a BSC is not enough—the objectives and overall vision will only be achieved if someone actually does something to cause them to happen. A core part of the development process is to work out how the organisation will be mobilised to deliver the selected objectives—an activity that involves communication, resource allocation, and project prioritization. A good way is to do the planning while all the ideas are fresh in your mind, i.e., as a part of the BSC development process. Having a plan also helps in subsequent communications about what needs to happen and when.

(f) Review on Regular Basis

Using the BSC creates a reference point for management discussions that can promote more objective and analytical discussions based on a shared view of what needs to be done, and factual information about what is happening, enabling management teams to become more efficient and effective at implementing strategies. The most effective use of this type of BSC is simply to review it on a regular basis. Typically as part of these review meetings, improvements to the overall strategic vision and goals are identified, and changes to the measures used to track performance are requested. The review meetings become a forum for continually updating and refreshing the BSC design, which is essential if the tool is to have long-term value (see Figure 5.4).

Benefits of Using BSC in Business Affairs

- Alignment of customer priorities and business priorities.
- Ability to track progress over time.
- Evaluation of progress changes.
- Identify opportunities for initiatives and partnerships.
- Accountability to constituents.
- Develop action plans and set strategic direction.

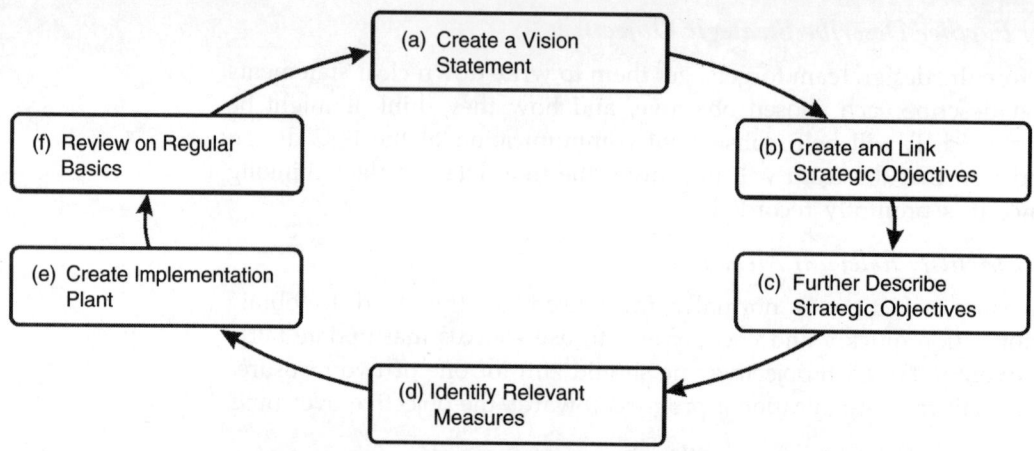

Figure 5.4: The Development and Reviewing of a Balanced Scorecard

Can We Link the BSC to other Processes?

One of the strengths of the BSC is its ability to work well in conjunction with existing management process. Balanced Scorecard is often used as the strategic centre of a strategic management system (see Figure 5.5) as it provides an easy way to use mechanism for the selection and co-ordination of other management tools being applied in the pursuit of strategic goals. When used in this way, the BSC has two roles. First, to inform and prioritise the selection of which other tools to use. Second, to report the outcome of the application of these tools when used to achieve strategic objectives.

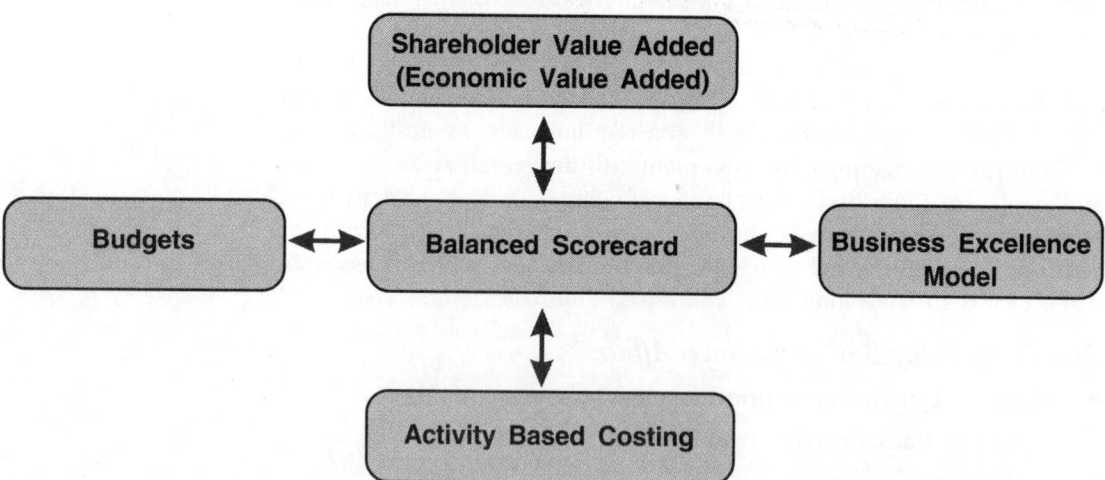

Figure 5.5: Balanced Scorecard—Central Component of the Strategic Management System

There is measurement renaissance afoot in the network economy. Industry leaders have discovered that measurement plays a crucial role in translating business strategy into results. Organisations which are toppers in their industry, stellar financial performers and adept change leaders, distinguish themselves by the following characteristics:

- having agreed-upon measures that managers understand;
- balancing financial and non-financial measurement;
- linking strategic measures to operational ones;
- updating their strategic 'scorecard' regularly; and
- clearly communicating measures and progress to all employees.

For those executives who assess the pivot points of their company's strategy—from how well customer's expectations are met to the ability to manage relevant environmental and regulatory forces, and to how adaptable the organisation is—the BSC effort will yield ongoing results to the bottom line.

A Case Study on ICICI Bank's Universal Banking Strategy

The desirability of a balanced picture of organisational performance is not really a new idea. Since the 1970s the academic literature on management control has been emphasising that:

- non-financial indicators of performance should supplement financial measures;
- non-financial measures of performance should include qualitative parameters;
- multiple parameters should be selected;
- some of the parameters must help in assessment of performance from the long-term perspective while others should enable performance valuation from the short-term perspective;
- selected parameters must facilitate measurement of effectiveness as well as efficiency at the organisational and sub-unit level; and
- established performance measures should help accomplish corporate strategic objectives.

The BSC framework measures organisational performance using financial and non-financial measurements in four perspectives: financial, customer, internal business process and learning and growth. The approach quickly evolved into a new system for describing and managing strategy. Many organisations in the USA that adopted the approach enjoyed breakthrough improvements in performance. The BSC approach was evolved by Kaplan and Norton when financial measurements became insufficient for contemporary organisation's strategies for creating value. The approach was shifted from managing tangible assets to knowledge-based strategies that created and deployed an organisation's intangible assets, including customer relationships innovative products and high quality services, responsive operative processes, skills and knowledge of the employees. Information technology supports the workforce and links the organisation to its customers and suppliers and the organisational climate which results in encouraging innovation, problem-solving and improving framework links like corporate vision, mission and strategy with the key organisational relationships of its stakeholders, employees, customers, suppliers and communities with commitment.

The Strategy Map and BSC Framework

The BSC framework describes strategy with strategic objectives measures, targets and initiatives (see Figure 5.6). Strategic objectives and measures can be imbedded in a general framework or a 'strategy map' as complementarily linked with the BSC framework to describe and visualise the hypotheses and interrelationships that form the hardcore of the strategy. The strategy map enables leaders to communicate clearly to employees what business the organisation is in, and how it intends to succeed and outperform its competitors (see Figure 5.7). It envisions the following critical elements for the growth strategy:

- objectives for growth in shareholder value;
- target customers where there will be profit;
- value propositions that lead customers to do more business and at higher margins with the company;
- innovation and excellence in products and processes; and
- the capabilities and alignment of employees and system that enhance performance.

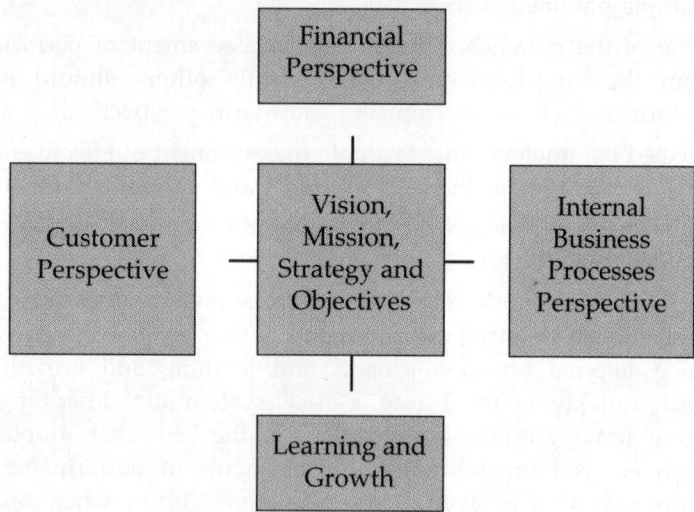

Figure 5.6: BSC Framework

For important internal processes and customer relationships to generate and sustain growth, the Strategy Map and BSC framework is used as a communication vehicle for identifying a vision to the employees, and to encourage new ideas and approaches that promote growth. Employees can become inspired with their understanding of how their organisation creates value and intends to be a healthy growing entity.

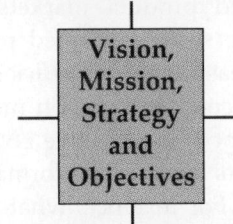

Figure 5.7: Strategy Map

Having created the high-level strategy map and scorecard, organisational leaders cascade the strategy down to the decentralised divisions, business units and support functions. Rather than dictating the company level measures down to operating units to define their own strategy based on local market conditions, competition operating technologies, and resources Unit managers choose local measures that influence, but are not necessarily identical to the corporate scorecard measures. The most significant transformations and partnerships occur in support functions and shared services, such as human resource, information technology, finance and purchasing departments. The process transforms these from functionally oriented cost centres into strategic partners with the line operating units and the company. This process aligns all the decentralized units into a strategic partnership with each other and the corporate parent to deliver integrated strategy corporate level synergies emerge in which the whole exceeds the sum of individual parts.

Application of BSC in a Bank

The Balanced Scorecard can be used very effectively to develop, communicate, as well as implement strategic choices in banks. A precondition, however, is that the different measures under each of the possible perspectives are chosen based on a cause–effect model that relates efforts (enablers) to output from stakeholders' viewpoint. The main advantage of using the BSC for a bank is that it can help build specific performance parameters for each of the markets (geographical as well as) in which the bank is operating and set specific benchmarks depending on the operating conditions in each of its markets. For example, the performance of a corporate banking unit must be measured differently from that of a retail banking unit and the performance of service oriented product markets from that of fund-based product markets. In the service-oriented product markets, the most important factor is the measurement of efficiency, whereas in a fund-based market, the primary focus has to be on measurement of risk.

Development of an effective BSC requires that the bank understands the drivers of its business performance—both at macro as well as at the industry level. For instance, what is the extent to which technology is providing value addition to the bank's customer or is it mainly a tool for bringing in operational efficiency? Who is the existing potential competitors of the bank and what is the basis of the competition, that is, the price, service, quality, choice of distribution channel or the product range? The most crucial question here is about the sources of competitive advantage, which the bank would like to build for itself. Finally, what would the bank be willing to trade off—profitability or growth? The next step is to choose the performance parameters and fix the targets that each business unit or manager is expected to achieve. The key success factor here is choice of performance parameters that are consistent with each other. For instance, a bank, which takes pride in the quality of service, must be able to allocate sufficient resources for training its staff and providing them technological support for bringing in customer acquisition but does not invest enough in back office processing capacity or its counter staff, or is able to gain market share in the credit market, but the credit management process is not reliable enough to distinguish good credit from marginal credit. Figure 5.6 presents the BSC for a typical bank. Further, the BSC concept needs to be applied not only at the bank level but also at each operating level. In other words, the performance measures should be developed, understood and evaluated at the zonal, regional and branch levels.

A Brief History of ICICI and Its Strategy of 'Universal Bank'

The ICICI group, which comprises of ICICI, its subsidiaries and other affiliate companies, is a diversified financial services industry. The ICICI was formed in 1955 at the initiative of the World Bank, the Government of India and representatives of the Indian industry. The principal objective was to create a Development Financial Institution (DFI) for providing medium- term and long-term project financing to Indian business. Until the late 1980s, ICICI primarily focused its activities on project finance, providing long-term funds to a variety of industrial projects. With liberalisation of the financial sector in 1990s, ICICI transformed its business from a development financial institution offering only project finance to a diversified industrial services provider that along with the subsidiaries and affiliates offers a wide variety of products and services. ICICI has set up independent operations through incorporation of subsidiaries and affiliates in the areas of venture capital financing (1988), asset management and management of mutual funds (1993), commercial banking (1994), brokering and marketing (1994), personal finance (1997), Internet stock trading (1999), home finance (1999) and most recently insurance (2000).

The ICICI group draws its strength from the core competences of its individual companies to lead the financial services industry into the new millennium. The group is now truly positioned as a virtual universal bank. The liberalisation of the financial and banking sector of Indian economy in the 1990s offered an opportunity for a wider range of financial services. The issue of universal banking, which in the Indian context means conversion of long-term development financial institution into commercial bank, has been discussed at length over the past few years. The Reserve Bank of India in its policy documents has formulated and developed an approach to universal banking by harmonising the role and operations of the development of financial institutions and banks (January 1999). The RBI announced in April 2001 that it would consider proposals from DFIs (like ICICI) wishing to transform themselves into banks on a case-by-case basis in its mid-term review of monetary and credit policy for the fiscal year 2002. The RBI encouraged financial institutions to submit proposals for their transformation into a bank.

As a bank, ICICI would have the ability to accept low-cost demand deposits and offer a wide range of products and services and greater opportunities for earning non-fund-based income in the form of banking fees and commissions. In view of the benefits of transformation into a bank and the RBI's pronouncements on universal banking, ICICI explored various corporate structuring alternatives for its transformation into a universal bank. ICICI also held discussions within an appropriate transition path and compliance with regulatory requirements. The ICICI Bank also considered various strategic alternatives in the context of the emerging competitive scenario in the Indian banking industry and the move towards universal banking. ICICI Bank identified a large capital base and sized up the scale of operations in the Indian banking industry. The strategic alternatives examined by ICICI and ICICI Bank included an amalgamation of the two entities in view of ICICI's significant shareholding in ICICI Bank, the existing strong business synergies between the two entities. ICICI also considered the reorganisation of the subsidiary companies.

The discussion of senior management of ICICI and ICICI Bank which commenced in July 2001 have led to the view that amalgamation of ICICI and ICICI Bank would be the optimal strategic alternative for both the entities and would create the optimal legal structure for ICICI group's universal banking strategy. In arriving at its decision, the two institutions have examined the recommendations and opinions of JM Morgan Stanley and Deolitte, Haskin and Sellers and DSP Merrill Lynch on the benefits of proposed amalgamation, the move towards universal banking and the RBI's policy statements and guidelines, the corporate relationship between the two entities and the advantages of ICICI group's strategy over the past few years of operating as a virtual universal bank. The merger of the Bank of Madura with ICICI Bank has lent support to the expansion of branch network, asset and clientele base for ICICI and ICICI Bank. The strategic benefits, regulatory issues and other macroeconomic issues of the merger of ICICI with ICICI Bank have been discussed by the author in another paper published earlier (*SEBI & Corporate Laws Weekly*, 8 April 2002).

The financial year 2002 marked a turning point in the corporate history of the ICICI group, as it witnessed the culmination of ICICI's group strategy of becoming an integrated financial services provider—the merger of ICICI Limited (ICICI) with ICICI Bank. The merger was a path-breaking initiative, which created India's first 'universal bank' and the second largest bank in the country. As part of the reorganisation two of ICICI's wholly owned retail finance subsidiaries viz., ICICI Personal Financial Services Ltd. and ICICI Capital Services Ltd. were also merged with ICICI Bank in order to integrate and consolidate the retail business.

Facets of BSC Approach and ICICI's Performance Evaluation

In this section an attempt is made to relate the facets of BSC approach to ICICI's performance evaluation in the following aspects.

Partnering with Employees

Several forces highlight the importance of partnering with employees. People want to feel that they are working for an organisation that is contributing value to the environment/society in which it is operating. Employees want to know that society benefits from the mission and strategy of their organisation and its products and services. They should understand how the success of the organisation not only benefits its shareholders but also its customers, suppliers and the communities in which the organisation operates. Employees also want to know where they fit within the organisation and how they can contribute to help the organisation achieve its mission and objectives. Organisational leaders also recognise that their strategies, however brilliantly they may be formulated, will be successful only if every individual in the organisation understand the strategy and helps the organisation to achieve it. With such an understanding, employees can link improvements in their daily processes to the achievement of high-level objectives.

ICICI Bank views its human capital as a key source of its competitive advantage. Consequently, the development and management of human capital is an essential element of its strategy and a key management activity. Human resource management in the fiscal year 2002 focused on smooth integration of the employees and human resource systems in the context of the merger, as well as on continuous improvement of recruitment, training and performance management processes. The process of integration of ICICI with ICICI Bank involved defining the organisational structure of the merged entity, people placement in various positions across the business and corporate groups, and integration of the grade and remuneration structure for the employees of ICICI, ICICI Bank, ICICI Capital Services and ICICI Personal Financial Services. The organisational structure was announced in February 2002 and became effective on 3 May 2002. The people placement process was based on appropriate competency profiling tools and matching employee profiles to job specifications. The grade integration process has also been completed, using job evaluation techniques. While ICICI Bank is India's second largest bank it had just over 7,700 employees is 31 March 2002, demonstrating its unique technology-driven and productivity-focused business model.

The recruitment process has been streamlined and a uniform recruitment policy and process implemented across the merged organisation. Robust ability—testing and competency— profiling tools are being used to strengthen the campus recruitment process and match the profiles of employees to the needs of the organisation. The ICICI Bank continues to be a preferred employer at leading business schools and higher education institutions across the country, offering a wide range of career opportunities across the entire spectrum of financial services. In addition to campus recruitment, ICICI Bank also undertakes lateral recruitment to bring new skills, competences and experience into the organisation and meet the requirements of rapidly growing businesses.

The rapidly changing business environment and the constant challenges it poses to organisations and businesses make it imperative to continuously enhance knowledge and skill sets across the organisation. ICICI Bank believes that building a learning organisation is critical to being competitive and growth oriented to meet customer expectations.

ICICI Bank has built strong capabilities in training and development to build competences. Training on products and services is imparted through web-based training modules. Special programmes on functional training and leadership development to build knowledge as well as management ability are conducted periodically appropriately as per the requirements of employees.

ICICI Bank seeks to build in all its employees a total commitment towards exceptional standards of performance and productivity, adaptability to the changing organisational needs and the demands of the business environment and a willingness to learn and acquire new capabilities. ICICI Bank believes in defining clear performance parameters for employees and empowering them to achieve their goals. This has helped to create a culture of high performance across the organisation.

ICICI Bank also has a structured process of identifying and developing leadership potential. Thus ICICI Bank has focused on human resource management as a key organisational activity and adopts efforts to integrate its employees as partners.

For all these scorecards to be effective, however, everyone in the organisation must understand the strategies for their unit, division and the overall corporation. The CEOs understand that they cannot implement strategies by themselves. They need contributions/actions and ideas from everyone. Individuals far from corporate and regional headquarters create considerable value by finding new and improved ways of doing business. This is not top–down direction. This is top–down communication, helping employees to learn how they can contribute to successful strategy implementation. Leaders use many different channels to communicate the strategic message. The strategy map and the BSC gets communicated though newsletters, brochures, bulletin boards, speeches, videos, training, education programmes and the company intranet. A final component occurs when the company finally implements the learning and growth objectives to upgrade the skills and capabilities of its employees. Employee skills and capabilities enhance internal business processes and customer value relating to outcome to other critical corporate processes.

ICICI's top management believes that all employees should have access to complete information regarding its strategy and positioning so that with the support of internal business processes and information technology tools take daily business decisions in a judicious manner. ICICI has made large investments in computers and intranet data base oriented information base that enable the employees to act in the decision-making situations appropriately.

Partnering with Customers

The customer perspective is at the heart of corporate strategy. Almost all companies want to grow revenues and reduce costs, so the objectives in the BSC's financial perspective are fairly generic across organisations. What differentiates them is how they define their customers and their value proposition for targeted customers. Often this process leads to strategic partnerships with targeted customers.

Over the past few years, ICICI Bank has transformed its business model and operating strategies. ICICI while being a virtual universal bank itself, derisked traditional asset portfolio by diversifying into retail finance. It capitalised on the opportunity for sustainable growth created by upward migration of household income levels and increasing awareness of retail financial services among consumers. Its successful implementation of this strategy is demonstrated by rapid progress towards market leadership in all retail products. The key dimensions of its retail strategy are products, channels and processes, underpinned by a strong customer focus. Its retail asset products include mortgages, automobile and two-wheeler loans, commercial vehicles and construction equipment financing, consumer durable loans, personal loans and credit cards. ICICI Bank has pioneered a multi-channel distribution strategy in India, giving its customers 24×7 (hours×day) access to banking services. The enhanced convenience that this offers to the customer has supported its customer acquisition efforts and migration of customer transactions from branches to lower cost technology enabled channels. ICICI Bank has also focused on the call centre as a key channel. With the latest information technology, the call centre is now evolving into a complete relationship management channel not only for the complaint resolution but also for cross-selling on in-bound calls.

ICICI Bank's Corporate banking strategy is based on providing customised financial solutions to clients, tailored to meet their specific requirements. The corporate banking strategy focuses on careful management of credit risk and adequate return on risk capital through risk-based pricing and proactive portfolio management, rapid growth in fee-based services and extensive use of technology to deliver high levels of customer satisfaction in a cost-effective manner. ICICI Bank's focus was on expanding the range and depth of corporate relationships.

By acquiring new clients and cross-selling all corporate banking products and services to the existing client base, ICICI Bank continued to focus on working capital finance for highly rated clients, structured transactions and channel financing. In longer-term loans, in the absence of traditional capital expenditure financing opportunities and limited corporate credit growth, ICICI Bank has taken advantage of emerging opportunities in the public sector disinvestments process, through structuring and advisory services. ICICI Bank has also emerged as pioneers in securitisation in India, by creating a market for a securitised corporate debt, which would help in expanding and deepening the debt markets.

ICICI Bank has made large investment in information technology with a view to gain competitive advantage by providing customer convenience and improved service as well as improving productivity and efficiency. This aspect can be considered as a contribution to enhance the level of internal business practices as well. Thus by adopting a partnership approach with customers, ICICI Bank is emerging as a leading player in financial services industry.

Partnering with Suppliers

When strong supplier relationships are part of the strategy leading to breakthrough customer and/or financial performance then outcome and performance driven measures for supplier relationships get incorporated into the BSC model. Further, by understanding and communicating the BSC approach effectively to employees in an organisation, employees recognise the importance and value of forging strategic relationships with key suppliers. This recognition and understanding provides the context for initiatives resources and performance feedback on the most critical elements of the supplier relationship.

The international institutional agencies like World Bank, International Finance Corporation, Asian Development, etc., and the domestic capital market institutions/markets are the principal suppliers/sources from where foreign exchange and domestic currency and lines of credit / fund requirements are mobilised. The principal focus of ICICI Bank's universal bank strategy was on the challenge of meeting regulatory reserve requirements on ICICI's liabilities prior to the merger. This posed the dual challenge of raising resources for meeting the reserve requirements and managing the interest rate risk arising from the acquisition of government securities in an environment of low interest rates. Yields on the government securities reached a historic low during 2001–2 as a consequence of the easy liquidity environment and RBI's soft interest rate policy. To minimise the risk of adverse mark-to-market impact on any rise in interest rates, ICICI Bank adopted a strategy of acquiring securities of lower duration. A significant portion of the requirement of government securities was acquired through active participation in primary auctions of floating-rate bonds and short-maturity treasury bills.

ICICI Bank has continuously emphasised on risk management and achieving appropriate trade-offs between risks and returns. All credit exposures are classified as per Reserve Bank of India (RBI) guidelines into performing and non-performing assets (NPA). Non-Performing Assets are further classified into sub-standard, doubtful and loss assets. From the fiscal year 2001, ICICI (while being a virtual universal bank) had adopted an accelerated provisioning policy whereby provisions aggregating 50 per cent of the secured portion of NPA are made over a three-year period instead of a five-and-a-half year period prescribed by RBI. Subsequent to the merger the ICICI Bank has also adopted the same provisioning policy. Loss of assets and the unsecured portion of the doubtful assets are fully provided for/written off. Additional provisions are made against specific NPAs if considered necessary by the top management. The NPA and risk management and other management control aspects of ICICI have been discussed by the author in a paper published earlier (*SEBI & Corporate Laws Weekly*, 10 and 17 December 2001).

ICICI had always laid importance on securing and maintaining high credit ratings by the national and international credit rating agencies not only for the necessity of obtaining funds from the national and international sources/markets but also as a matter of seeking and maintaining the funding agencies'/stakeholders' faith and trust. During the year 2001–2, ICICI became the first Indian company to be rated higher than the sovereign rating for India by Moody's Investor service when its senior and subordinated long-term foreign currency debt was rated Ba 1, i.e., one notch above the sovereign rating for India. The same rating has been assigned to post-merger ICICI Bank. ICICI Bank has maintained high profits and dividends to shareholders over the years and also forged a good relationship with RBI, Government of India and international financial agencies/markets throughout the process of adopting universal banking strategy.

Partnership with Communities

As in the case of utilities, banking/financial services institutions, whose prices (interest rates) and operations are regulated to some extent by governmental authorities/agencies, should have excellent relationships with these authorities and legislatures. Besides maintaining compliance with the requirements of governmental authorities and regulatory agencies, a corporate needs to achieve a reputation as a leader, by being a good employer and good corporate citizen.

ICICI Bank's corporate governance philosophy encompasses not only regulatory and legal requirements such as the terms of listing requirements with stock exchanges, but also several voluntary practices aimed at a high level of business ethics, effective supervision and enhancement of value for all stakeholders. ICICI Bank has established a tradition of best practices in corporate governance. The corporate governance framework in ICICI Bank is based on the executive management and the constitution of Board Committees, comprising a majority of independent directors and chaired by an independent director, to oversee critical areas. During the fiscal year 2002, ICICI Bank received several prestigious awards in recognition of its business strategies, customer services, human resources practices and transparency in financial reporting.

The merger strategy of India's largest financial institution, ICICI, with its largest private sector bank ICICI Bank, also involved significant accounting complexities and adhered to the internationally accepted accounting standards and the requirements of the Institute of Chartered Accountants of India.

ICICI Bank believes that as one of India's largest business enterprises and one of the largest participants in the financial system, it needs to make focused efforts towards contributing to economic and social development in India. This complements its business operations of providing financial services to government, industry and individual customers. ICICI Bank's community development initiatives are channelised through a dedicated not-for-profit group, the Social Initiatives Group (SIG) which seeks to identify and support cost-effective, time-bound, scalable and replicable initiatives designed to improve the capacity of the underprivileged to participate in the larger economy. ICICI Bank supports initiatives that have both near and long-term impact. In this context, health, education and availability of financing have been identified as the three key areas. Within these, infant health at birth, elementary education and micro-financial services has been identified for focused attention.

Conclusion

Benefits from adopting BSC framework to a live example of organisation as described earlier in the case of ICICI Bank are significant.

The BSC helps in translating the vision, mission and objectives of the organisation into short-term operational parameters and action oriented programmes towards achieving the desired goals in the current environmental context. It promotes goal congruence between the subunits and the organisation. The BSC links performance measures at the subunit level to the organisational strategic intent. BSC measures must therefore, be organisational strategy-specific. BSC ensures integration of financial measures and non-financial measures of performance. The BSC framework gives a balanced view of the company's performance and enables managers to keep a track of achievements on different parameters.

The value creation arises from mobilising and managing the organisation's intangible resources, especially loyal and profitable customer relationships, high quality and responsive operating supply chain processes, information systems and knowledge, and motivated, skilled and empowered employees. Leaders need new evaluation measures and management systems to align their tangible and intangible assets to deliver a coherent and integrated strategy. The strategy gets communicated in the above-mentioned BSC framework to the critical constituents—employees, customers, suppliers and the community—and focus their entire organisation on enhancing the strategic partnerships with these constituents that drive and sustain long-term value creation. The illustration of ICICI Bank as given here in the BSC framework is an attempt to throw new and innovative insights to its adopting universal banking strategy.

References

Balasubramaniam, C.S. 2001. Management Control Systems in Development Finance Institutions—Recent Developments and Issues, *SEBI & Corporate Laws Weekly*, 10 and 17 December.

Bradach J., 1996. 'Organisational Alignment: The 7-S Model', HBS Case 9-497-045, 12 November.

Deming, www.deming.org.uk.balancescorecard 'Harmonizing the Role and Operations of Development Financial Institutions and Banks', a discussion paper, Reserve Bank of India, January 1999.

ICICI Bank's 8th Annual Report and Accounts 2001 – 2002.

Kaura Mohinder N. 2002. *Management Control and Reporting Systems*, New Delhi: Response Books.

Kaplan, R.S. and D.P. Norton. 1992. 'The Balanced Scorecard Measures that Drive Performance', *Harvard Business Review Paperback*, MA: Cambridge.

SEBI and Corporate Laws Weekly, 8 April 2002.

Waterman R., T. Peters and J. Phillips. 1980. 'Structure is Not Organisation', *Business Horizons*, June.

6

Government to Citizen Relationships Gyandoot—Tales and Travails A Three Year-E-governance Experience

Sanjay Dubey

Abstract

Gyandoot is a world acclaimed ICT project. Much has been written about it and how it helped the rural populace access some of the government information; how its usage helped farmers increase their returns from agriculture produce; and how various government services were extended to citizens without involving the drudgery of meeting the government officials. However, since its launch, the project needs critical scrutiny. It is time to reflect back and assess as to what has been its achievements. Is Gyandoot a sustainable model or does it require further upgradation? What were its shortcomings? Can there be a better model? Is it replicable and scalable particularly with very low levels of teledensity[1] in rural areas? Is it possible that these kiosks can be converted in mobile information kiosks[2]? It is exactly these questions that this chapter tries to answer. This chapter gives the details as to how the synergies generated by Gyandoot has been further utilised in the past four years to augment the system and in turn give more benefits to the citizens.

Introduction

District Profile

Dhar is a tribal district situated in western Madhya Pradesh, India. Out of total population of 1.7 million, 40 per cent of them subsist below the poverty line and only 48 per cent of them are literate. Spread over an area of 8,195 sq.km, the district is administratively divided into 13 development blocks, 668 Gram Panchayats, 10 urban areas and 1,543 villages. The economy is agriculture based and the main crops are soyabean, cotton and wheat. Road connectivity being low (27.20 km per 100 sq. km) and with no rail head, it is a district which lacks the basic infrastructure.

Present Scenario

Presently, relationship between government and citizen is more of a benefactor–beneficiary one. Despite poor backgrounds, citizens are becoming more demanding. They argue the logic of standing in queues for depositing the electricity bill. They question, and rightfully so, about the need of spending money and time for lodging a routine complaint as of a faulty hand pump in the neighborhood, and so on. There could be counter arguments from the side of governments for not being able to provide these services, but it is very difficult if not impossible for the governments to 'immunise' itself from this issue any more. Local government should be at the heart of community, not at its margins (Budhiraja, 2003).

Right to information and citizens charter (M.P. Govt. Act: 2000) have made it mandatory on the part of the government to divulge the information pertaining to the matters of citizens. State governments with their best intentions cannot provide solution to this, if the information remains in the hands of few individuals. More often than not the officials have vested interest in not disclosing this information. Hence, if we are keen to allow every individual to play its role, it becomes essential that we make information available at multiple sources and involve multiple players. In short, the system should be SMART[3]. But before any system can successfully achieve this, the following issues should be resolved:

- should it be government funded or should it be community owned?
- should there be user charges and if yes then on what basis?
- who shall run these kiosks and what should be the timings for kiosks?
- should the kiosk be open on holidays?
- where should these kiosks be housed to protect the hardware and at the same time make it easily accessible?
- which shall be the services on offer to citizens?
- should it be intranet or internet based? and
- which should be the language of interaction?

Gyandoot for the first time tried to address these issues. It was launched with the aim of providing various services (see Annexure). The services on offer ranged from e-commerce to e-governance. The rural population is serviced through kiosks which are situated hundreds of kilometres away from the district headquarters. The village councils provided the seed capital for establishment of kiosks, while the local rural youth, passouts from high school, were identified and trained to manage the kiosks. For managing these kiosks, the manager is not paid any salary or stipend. He/she is supposed to earn his livelihood from the user charges. He/she depending upon the response from the citizens can remain open all days a week and 24 hours a day.

All this was made possible, while different state governments and institutions were trying to figure out answers to some of the above questions. No sooner was it launched did it win the national and international acclaim in the form of 'TCS–CSI' award and 'Stockholm Challenge Award'. Media, international institutions and personalities showed interest and it is at this time that skeptics also started questioning the sustainability of the system. People feared that it will be yet another innovation which will die its natural death after the transfer of the officials who planned it. Alas! These predictions did not turn true.

Achievements So Far

Doubts may be raised that there are not enough kiosks that are making money as they were earlier expected to do (Brij Kothari: 2002). There are some services, which are not getting enough traffic. Well, I have no hesitation in admitting it but then can I ask this question? Is it not the strength of the model that automatically culls out the worst performers and non-innovators? Why should they become the committed liability to the system when all of us loathe it and talk about fair competition and fair market economy. There are kiosks offering almost the same services as other kiosks yet they are making money to the tune of more than Rs 7000 a month. They have added systems, web cams, photocopiers, etc., in their initial inventory. If the problems as the skeptics point out are so immense then what is that, that is keeping them in business? Why do they still open the kiosks on all days and even on non-working hours? Have we been able to evolve any system other than Gyandoot, which gives services to all on all days? Have we really looked into the fact that, if these kiosks were to be operated by would have been immense? This single wrong decision alone would have wiped out the faith of its customers, i.e., citizens.

Whenever we evaluate Gyandoot, we always assume Gyandoot as a static system in the dynamic world. When every third month we have different models of computer that is being rolled out of computer

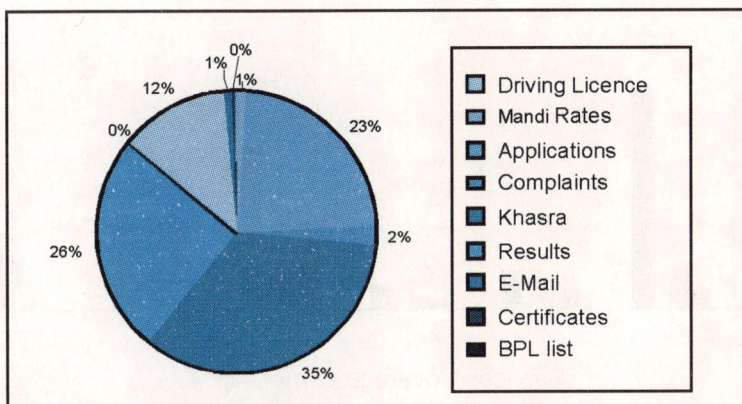

Figure 6.1: Usage Pattern

companies it is naïve to assume that Gyandoot should continue to offer the same set of services as it did at the time of launch. One of the major strengths of Gyandoot is its simple mechanism of adding facilities and services. It is more a demand based system than technology dependent. I admit that there are services, which are more revenue generating than others, but there are services, which are essential from the utility point of view rather than from the revenue angle. There were services, which have been added, worked very well and got phased out because of the change in policy of government. Driving license is one such example. Our perspective will change once we see it as a system that is evolving and innovating continuously.

The world has changed since its launch and so has the original services in Gyandoot. Mandi rates, which was one of the most sought after service at the time of launch, gradually lost it charm since mobile phones penetrated the markets. Issuance of driving license through kiosks was another service which was not offered at the time of the launch, but received massive response when it was launched in December 2002. It continued to remain so till 'smart card' system was introduced by the government for issuing driving license. There were some such

Table 6.1

Year	No. of Services	Coverage area			Ownership	
		Blocks	Tehsils	Kiosks	Community Owned	Private
	1	2	3	4	5	6
2000	5	5	3	21	21	0
2001	10	5	4	24	21	3
2002	35	10	5	39	21	18
2003	54	11	7	40	22	18

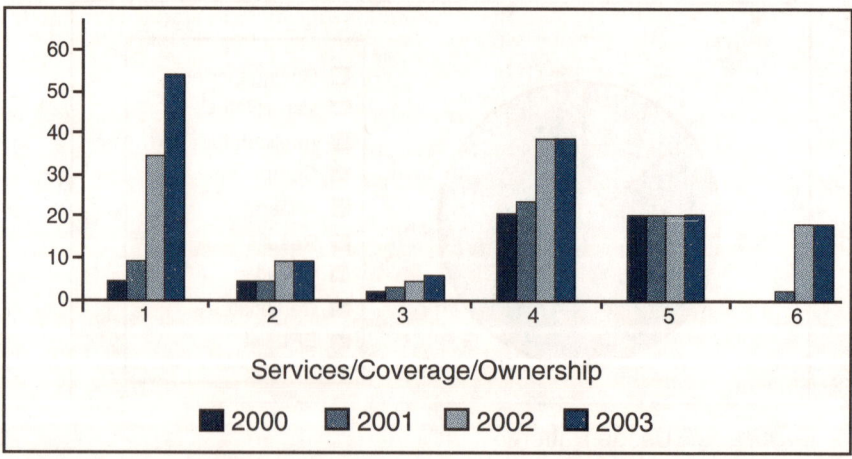

Figure 6.2: Growth of Gyandoot

similar services which were not able to generate enough traffic. However, continuous upgradation of the system and services, kept it kicking and alive. Connectivity and power backup were the speed breakers in sustainability and expansion of the network. To overcome these hurdles we forayed in the field of WiLL for connectivity and data transfer and providing solar panels in kiosks for power backup. In short, the system could not have survived if the continuous upgradation and innovation of system was not addressed. Details (see Table 6.1 and Figure 6.2) of various services, coverage and ownership of kiosks only highlight the fact that Gyandoot have grown from strength to strength.

JAN MITRA— a New Concept

Citizens having tasted the power of information expected that we should be more transparent in exercising the so-called discretionary powers. In other words, they should have the right to critically examine our decisions. We accepted the challenge and 'Jan Mitra' the Common Facilitation Centre (CFC) was launched in January 2005 on the third anniversary of Gyandoot. The idea is to complement Gyandoot's spread along with the office automation and file tracking system. Decisions which were hitherto shrouded in mystery are now open to every citizen. The stress now is on bringing a transparent and responsible system, thereby improving the visibility and viability of Gyandoot.

Working of Jan Mitra

Jan Mitra functions as 'one stop shop' extending all kinds of services to the citizen under one roof. The application before being accepted at the centre is screened for any possible faults or missing papers so as to ensure that the application submitted is not rejected on frivolous grounds. Once the application is accepted the applicant is sure of getting his request decided on merits. The centre has the facility of receiving applications, disbursing all kinds of forms, tender documents and to track the movements of his/her application without approaching 'baboos' of the collectorate. Jan Mitra (CFC) has made this possible as all the sections and departments of collectorate are connected through Local Area Network (LAN). The remote computers in *tehsil* and block offices are connected through dial-up facilities. When an application is submitted to the Jan Mitra (CFC), a unique token number is generated which can be used for future reference to know the status of the applicant's file. This facility can be availed not only from the CFC but also from any of the remotely located Gyandoot kiosks physically hundreds of kilometres away from district headquarters. In all 40 government departments in Dhar collectorate are connected through CFC and Gyandoot server. Introduction of Jan Mitra reduced the offline movements of application from Gyandoot server to the government offices. Now all applications and requests made from rural kiosks move online from one section to another.

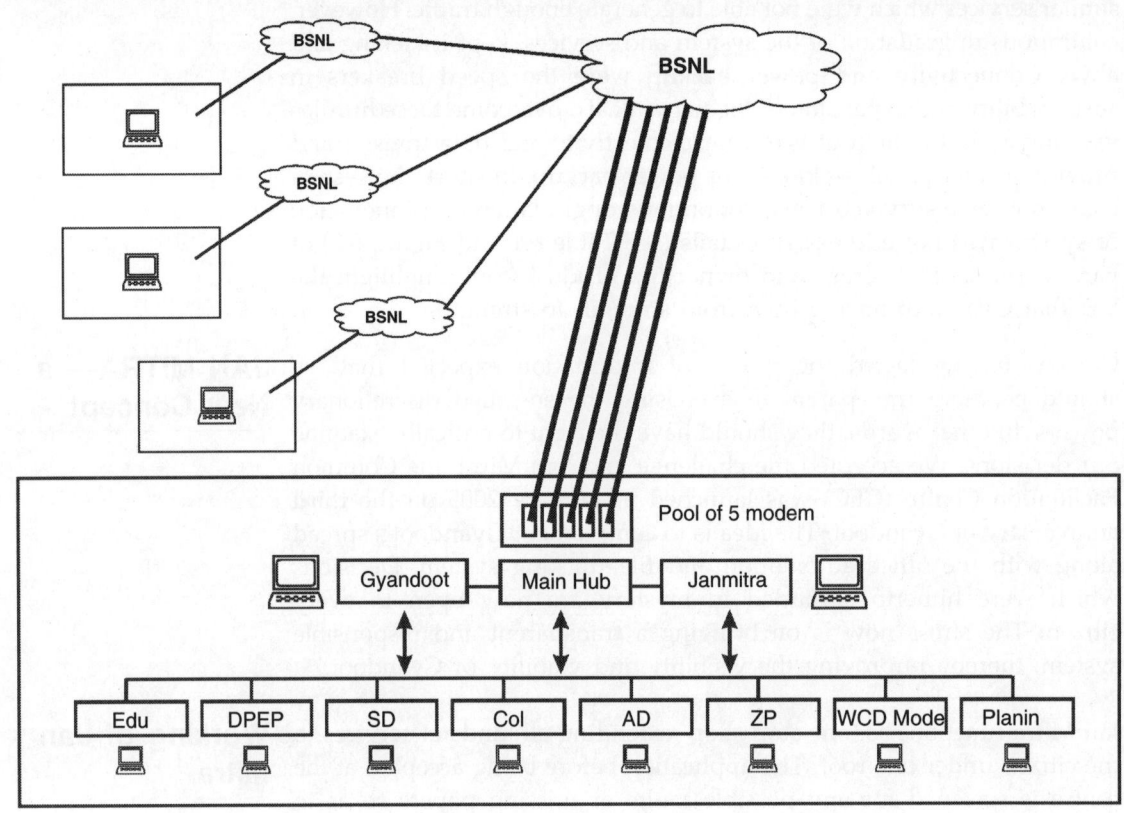

Figure 6.3: Gyandoot Intranet Network

Services

District and local governments have traditionally aimed their e-governance efforts in extending facilities to citizens. These efforts have always stopped short of touching the domain of District Magistrates 'discretionary' powers. Overawed with the zeal of improving interface for citizens we often forgot our employees. The mundane matters of getting GPF (Group Provident Fund), pension cases sanctioned have frustrated and demotivated the employees. It is for the first time through 'Jan Mitra' that we decided to address some of these issues which were strictly the prerogative of the district magistrate's power.

Disposal of personal claims of government servants, viz., GPF, GIS, Gratuity, FBF and pension cases is now handled online. Government officials can make a request from rural kiosks located in their village, for their personal claims and they are informed back about the sanction/rejection of their application in their respective kiosks. This not only reduces the waste of time but acts as a great motivating factor.

This also functions as a centre, wherefrom all kinds of forms and tender documents are dispensed and accepted. Challans, which are hitherto being deposited in banks, are also deposited here. Services that are provided from Jan Mitra centre are listed below (Table 6.2).

Table 6.2. List of Services Provided by Jan Mitra

S. No.	Facilities	Charges Limit	Time	No. of Applicants
1.	Agricultural license application/renewal	Rs. 10	1 month	078
2.	Arms license application/sanction	Rs. 10	3 months	423
3.	Application for recognition of new school/renewal/extension	Rs.10	1 month	349
4.	Application for licenses like petrol/diesel/kerosene	Rs. 10	1 month	004
5.	GPF application	Rs. 10	15 days	015
6.	Application for mining license/renewal	Rs. 10	3 months	183
7.	Application for domicile certificate	Rs. 10	1 month	1410
8.	Application for verification	Rs. 10	15 days	
9.	Permanent caste certificate	Rs. 10	1 month	
10.	Temporary caste certificate	Rs. 10	15 days	
11.	Affidavit printing	Rs. 5	immediate	020
12.	Application for drug license/renewal	Rs. 10	1 month	004
13.	Application for registration of firms /renewal	Rs. 10	2 months	002
14.	Court cases, status	Rs. 5	immediate	020
15.	Tender process	Rs. 10	immediate	099
16.	Pension cases	Rs. 5	3 months	025
17.	Personal claims	Rs. 5	7 days	
18.	11-point programme	Rs. 2	immediate	005
19.	Bus Timings	Rs. 2	immediate	015
20.	Railway Timings	Rs. 2	immediate	025
21.	Khasra	Rs. 15	immediate	3358
22.	Exam Results	Rs. 10	immediate	259
23.	Others	Rs. 10	immediate	011
			Total	6,305

Court Cases

The revenue and judicial cases are tried on a regular basis. However, the applicants are not required to be present on every date in which the case is heard in the court. Earlier they have to depend upon their lawyer to get the information regarding the new date of hearing as also the status of the case. But with the introduction of 'Jan Mitra' now the client from any of the rural kiosks can find out the status and the next date of hearing. This has reduced their dependency on their lawyers and have also unburdened lawyer to a great extent. Presiding officers of the court are happy as it has resulted in better turnouts in their courts.

Arms Licence

District Magistrate is authorised by the government to issue arms license to the residents of the district. Earlier anybody in need of arms license has to fill the form and submit it in the concerned section. This application was then processed and sent to Sub Divisional Magistrates/ Superintendent of Police for verification of antecedents of the applicant. On receiving the antecedent report, the District Magistrate decides

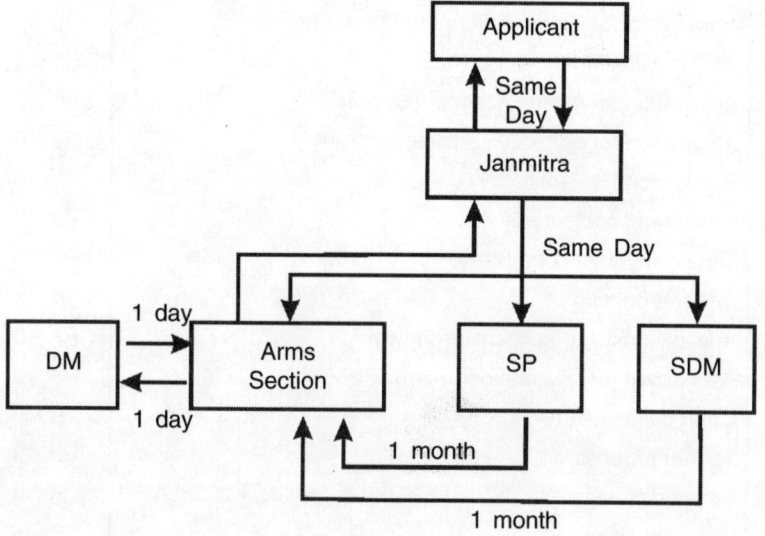

Figure 6.5: Manual process of issuance of arms license

about sanctioning/rejection of the application. This process earlier used to take somewhere between 3–8 months. However, after the introduction of 'Jan Mitra' not only the application can be processed at the earliest but also one can track the movements of his application along with the comments by the concerned officials for sanctioning/rejecting the case.

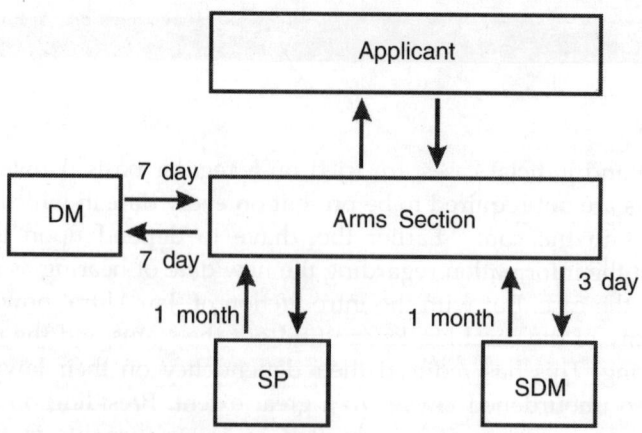

Figure 6.6: Improved Process of Issuance of Arms License

Fertiliser Licence

For getting fertiliser license one has to submit his application to the concerned SADO (Sub Area Development Officer). After scrutiny, the SADO forwards the same to the DDA (District Development Officer) within 15 days. In the DDA office the process takes about one month for issuing/rejecting his application. With the introduction of 'Jan Mitra' the applicant saves about 15 days for getting the results/status of their applications. During this time he can track the movement of his application.

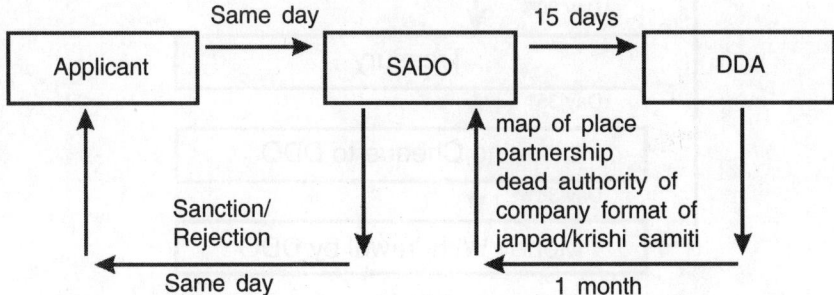

Figure 6.7: Manual Process of Issuance of Fertiliser License

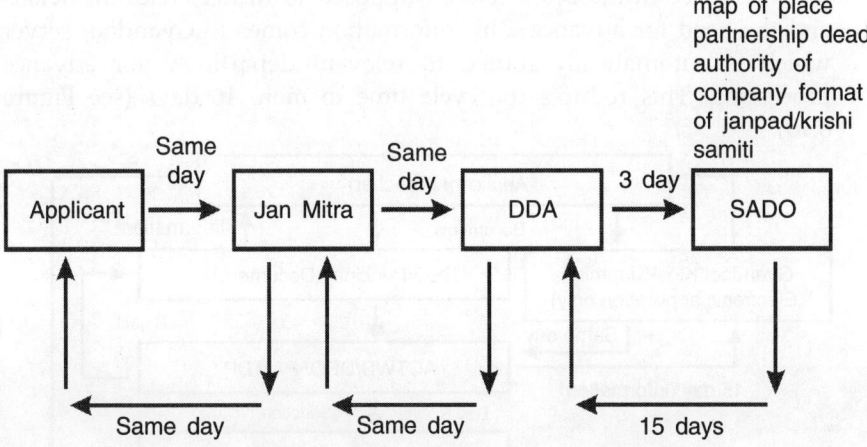

Figure 6.8: Improved Process of Issuance of Fertiliser License

GPF Sanction

In the earlier process if an employee posted in block has to withdraw GPF advance then he has to apply to his OIC and then what follows is the long wait (see Figure 6.9). Typically the whole cycle of getting the money paid takes 50 days often defeating the very purpose for which it was required. This too when everything moves 'smoothly'. We have tackled this delay by introducing Jan Mitra and Gyandoot in the process. Now an employee while making an application for withdraw of GPF advance also registers himself in one of the kiosks situated near

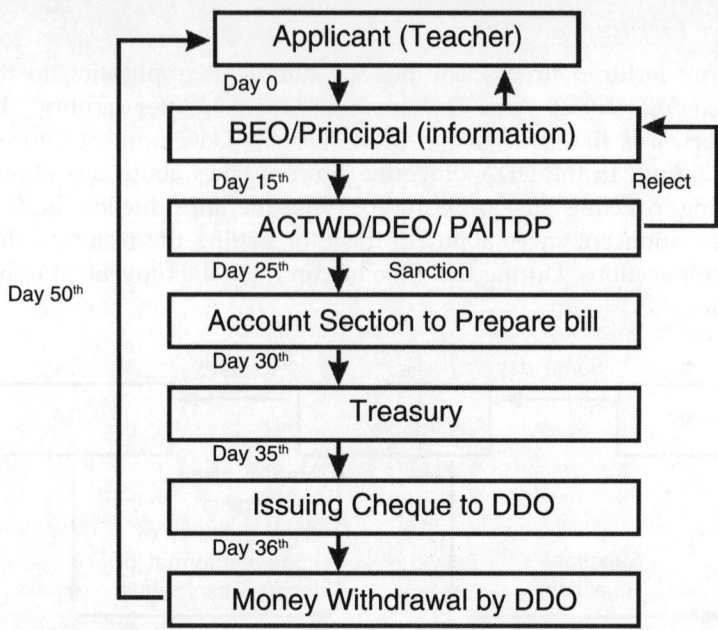

Figure 6.9: Manual Process of Issuance of GPF Advance

his workplace in the block. He is supposed to furnish relevant details and the need for advance. This information comes to Gyandoot server which is automatically routed to relevant department for advance processing. This reduces the cycle time to mere 16 days (see Figure 6.10).

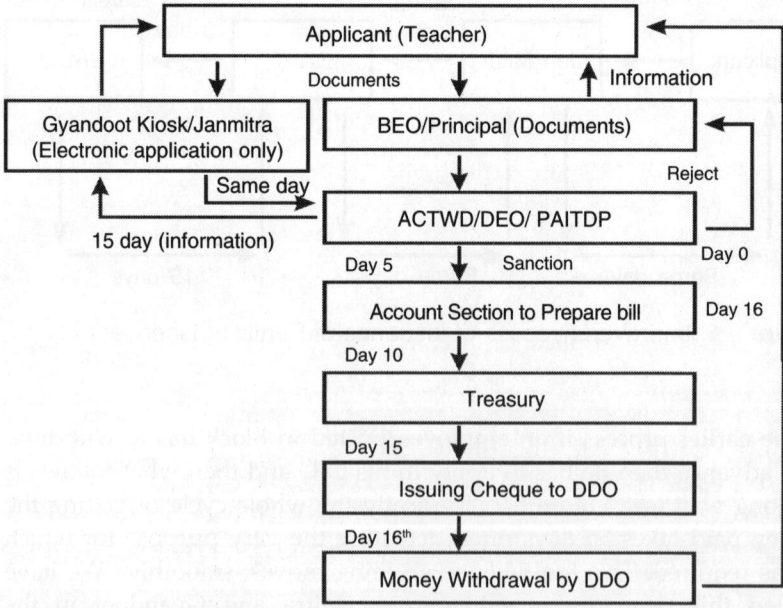

Figure 6.10: Improved Process of Issuance of GPF Advance

The difference between what we do and what we could do would suffice to solve most of the world's problem.

Mahatma Gandhi

Complex Problems—Simple Solutions

The question is how can technology help us to achieve this? The reaction to these ranges from degovermentalisation to reengineering the government processes. But there are some sovereign functions which any government has to discharge. So what is the way out? The answer lies in finding simple solutions. It is obvious from the flowcharts provided earlier that we have not done any reengineering of the processes or any change in flow of information. Besides reducing the slacks that are present at various levels by the application of technology (internal efficiency raising), we have also provided the services at the doorstep of citizens. We evolved the system which can lend itself for closer monitoring. This has resulted in considerable savings in time, facilitating the citizens to get assured and timely replies.

User Charges

Jan Mitra, the Common Facilitation Centre extends 20 services some of which are common to the services available in Gyandoot. Citizens accessing the services have to pay the user charges. These user charges are fixed on the basis of opportunity cost in terms of time and cost of travel. Each service has very stringent dead line within which his/her application has to be decided.

Strengthening of Gyandoot

The anticipated amount of traffic per year in Jan Mitra (CFC) by the proposed services is 15,000 to 20,000 per year. However, the number of applications and services received in the first four months itself has made it a successful venture. The average income per year is expected to be Rs 2,20,000. This ensures Jan Mitra's viability since the initial expenditure is incurred by the Gyandoot Samiti and the recurring expenditure is easily reimbursable by the earnings made by the centre.

Since *tehsils* are also connected through dial-up facilities, it will now be possible to give *Khasara, B-1* copies online in real time to any of the applicants from remote locations. The extension of facility of applying for personal claims through Gyandoot kiosks will itself generate immense amount of traffic from government servants to bolster and support Gyandoot.

Status of any application can be monitored from the offices of the Collector and CEO Zila Panchayat. It acts as a deterrent to the erring officers thereby ensuring timely disposal of cases. Online transfer of the application reduces the paperwork in the offices and consequent delays in decision making.

Proposed Services

The proposed services to be extended to the citizens include issuance of birth and death certificate, installation of photocopier, charging facility of Sims of all reputed mobile companies and installation of railway reservation counter at the centre. Incidentally, we have received sanction of a computerised railway reservation counter by the railway ministry which will soon be functional at the centre. From 9 June 2003 we have facilitated the citizens to deposit their electric bills at the centre. Till today a total of 6,305 people have utilised its services for depositing its electric bills.

Road Blocks and Speed-breakers

Launching and sustaining the system is not as simple as it sounds. Problems are faced on regular basis and impediments range from technological backlog to human element.

Technological Hurdles

Telecommunication infrastructure in Dhar is as good or as bad in any other rural area of the country. Often one has to constantly chase telecom officials for mending one snag or the other. Mix of copper cables and optical fibres creates barriers in smooth transmission of data because of the different bandwidths that they support. Vagaries of power availability (rather unavailability) during business hours (morning to evening) can't even be cured by providing UPS in the kiosks.

Human Factor

We have tried using solar panels in kiosks but initial capital cost and constant upkeep restricted its wide usage. Kiosk operators who often have no working knowledge of computers find it difficult to generate awareness amongst the rural people. At times simple citizens are at loss to distinguish between a computer terminal and a TV, further hindering its easy acceptance. Many are unaware of existence of this facility as they have never ventured out of their surroundings to visit any government office. Resistance have often come from those quarters from where you least expect them. Officials who are to facilitate the wellbeing of citizens are often the ones to discredit the system and try sabotaging it. They would be reluctant to accept any change that will reduce their discretionary powers and make them accountable. They would be the ones who would throw spanner in any initiative that the government takes and it is they who need to be convinced about the benefits of technology before they accept it. Training and motivating them needs to be done at regular intervals. Last but not the least, top leadership in the district and state play a vital role to keep the system functional and responsive.

Progress So Far

As on today, a total of 6,305 applications were received/and services provided through Jan Mitra, (see Table 6.2) while Gyandoot services continued to serve the public.

Conclusion

To extend government programmes in predominantly tribal districts with more than 60 per cent of its population belonging to Patilyas, Bhils and Bhilalas has always been a development challenge. Shrinking natural resources with persistent drought-like conditions in the district only lead to deprivation. In such circumstances, citizens look towards the government to support them. Information regarding new works have been opened in the government sector, repairs of hand pumps for safe drinking water, timely disposal of grievances, delivery of agriculture inputs and other professional services are the needs of the hour. In these circumstances, IT open up new vistas of development, empowering penurious people and equipping them with the services at their doorstep, leading to savings in their time and money.

A self-sustainable model, with a wide area coverage and scope for new addition of services, is the kind of model that is required in developing countries like India. It is cost-effective, easy to install and ideal to bring about transparency, efficiency, effectiveness and make 'responsible' governments respond in government functioning.

Annexure

Sl. No.	Name of Service	Retail tariff (in rupees)	Delivery time frame (in days)
1	Grievance Redressal	10	7
2	Caste certificate	10	15
3	Domicile certificate	10	7
4	Income certificate	10	7
5	Land records	15	Immediate
6	PMRY	10	15
7	Driving license	20	10
8	Online results of 10th/12th board exams	10	Immediate
9	Hindi e-mail	10	-
10	Employment registration	10	15
11	Social Security Pension	10	10
12	Old age Pension	10	10
13	Matrimonial	25	-
14	Auction site	25	-
15	Application forms	5/page	Immediate
16	BPL survey list	5/page	Immediate
17	Local employment news	5/page	Immediate
18	Registration of birth/death (urban area)	10	10
19	Social Security Pension	10	10
20	Expert advice on agriculture	10	7
21	Expert advice on veterinary	10	7
22	Expert advice on health	10	7
23	Expert advice on legal/administrative issues	10	7
24	Online booking of vermi compost	10	Immediate
25	Information on child marriage/bonded labour etc.	Free	-

26	Details of sanctioned works under Rural Development		
	Details of sanctioned works under MP/MLA	5/page	Immediate
27	Yellow pages	-	Immediate
28	Gyandoot course	50/student	Immediate
29	Property Registration guidelines	5/page	Immediate
30	Model question papers	5/page	Immediate
31	Personality tests	Free	Immediate
32	Online quiz	Free	Immediate
33	Sawaliram se puchiye (online answer to children queries)	Free	7
34	Gyandoot e-library	Free	Immediate
35	Details of allocations made to various Panchayats	5/page	Immediate
36	Details of allocations to various Public Distribution Shops	5/page	Immediate
37	Details of all the government schemes for development	5/page	Immediate
38	Opinion poll	Free	Immediate
39	Citizen charter	5/page	Immediate
40	Important telephone nos. of the district	5/page	Immediate
41	Railway/Bus time tables	5/page	Immediate
42	Agriculture Practices/Rates of certified seeds	5/page	Immediate
43	News on government tenders	5/page	Immediate
44	Tele-medicine	-	4

Source: District Collector's Office

End notes

1. As per 2000 figures by International Telecommunications Union's Information and Communication Technology Global Statistics, the teledensity in India was 3.20 overall and 0.4 for rural India.
2. Dean IIT Kanpur in one of his speeches in 2002 has remarked that the technology for kiosks should be so simple that it can be available even on *thela* (hand carriage).
3. SMART : Simple, Moral, Accountable, Responsive, Transparent.

Glossary

ACTWD : Assistant Commissioner, Tribal Welfare Department.

Bhils : tribal community of central India; considered to be one of the five most populous tribes of India; categorised by migrations and their aggressive nature.

Block : administrative unit for development.

BEO : Block Education Officer.

Collector : representative of the state government at the district who is vested with authority to administer the area.

Collectorate : campus of Collector office.

CFC : Common Facilitation Centre.

Gram Panchayat : administrative unit of a village or a group of five villages headed by the sarpanch; looks after the

	welfare and development of the panchayat areas; forms the lowermost rung of the PRI (Panchayati Raj Institution).
Gram Sabhas	: body comprising all adult members residing in a panchayat: considered to be the general body of the gram panchayat.
Gyandoot	: (literal meaning—purveyor of knowledge): name of the Intranet network.
Jan Mitra	: Common Facilitation Centre.
Khasra-B1	: land ownership record.
Kiosks	: place where computer system and other peripherals are installed.
Mandis	: auction centres for agricultural produce; few local traders bid for the produce; often managed by Agricultural Produce Marketing Committee.
PA, ITDP	: Project Administrator, Integrated Tribal Development Project.
Patwari	: village revenue officer; has all the land records with him, which he often keeps in a bag; manipulations in his records result in countless legal battles.
Samiti	: society/committee.
Sarpanch	: head of the village council; directly elected by the villagers; lowest and most critical rung of the elected representative in the PRI.
Soochanalayas	: (literal meaning: centre for information) information kiosk.
Tehsil	: administrative unit for the revenue officer.
Zila Panchayat	: district council; elected body comprising 15–25 members, which looks after the development and welfare activities in rural areas; controls block councils and village councils.

References

Bailie, M. and D. Winseck (eds). 1996. *Democratizing Communication: Comparative Perspectives on Information and Power*. Cresskill, NJ: Hampton Press.

Bhatnagar, S. and R. Schware. 2000. *Information and Communication Technology in Development: Cases from India*. London: Sage Publications.

Budhiraja. *Electronic Governance—A Key Issue in the 21st Century*.

Burns, D., R. Hambelton and P. Hoggett. 1994. *The Politics of Decentralization*. Basingstoke: Macmillan.

Dutton, W. H. 1996. *Information and Communications Technologies: Visions and Realities.* Oxford: Oxford University Press.

Gore, A. 1991. 'Infrastructure for the Global Village', *Scientific American*, 265: 108–11.

_____. 1993. *Creating a Government that Works Better and Costs Less.* New York and Harmondsworth: Plume Books and Penguin.

Graham, S. 1991. *Developing Community Teleservice Centres.* Manchester. University of Manchester.

Govt. of India IT Policy–2002.

Govt. of M.P. IT Policy–2002. Information Technology Mission.

Information Technology Mission. Govt. of M.P. IT Policy–2002.

Office of the Vice President. 1993. 'Re-engineering Government through IT', Washington DC: Government Printing Office.

Rajora, Dr R. 2001. *Bridging the Digital Divide: Gyandoot – the Model for Community Networks.* New Delhi: Tata Mcgraw Hill.

Smart Card – Transport Commissioner M.P. Order No. 736/tc/2002 dated 14.11.02.

Stoker, G. 1988. *The Politics of Local Government.* Basingstoke: Macmillan Education.

Third Human Development Report. 2002. Madhya Pradesh.

Zuboff, S. 1988. *In the Age of the Smart Machine: The Future of Work and Power*, Oxford: Heinemann.

Online Resources

Moving from Virtual to Real Benefits in Local Development UNCRD 2002: Reflections in an E-workspace.

Evaluating the Impacts of the Gyandoot Project: Naveen Prakash, Brij Kothari. http://www.uncrd.or.jp/ict/eworkspace/papers/cs_gyandoot.htm

Gyandoot: Community-Owned Rural Internet Kiosks: Subhash Bhatnagar and Nitesh Vyas. http://www1.worldbank.org/publicsector/egov/gyandootcs.htm

White Paper on Electronic Governance: http://egov.mit.gov.in/

E-governance Related Issues: http://egov.mit.gov.in/

What is Electronic Governance?: http://egov.mit.gov.in/

Minimum Agenda for E-governance: http://egov.mit.gov.in/

Department of Information Technology, Madhya Pradesh: http://www.mp.nic.in/dit/policy.htm

Ministry of Personnel, Public Grievances and Pensions

The Freedom of Information Act — 2002: http://persmin.nic.in/freedomofinfo1.html

Right to information — Madhya Pradesh: http://mpinfo.org/hindi/right/index.html

7
Enterprise Resource Planning

Anand Kr Tiwari

What Is an Enterprise Resource Planning (ERP)?

Enterprise Resource Planning (ERP), as it is called, is a multi-module application package which support the broad set of activities to help computerise and manage all the important areas of a company's business. It allows the company to replace individual, disconnected applications with an integrated system for planning, monitoring and controlling their business. The various ERP modules include production planning and management, sales and distribution, finance, material management, inventory management, plant maintenance, quality control, human resource, document management, etc.

Enterprise Resource Planning does a seamless integration between all the modules so as to maintain a smooth flow of information/data across the organisation and at the same time maintaining a horizontal integration of all these activities to financial activity and Expert Information System/Management Information System (EIS/MIS).

An ERP implementation is a major exercise. It is basically a 'Business Practice' rather than an 'IT Activity'. It should not be treated as 'panacea' but as an 'enabler for business'. It demands lot of business process reengineering, change management activity, change in work culture, and total commitment and involvement of both top management and end-user. That's why all ERP systems are said to be 'user driven' rather than IT driven. The IT people are there to provide technical support to the project.

The bottom line is that an ERP implementation is a true team effort involving users, IT personnel, ERP implementer and the top management.

ERP Component

The ERP should be implemented based on centralised server architecture. The server required for the ERP package shall be located at a central section mostly corporate office.

The ERP implementation has be done in two phases as detailed below:

Phase I
- Finance module

- Sales and distribution module
- Material management
- Production planning and management
- Costing
- Quality management

Phase II
- Human resources
- Maintenance

The implementation in each phase should have the following milestones:

(a) Business definition

(b) Prototyping/blueprint

(c) Master database creation

(d) Integration testing

(e) Implementation

(f) Post Implementation support

Let us take a live example and find out how ERP was implemented in a large Indian public sector company.

Table 7.1. IT Strategy Implementation Road Map

S.No	Activity	1st year				2nd year				3rd year			
		1*	2	3	4	5	6	7	8	9	10	11	12
1	BPR												
2	LAN												
3	Installing Hardware												
4	Traning												
5	ERP implementation												
6	Non-ERP Appl. Dev.												
7	Web server, internet and intranet application												
8	E-Business												

* Each cell represents a Quarter (3 Months)

Introduction

Objectives of the Study

(a) To infer that Information Technology (IT) can be a strategic tool for the sustained business growth of Metals Ltd in this highly competitive environment.

(b) To evolve an effective IT centric strategy that Metals Ltd can adopt.

(c) To suggest the prerequisites for implementing the recommended IT strategy.
(d) To give the action plan including infrastructure requirement for implementing the recommended IT strategy.

Scope of the Study

The scope of this research report is to give a broad IT strategy for the organisation of Metals Ltd to enable it to improve upon its performance. The report also recommends the new IT infrastructure requirement, estimated total cost of implementation, as well as the road map for implementation of the IT plan.

Introduction to the Organisation

Mishra Dhatu Nigam Limited (Metals Ltd), Hyderabad, is a Government of India enterprise under the ministry of defence. It was incorporated in 1973 as a public sector undertaking for the manufacture of special metals and superalloys. Presently, Metals Ltd is an ISO 9001–2000 organisation of worth Rs 133 crore and an annual turnover of around Rs 100 crore, an employee strength of around 1,300, and a market share of around 30 per cent serving strategic sectors like defence, atomic energy, aerospace, as well as general engineering industries.

For setting up Metals Ltd technical collaboration with companies from France and Germany has been entered into with a view to achieve self-reliance in special steels, superalloys and titanium and titanium-based alloys needed for strategic sectors. For nearly two decades now, Metals Ltd has been handling challenging production tasks, taking lead positions in indigenisation of critical technologies and products to render support to several programmes of national importance and hi-tech segments of the Indian industry.

Mission of Metals Ltd

To achieve self-reliance in the development, production and supply of strategic materials and products for critical and hi-tech engineering application.

Products

The product range of Metals Ltd can be divided into five major categories:

Superalloys: nickel-based, cobalt-based and iron-based alloys.

Titanium and Titanium Alloys: commercially pure titanium and titanium alloys.

Special Purpose Steels: maraging steel, armament steel, nuclear grade steels, cryogenic steels and special stainless steel.

Special Products: weld consumables, magnesium alloy, titanium tubes and molybdenum wire and plates.

Alloys for Electrical and Electronics: resistance alloys, controlled expansion alloys and soft magnetic alloys.

Quality

Metals Ltd has ISO 9001-2000 Certification as well as international certification by quality regulatory and monitoring agencies like Director General of Quality Assurance, Director General of Civil Aviation, Department of Space and Atomic Energy, and Source Approval of Boing Co., USA and a successful Quality audit by EADS-AIRBUS.

Customers

Metals Ltd has in its clientele customers from all strategic sectors like

Space Sector	:	VSSC, LPSC.
Atomic Energy	:	Department of Atomic Energy, NPCL, NFC.
Defence Sector	:	Ordnance Factories Board, HAL, BDL, Defence Research Development Organisation.
Commercial Sector	:	Bharat Heavy Electricals Ltd., Railways, Lamp Industries, Reliance Industries, Bajaj Tempo, Crompton Greaves, etc.

Metals Ltd has its head office based in Hyderabad with commercial offices at

- New Delhi,
- Mumbai,
- Chennai, and
- Kolkata.

The manpower strength of Metals Ltd as on 1 April 2003 was 1,288 comprising 256 executives and 1,032 non-executives.

Research Methodology Used in the Study

Data Type and Sources

The sources of internal secondary data are:
- annual reports of Metals Ltd;
- performance review reports; and
- corporate plan document of Metals Ltd.

The sources of external data for the study are:
- periodicals like *Metal News*; and
- data published on Internet/websites like www.infoline.com of major metallurgical companies like SAIL, TISCO, Kalyani Steels, etc.

Data from presentations made by IT consultancy organisations like HCL Infosystems, OAK Brook Technology, Aptech Consulting, etc., on the computerisation of Metals Ltd is used. This secondary data has been collected for the past five years.

Primary data collection is here required for conclusive research and will be the one collected for the very purpose of this research study.

The major sources of primary data are stakeholders of Metals Ltd—heads of various departments/sections, employees/users, etc. Also functional-in-charges of some such organisations like BDL Ltd., DMRL,

Godavari Fertilisers, etc., where similar kind of study has been done and who have already implemented IT, have been interviewed.

Again study has been made regarding the IT technology available in the market.

Methods of Data Collection

The major collection method used is the communication method, which is by way of direct/indirect dialogue with the respondents in verbal/written fashion using questionnaires, structured formats, etc.

At the same instance, observation method of data collection, which is actually observation of various phenomenon/business processes, is also employed so as to get an insight into the real situation and learn user as well as organisation behaviour.

In communication methodology the techniques included are:

Data Sampling

The major sampling methodology used are simple random sampling and judgement sampling based upon such vital parameters about the respondents like knowledge and experience of respondent about the organisation, functional knowledge, IT savvyness, open mind, attitude/approach about problem solving etc. All efforts have been made to confirm the representativeness of selected sample.

Data Processing and Analysis

Data so collected, are then processed and edited for any error, omission and inconsistency. After through processing, it is summarised in various tables and presented in graphical/pictorial formats like bar chart, pie chart, line graph, etc., so as to bring out the relative importance of various components of data and to represent variations/exceptional behaviours.

Such tools like signed test, regression analysis and model building used do analyse the data and come out with some conclusion.

Observations about the Organisation

Metals Ltd was initially envisaged as an R&D centre for development of special metals and alloys of strategic importance. The foreign technical collaborations ended by 1989 and thereafter, Midani pursued the development and production activities on its own. It has developed more than 100 alloys through in-house R&D efforts constituting major parts of the present turnover.

But over a period of time, the objective of the company transformed from being a R&D organisation to a profit-making, self-reliant manufacturing facility and therefore, the futuristic position of the organisation on the world business map has to be visualised in that context.

Performance of Metals Ltd

On one hand Metals Ltd is successfully developing and manufacturing high quality superalloys and special metals and holding a position of repute among the defence PSUs, enjoying consistent clients from all the strategic sectors.

On the other side, the performance of Metals Ltd has slipped over the period. The following trend depicts the slipping performance of Metals Ltd:

- sales has declined,
- profit margin has shrunk to unviable level,
- order booking position is not satisfactory,
- value addition and employee productivity indices are extremely low,
- export earning are meager,
- earning per share is low.

The following graphs (Figures 7.1–7.3) depict the declining performance of Metals Ltd in the past *five years.*

Figure 7.1

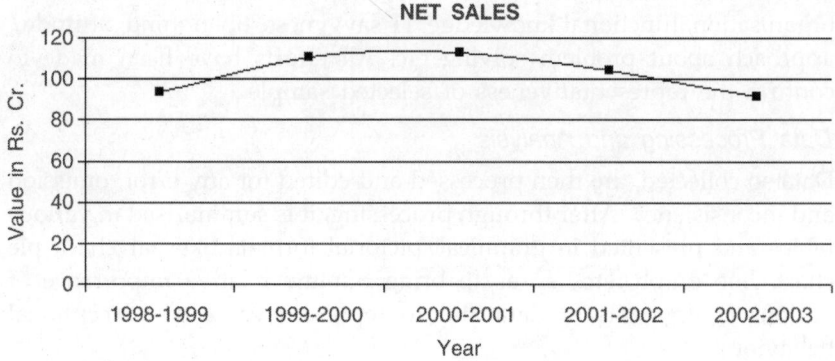

Figure 7.2

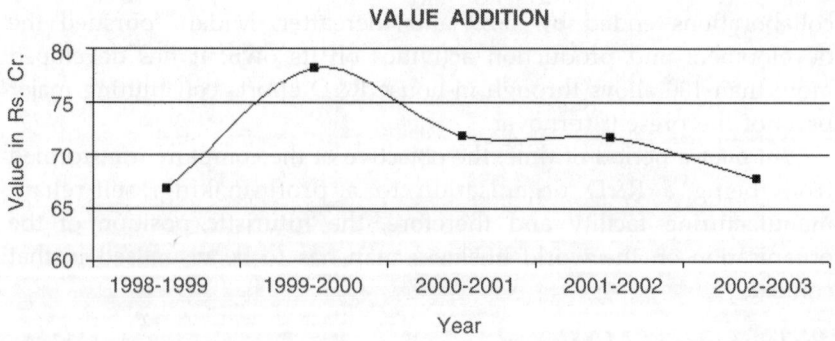

Figure 7.3

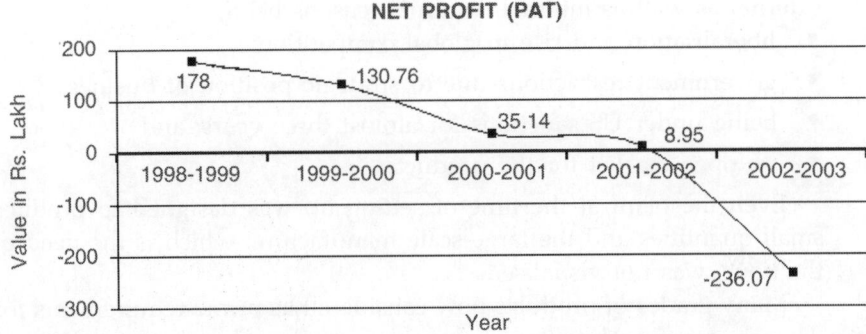

Some of the other major non-conformance in Metals Ltd are:

Figure 7.4

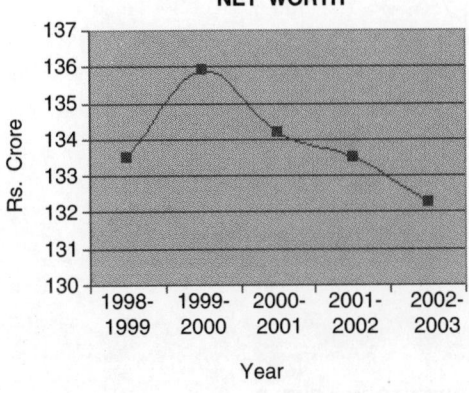

Figure 7.5

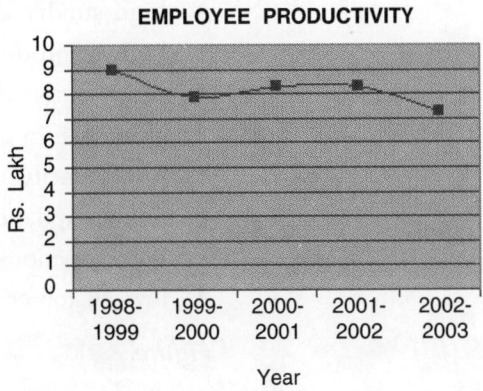

Figure 7.6

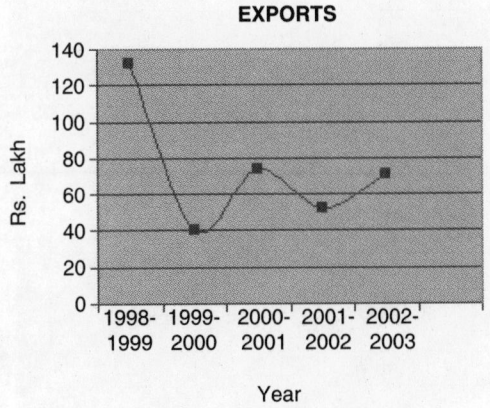

Figure 7.7

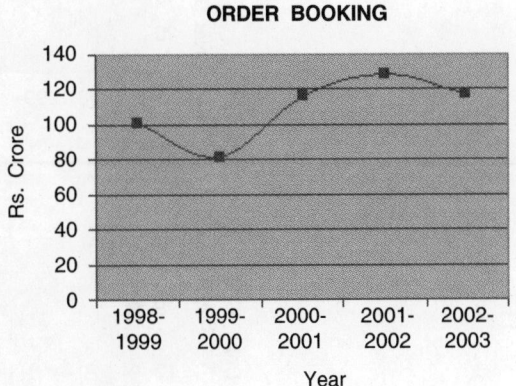

Source: Metals Annual Report and Department of Defence Production Annual Reports.

The discussions with the stakeholders of the organisation have led to the conclusion that the cause of this unpromising performance is both external as well as internal. External reasons being:

- liberalisation and rise in global competition;
- government restrictions due to strategic position of business;
- being under US sanctions for almost three years; and
- no open market for the products.

Even the plant at the time of setting up was designed to produce small quantities and the large-scale manufacture, which is the need of the hour, was not visualised.

Many grades of products now considered as prime requirements for defense, space and nuclear energy programme were not visualised at the beginning.

The major cause of performance degradation are internal which include (see Figures 7.8–7.11):

- very high inventory;
- high sundry debtors;
- high in production cost;
- high overheads;
- steep rise in employee cost;
- low capacity utilisation;
- non-compliance to delivery schedule;
- high rejections; and
- low customer satisfaction.

Figure 7.8

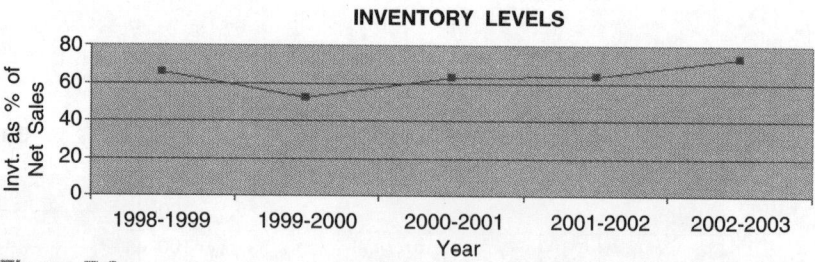

Figure 7.9

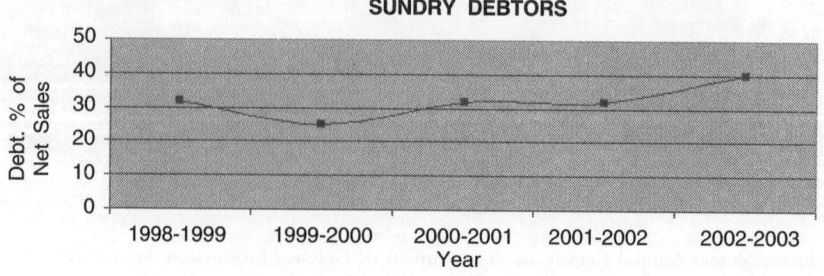

Figure 7.10

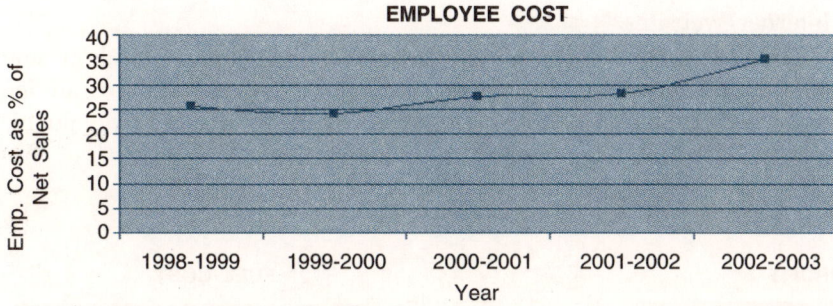

Figure 7.11

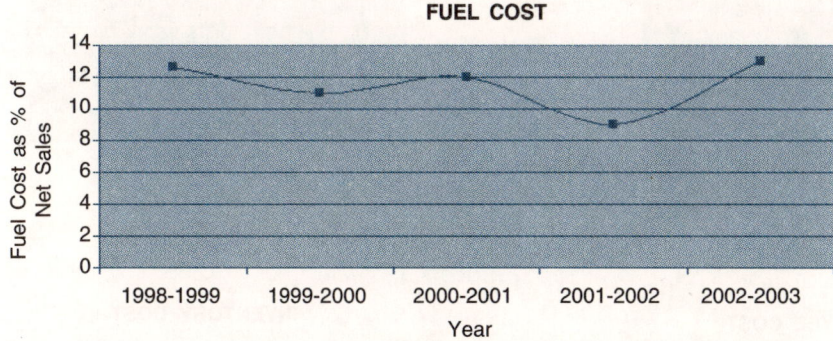

Source: Metals Annual Report and Department of Defence Production Annual Reports.

Industry Measurements

As part of the study, the performances of Metals Ltd on various financial and operational figures are compared with that of well-known companies in metal and alloy industry. The parameters that are compared are:
- inventory as percentage of net sales;
- debtors as percentage of net sales;
- fuel cost as percentage of net sales;
- employee cost as percentage of net sales; and
- PAT as percentage of net sales.

Companies that have been included for comparison with Metals Ltd are:
- Steel Authority of India Ltd. (SAIL)
- Tata Iron & Steel Co. (TISCO)
- Kalyani Steels
- Ispat India Ltd.(IIL)
- Jindal Vijaynagaram Steel (JVL)

Comparison has been done taking the average of performance figures of each company over a period of five years as available on the Internet/websites.

Though there is difference in processes, levels of technology and automation, turnover, ownership, etc., (see Figures 7.12–7.16) among these companies and Metals Ltd, it is worthwhile to draw valuable insight from this comparison.

Figure 7.12

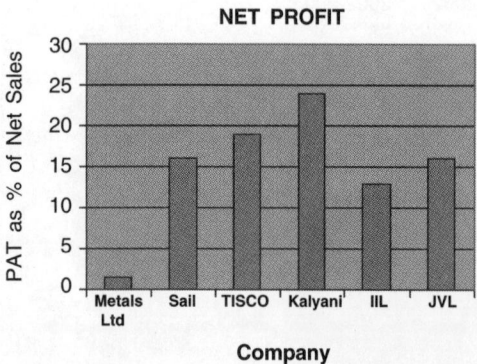

Figure 7.13

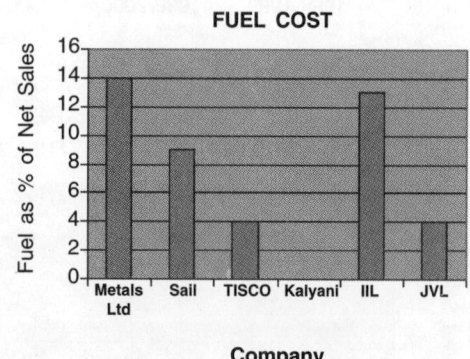

Figure 7.14

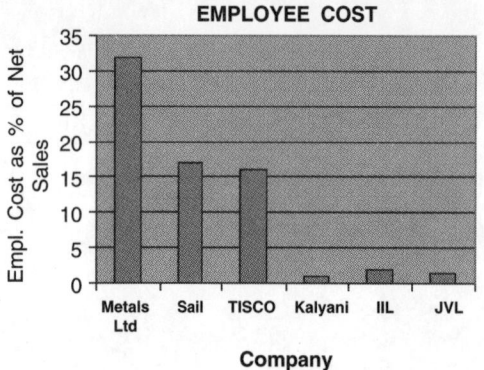

Figure 7.15

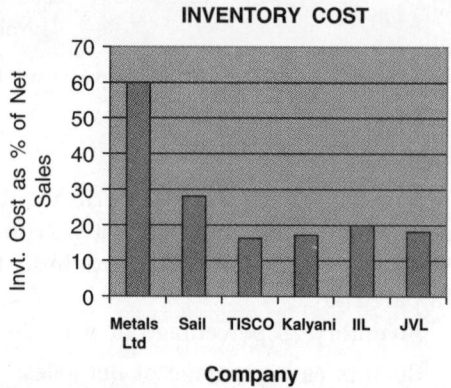

Figure 7.16

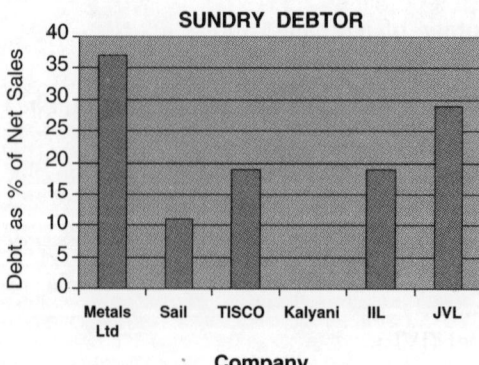

Source: Metals Annual Report and Department of Defence Production Annual Reports.

Swot Analysis for Metals Ltd

The Strength, Weaknesses, Opportunities and Threats (SWOT) perception for Metals Ltd as concluded from the discussions with the stakeholders of organisation is given (see Table 7.2) here.

Table 7.2

STRENGTH	WEAKNESS
1. In the whole country, Metals Ltd only has such specialised facilities like Vacuum induction melting and refining, vacuum arc remelting, electro-slag refining, vacuum annealing, etc., on industrial scale. 2. Highly skilled manpower. 3. Product and quality acceptance by national and international organisations of repute. 4. Involved in the manufacturing of high performance products of high strategic requirements.	1. Lack of conversion facilities for value added products like rings of missiles and rockets, close die forging, net shape castings, etc. 2. Manpower also relatively old and seasoned. Lack of fresh blood. 3. Small capacity equipment, small batch size production, compared to international players leading to uneconomic production and longer delivery time. 4. Facilities/equipments are very old and some are very low productive.
OPPORTUNITY	**THREAT**
1. Many national projects are maturing into production phase, viz., LCA, MBT, missile systems, PSLV, GSLV, etc. 2. Many of the Metals Ltd products are still relevant and have universal appeal. 3. Sanctions/restrictions under MTCR and NPT regimes. 4. New opportunities in the field of products like bio-medical implants and Body Amours.	1. Unfavourable duty structure on imported raw materials and equipment. 2. Liberalisation. Growing competition — internal and external. 3. Regular government customers shifting to foreign companies/MNC for sourcing their supplies.

Source: Metals Annual Report and Department of Defence Production Annual Reports.

Projected Performance of Metals Ltd

The projected performance for Metals Ltd as reflected in the five-year Perspective Plan (see Figures 7.17–7.18)

Figure 7.17

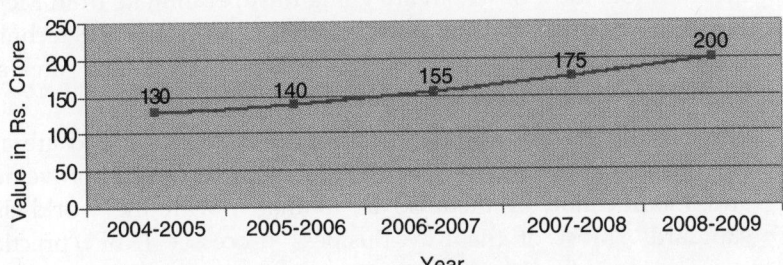

Figure 7.18

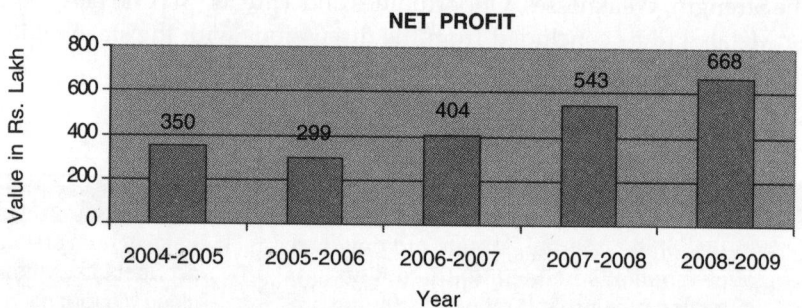

Source: Metals Annual Report and Department of Defence Production Annual Reports.

Why Computerisation for Metals Ltd?

(a) The existing equipment, machinery and facilities at Metals Ltd have been in operation for the past 20 years and most of them have worn out beyond repair. It is nearly impossible to achieve any higher level of efficiency from the existing set of machinery. Upgradation of these equipments as well as procurement of new equipments with higher capacity and capability to new grades/products is needed. This requires heavy investment (nearly 100 crores) by the organisation in the coming 2–3 years. But keeping in view the marginal profit earned in the last so many years, Metals Ltd is not in the position to invest heavily for equipments/facilities. And the government is also not keen to release any substantial fund or grant.

(b) Even the manpower in Metals Ltd, which is considered to be the most important resource for any organisation has been seasoned and grown old. The average age of Metals Ltd employee is presently 45 years. There is lack of young professionals who can learn fast and work more efficiently. It is highly unpractical to expect the existing workforce of Metals Ltd to learn new skills and drastically improve upon their performance and efficiency, so as to cope up with the fast changing business environment. Again, there is fear of loosing the vast amount of technical and management knowledge/experience available with the seniormost personnel of the organisation, most of whom are going to superannuate from Metals Ltd in a year or two. The only solution is to codify the technical information available with them, using IT tools and create a knowledge bank for future application.

(c) The existing business processes/procedures of Metals Ltd are also too old and inefficient. There is little room for any improvement and modification in them so as to match with the world-class standards. Most of the Key Business processes (KBP)/practices have to be benchmarked with the standard procedures being practised around the globe and these require Business Process Reengineering (BPR) activity.

It is very clear that the strengths of Metals Ltd are not fully transformed into global competitiveness, business excellence and leadership. The performance of organisation has reached a stagnant stage in all areas and it has to outperform in the forthcoming days in order to maintain its smooth existence in the highly competitive market and achieve the projected performance.

However, the existing systems/processes including machinery and manpower cannot support operational efficiency beyond a certain level.

Therefore, this situation demands interference of such inanimate tools/systems, which can prompt actions and corrective steps till the route cause of failure is eradicated. Information Technology can prove to be a miraculous enabler in this direction. Here comes intensive computerisation and implementation of IT enabled business processes/systems as the only means to achieve the expected level of competency.

Therefore, this research study concludes that IT can be a strategic tool for the sustained business growth of Metals Ltd and seeks to suggest an IT Strategy for the organisation.

Some of the major benefits that Metals Ltd can get from computerisation are summarised below.

(a) Online availability of updated information and a speedy information exchange between shops/departments.
(b) Record large volume of data accurately and precisely. Compiled knowledge in the form of database will help executives to take better, faster and informed decision.
(c) By implementing standard IT package standard business practices can be introduced—automatic BPR.
(d) Improved control over consumption of material, fuel, equipment hours and other critical resources and proper accounting for the resource consumed.
(e) Improved quality-time-cost in an Integrated manner.
(f) Improved customer satisfaction.
(g) Reduce data redundancy and paper work.
(h) Record non-conformance and prompt corrective actions.
(i) Avoid non-value addition activities. More transparency in work.
(j) Check on absenteeism and overtimes.
(k) Benchmarking analysis of crucial processes.
(l) Using expert IT system, even less-experienced personnel can handle routine cases, freeing the more experienced to handle special complex cases.

IT Strategy for Metals Ltd

Key Design Issues

Integrated Approach

Metals Ltd needs a completely integrated computerised system including every department/section and centralised database and all sections interlinked through an integrated network. This is very essential for effective coordination and interactive information exchange among the departments/sections. There has to be an integration in information flow from the stage of receipt of customer enquiry, sale order placement, production planning, receipt of raw material, production processes up to the sale of finished product along with a horizontal integration to the MIS system.

Data Capture

Every small bit of data can be of immense importance to the organisation and has to be captured. Any significant data has to be timely captured and fed to the computer system. Since the data is generated once, it is most pure, valid and accurate if captured at the place of generation, i.e., at the work centre. Hence, we need to provide data entry facility at all the work centres, as well as some of the critical equipments, e.g., melting furnaces, forging press/hammer and weighbridges, and quality testing equipments at quality labs to be interfaced to the main server of online data capturing. This will help get rid of any manual data entry error committed deliberately or unknowingly.

Management Commitment

The top management involvement in IT planning becomes necessary especially in large organisations like Metals Ltd since the company's business plane needs to be aligned with the IT system. Some very drastic changes may have to be brought into the work culture and greater discipline has to be practised. Again management has to fix a timeframe for the IT project. It has to set a deadline for completing IT implementation so that by the end of that period all the data which is of some importance for the enterprise has to be fed to the computer and all the reports of corporate significance has to be extracted from the IT system only. If this is done, only then can we achieve timely results from an IT plan.

User Involvement

It is absolutely essential that the user is involved in the IT planning right from the beginning. The user has to consider IT implementation as his assignment instead of perceiving it as simply an IT project. User involvement in IT implementation has the following advantages.

(a) It confirms user's, expectations out of computerisation.

(b) Improves the chance of system meeting their needs.

(c) Leads to consensus building. Leaves no room for excuses.

(d) Instills more confidence in effectiveness of the solution bringing about desired improvement.

(e) Users have the best understanding of organisation/processes/practices as well as the importance of relevant data.

IT Expenditure

Mostly IT costs run quite high in many organisations in India partly because of its pride of place in the corporate budget and partly due to lack of IT awareness.

An average IT budget in Indian industry is 4–5 per cent of revenue. People always have the feeling of being left behind in the technology race if they spend less on IT. But a decision regarding suitable IT system and IT expenditure has to be made based on the cost-benefit analysis, otherwise it increases the risk of failure to realise the anticipated benefits.

Again in order to achieve total integration and efficient computerisation, the management has to be prepared for reasonable high IT expenditure. The benefits of this expenditure has been realised in terms of better information availability, assistance in business flow and integration, improvement in all performance parameters, removal in non-conformance, improved cost-time-quality leading to customer satisfaction and finally leading to improved productivity. Return on IT investment can be realised in terms of controlling and reducing the losses in all the areas of business that will otherwise be unavoidable.

Constraints in IT Implementation

- Lack of exposure to working in computerised environment.
- Scarcity of IT skilled manpower in the organisation.
- Unavailability of modern IT infrastructure.
- Fear among organisation personnel of getting exposed due to the inherent transparency imposed on their day-to-day activities by the IT system.
- Resistance of personnel to change their old practices, way of working and adapt to the standard business practices.

Department/Sectionwise Observations

As part of study I have interacted with different departments/section personnel, departmental heads and workers with an aim to understand their idea about computerisation and requirement for the same, present computerisation status, information availability, user expectation, commitment and constraint in computerisations, etc. The interaction has taken in the form of direct interviews, use of questionnaires to provide response and onsite observation of shop-floor activities/processes.

The following are the observations at various departments/sections of Metals Ltd:

Melt Shops, Titanium Shop and Scrap Management

At present Melt Shop I & II, Titanium shop and Scrap Management Group have collectively got a total of 5 PCs in standalone mode and one data-entry terminal connection to the main server. Besides office documentation few of the processing jobs like raw material consumption, scrap generation, etc., are being done on the computer facility provided there. Computer literacy is also low.

Areas to computerise:

(a) process sheet, PCP, route card, melting plan—yearly/quarterly/monthly;

(b) daily melting details;

(c) material transfer to upstream shops;

(d) raw material consumption and scrap utilisation;

(e) fuel consumption furnacewise;

(f) stock of raw material and scrap as well as consumables in sub-stores/pipeline;

(g) chemical analysis of the melting process and yield analysis;

(h) attendance/shifts record/OTs/employee information; and

(i) MPR/CPR/other procurement requisition process.

For achieving it melting shops require online information from other production shops, technology department, stores, PPC, purchase, marketing and finance department.

The optimal number of data-entry terminals required is ten.

With full computerisation it is expected to reduce raw material consumption as well as power/fuel loss; better accounting for material; reduced melt losses; improved scrap utilisation and controlled deviation, etc.

The personnel department are fully committed towards computerisation and any accompanying changes. The only constraint is lack of exposure to computers which can be overcome with training.

Forge Shop, Hot Rolling Mill, Cold Rolling Mill, Bar and Wire Shops

At present the above-mentioned shops have a total of 3 PCs in standalone mode and one data entry terminal connection to the main server. Mostly the computers are being used for office documentation and for generating MPR/CPR and internal notes. There is no data processing application available at these work centres.

Areas, which can be computerised are:

(a) production plan—yearly/quarterly/monthly;

(b) daily production details;

(c) material transfer to downstream shops;

(d) machine hours and LPG fuel consumption;

(e) finished goods and work-in-progress;

(f) attendance/shifts record/OTs/employee information; and

(g) MPR/CPR/other procurement requisition process.

For achieving it the above-mentioned shops require online information from melting shops, technology department, stores, PPC, purchase and finance department.

The optimal number of data-entry terminals required is eight.

With full computerisation it is expected to reduce fuel consumption, complete knowledge of finished product and work-in-progress activities, better accounting for material and machine hours, reduced rejections and scrap generation, etc.

The department personnel are interested in computerisation and any accompanying changes. The constraint is lack of computer knowledge.

Quality Control Lab (QCL)

The Quality Control Lab department is making use of computers since long for maintaining test records and test reports. The Stage control lab, which is closely associated with QCL has computerised all its testing procedures except mobile testing along with interfacing between test equipments and computers. They are providing critical inputs to QCL. There are a total of 12 computers available with these two departments and a data entry terminal facility at QCL department.

The major activities, which are yet to be computerised at the Quality Control Lab department are:

(a) route card, PCP;

(b) field inspection report;

(c) raw material inspection report;

(d) test reports, test certificates and dispatch clearance;

(e) rejection report; and

(f) process control/scheduling of testing processes.

Online integration with all the production shops, PPC, marketing department, stores section; and technology is a must for effective computerisation.

The required number of data entry terminal is eight.

The department expects streamlining of testing process and improvement in product quality compliance as well as maintaining delivery schedule.

The department personnel are fully committed towards computerisation. With a good level of computer proficiency among personnel there is no constraint in implementation of IT system.

Maintenance Services (R&M–Mechanical, Electrical, Instrumentation and Civil)

At present none of the processes/activities in any of the maintenance departments is computerised and PCs provided at each section is being used only for office documentation activities. There is no data entry terminal provided.

The areas required to be computerised are:

(a) equipment/spare parts history;

(b) proper codification of equipments, consumables, spare parts;

(c) breakdown and maintenance history;

(d) spare parts stock as well as rotational requirement;

(e) preventive maintenance schedule;

(f) maintenance as job status;

(g) product design, troubleshooting charts, equipment circuitry;

(h) attendance/OTs/shift schedule;

(i) equipment procurement plan—periodic; and

(j) information related to construction and installation activities.

An online integration with different production shops, stores, purchase and finance.

A department is required.

The total number of terminals required to support maintenance activity is 14 located at various places.

Lack of exposure to computers is the biggest drawback for this section and a major constraint towards computerisation. Intensive training on computers is required.

Along with this, benefits of computerisation have to be clearly explained to the users in order to help them accept computerisation.

Marketing Department

The marketing department is making use of computers since long for maintaining sale order records, invoice information, DC records and TC reports. It is the only marketing department of   , which has a history of registered sales of more than 15 years. There are a total of eight computers available with the departments and two data entry terminals.

The major activities, which are yet to be computerised at the marketing department are:

(a) route card, PCP;

(b) link-ups with test reports, test certificates and dispatch clearance;

(c) rejection information;

(d) customer enquiry processing system;

(e) enquiry—offer–sale order flow;

(f) sundry debtors information;

(g) customer database.

(h) customer relationship management and complaint redressal system.

Online integration with all the production shops, PPC, QCL, stores section, finance, technology is a must for effective computerisation.

The required additional number of data entry terminal is 16.

The department expects streamlining of Enquiry-Offer-Order system as well as customer relationship management and application engineering for products and improvement in delivery schedule, after the implementation of complete IT.

The department personnel are fully committed towards computerisation. With a good level of computer proficiency among personnel there is no constraint in the implementation of IT system.

Finance and Accounts Department

Like the marketing department the finance and accounts division of Metals Ltd is also making use of computers since the inception of Metals Ltd for the processing information about invoice, bills receivable, bills payable, budgeting, payrolls, PR trust, etc. The finance department also owns a huge financial data in coded form.

A total of six computers are available with the departments and four data entry terminals.

The major activities, which are yet to be computerised at the finance and accounts section:

(a) online costing system;

(b) material accounting;

(c) better pricing system;

(d) online balance sheet and cash flow statements; and

(e) improvement in payroll processing.

Online integration with all the production shops, PPC, marketing, purchase and stores section is a must for effective computerisation.

The required additional number of data entry terminals is six.

The department expects streamlining of costing system as well as material accounting system with the implementation of complete IT.

The department personnel are fully committed towards computerisation. With good level of computer proficiency there is no constraint in implementation of IT system.

Stores Department

The stores and material section of Metals Ltd is using computers for quite some time for the purpose of delivery challan, invoice, goods receipt, etc.

There are two computers available with the department and three data entry terminals.

The major activities, which are yet to be computerised at the stores are:

(a) improved material coding;

(b) equipment/spares codification;

(c) computerisation of bills of material;

(d) computerisation of CSRV/GR;

(e) material management; and

(f) raw material stocking, consumption and pipelining.

Online integration with all the production shops, PPC, marketing, finance, purchase section is a must for effective computerisation.

The required additional number of data-entry terminals is seven.

The department expects streamlining of material accounting system with the implementation of complete IT.

The department personnel are fully committed towards computerisation.

But there is lack of computer proficiency.

Objectives of IT Strategy

Keeping in view with the above-mentioned issues and observations, the following should be the objectives and goals of an efficient IT strategy for Metals Ltd.

(a) Provide an integrated, online system, which should remove data redundancy and obviate the need for any reconciliation among concerned sections/departments and also facilitate the sharing of information among departments and monitoring of various performance parameters.

(b) Provide a robust and user-friendly system to end-users meeting their business needs.

(c) The proposed system should be of open architecture, modular, scalable, adaptable and available for operation on 24×7 basis.

(d) The proposed system should do automatic BPR by standardising Metals Ltd processes and providing solutions for those areas where there is no system.

(e) The system suggested should use the latest technology, without any risk of obsolescence for a substantial period of time.

(f) The system should ensure that no single component failure would have a major impact on operations. The system should guard Metals Ltd against data loss, corruption, duplication, etc., and give pre-failure warning.

(g) Enable e-business.

IT Options for Metals Ltd

Looking at the present technology trend there are three options available to Metals Ltd for computerisation:

(a) computerisation through in-house application development;

(b) computerisation by outsourcing application package from reputed software development companies; and

(c) implementing a standard enterprise resource planning (ERP) package.

The advantages and disadvantages of the three computerisation options are summarised below (see Table 7.3).

Table 7.3

In-house Development	Outsourcing from Software Company	ERP Package Implementation
ADVANTAGES 1. Maintenance of applications will be easier as they have been developed in-house.	1. Development and implementation is faster as against in-house development	1. ERP only is a pre-packaged application for all the vital business activities of a corporate with 100 per cent integration possible between individual modules. 2. Automatic BPR possible by ERP as it incorporates best business practices. 3. With very limited customisation ERP implementation can be started instead of spending time on development, testing, etc. Early results can be achieved. 4. ERP is an open system, i.e., OS (Operating System), hardware and database independent. It is modular in architecture, immune to technological changes, and any future upgrades is free. 5. ERP implementation is a one-time investment and involves no hidden or indirect cost. 6. ERP is least dependent on human behaviour and organisational practices and thereby does not demand any futuristic alteration based on organisational changes.
DISADVANTAGES 1. Hundred per cent integration and completion of application development cycle are never achieved. 2. Requires large number of IT skilled personnel, which demands high expenditure in terms of salary/wages. 3. Skills of existing personnel need to be upgraded through extensive training. 4. Computerisation of the existing non-standard practices will lead to a worse effect, as existing outlived practices can't support ope-rational efficiency beyond a certain level.	1. Huge expenditure to be incurred in terms of development charges. 2. Requires a long time for study, development and imple-mentation. Huge delay in getting results. 3. Future changes in technology as well as changes in users and management demand, and in developed application. Leads to an unending process of development, custo-misation and improve-ment, thereby involving lot of hidden cost and time.	1. Resistance of organisational personnel to change their basic practices and adapt to new standards of business practices/process as demanded by the ERP package. 2. Resistance by the users to enter voluminous data into the system, which is the basic requirement of an ERP system. 3. Resistance to change management.

Source: Metals Annual Report and Department of Defence Production Annual Reports

Option 1

The IT department of Metals Ltd presently does not have sufficient number of skilled staff to take up the enormous job of software development for the whole organisation. It requires a minimum of 20–25 skilled developers to complete the job of developing, testing and implementing application for all the sections/departments/business activities of Metals Ltd in a reasonable time. This will involve a huge expenditure in terms of salary/wages and other staffing expenditure.

Option 2

If the job of developing and implementing software applications for all the sections/department/business activities of Metals Ltd is offloaded to some reputed software development company, it will take a long time to develop and still longer time to implement, and by that time, some new advanced IT technology may come up. Also the outside agency would not be able to fully/clearly understand our business requirements.

Option 3

Metals Ltd primarily needs business process improvement which can be achieved by implementation of an ERP package as it is designed around the world's best business practices/processes. We can immediately start implementing the system and can expect early results from the ERP implementation.

IT Solution for Metals Ltd

Taking into consideration all the vital aspects of IT implementation including available IT technology in market, IT options before Metals Ltd, user's expectation from IT system, level of integration and assimilation required among the various sections/departments in terms of information flow, the existence of non-conforming business practices in the organisation, experience opinion of IT consultants, kind of IT systems implemented in similar organisations, the following IT solutions are suggested for the organisation of Metals Ltd (see Figure 7.19):

(a) implement a Standard ERP Package, which can meet Metals Ltd requirements. All the major modules of the ERP has to be implemented in a phasewise manner;

(b) develop in-house certain customised applications for those business areas of the organisation for which there is no ERP module available, and integrate it with the ERP system.

(c) The ERP implementation practices has to be preceded by BPR activity aimed at reengineering and realigning all the vital business processes of Metals Ltd as per the world best business practices. The BPR consultants, help should be sought in this direction.

(d) A complete organisationwide network including factory-site and corporate office is a prerequisite for any efficient IT solution. Therefore, a separate LAN project has to be started immediately and it has to be completed before the ERP implementation.

Figure 7.19 **IT Set-up Design for Metals Ltd**

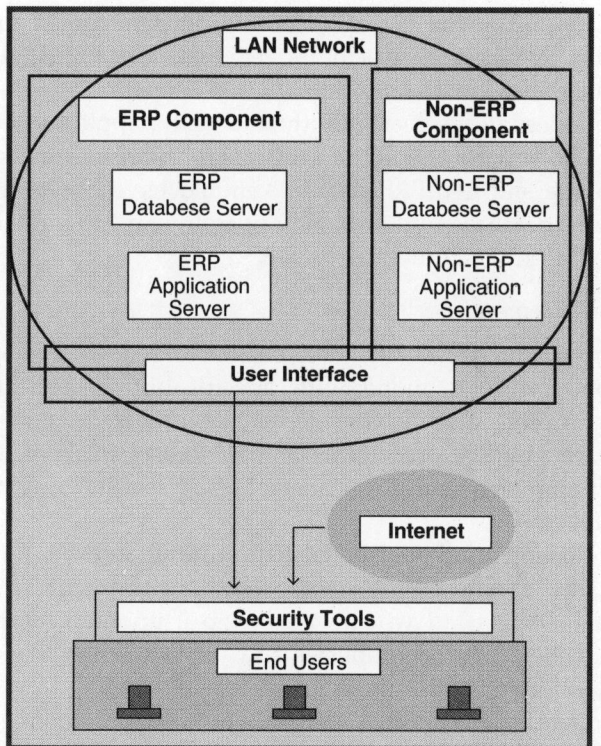

Source: Metals Annual Report and Department of Defence Production Annual Reports

Metals Ltd needs to employ a reputed ERP implementer through the regular process of tendering, evaluating and selecting a suitable party. The ERP implementation vendor must be using standard ERP systems to implement the processes, mentioned earlier, to meet the extent possible. In case where standard ERP practices are not meeting Metals Ltd business requirements and the existing process flow is critical for the business, programming and other techniques suggested by the ERP vendor should be used to address the following types of gap:

- functionality enhancements;
- data transfer requirements; and
- reporting requirements.

However, under no circumstance, the source code of the ERP package should be changed as the same may result in serious repercussions during integration and future upgrades.

Non-ERP Components

The processes, which are not supported by ERP, should form part of non-ERP component of the proposed IT system. This non-ERP component can be a fresh development or can be a customised software application.

The non-ERP components should also be implemented based on centralised server architecture. The server required for the project shall be again located at the centrally located department. In future when necessitated by business growth, the regional office should log-in to the server using VSAT connectivity.

The queries and screens in the non-ERP application should be adequate and reports should be available in the respective system. The ERP database and non-ERP database should have proper integration.

Any ERP database updating request from non-ERP system and vice versa should be put in a batch mode.

Intranet Component

An intranet site for Metals Ltd should be developed, wherein information on various products alone with specifications, applications, etc., significant events and achievements like orders bagged should be covered. All policies, procedures and notices/circulars in the area of personnel and administration can be hosted for the benefit of Metals Ltd employees.

These documents should be hosted on Intranet server for which the non-ERP server should be used. After the Intranet site becomes operational, Metals Ltd will have to keep it updating with the latest changes in their products, policies and procedures so that employees get the latest and valid information.

Subsequently, the intranet can provide a forum for free and frank exchange of ideas/comments/opinion on matters concerning Metals Ltd's business and thus can be an effective medium for easy and quick reach to employees.

E-Business Components

E-business includes five key ingredients:
- information;
- business software;
- computers;
- networks for communication; and
- creative vision or strategies applied.

When these components are combined to support the basic business processes, like purchasing or supporting a sales team, it amounts to e-business practices.

Getting the most out of e-business practices can entail exploring new relationship with suppliers or finding new ways for the employees' team to work together. A successful e-business strategy is not just developing internal e-business applications, but it also means evaluating and implementing externally developed solutions such as purchasing system, add-in information resources developed by a third party or applications hosted and managed by the external party.

The following e-business functionalities are relevant to Metals Ltd.
- *Communication and collaboration:* e-mails, document sharing, online product database, etc., inside the organisation.
- *Procurement:* explore online purchasing, evaluate new suppliers, seek larger discounts, use electronic marketplaces, etc.
- *Marketing:* build/upgrade/manage website for Metals Ltd, which will display details of products with specifications, characteristics, standards, applications, etc., and this website has to be periodically updated. In future it should allow the customers to register their queries/specify requirements.
- *Sales support:* track order execution status, manage proposals, lend information support through customer databases, etc. In future, online receipt of customer enquiry, quotation response, receipt of customer purchase order and booking of sale orders may be envisaged.

Most of the above-mentioned functionalities can be fulfilled by a web-enabled ERP solution.

User Interface

The following types of users are envisaged.
- End User;
- System Administrator;
- Database Administrator; and
- Power Users.

All users should have a common starting point. Access to relevant application should be based on authorisations guided by the role requirements.

Information Security

Metals Ltd should have a comprehensive Information System Security Policy. Through it the areas that we want to protect are clearly identified. The systems can be made secure by applying appropriate technology like anti-virus, hardware/software firewalls, intrusion detection system, perimeter security, encryption, digital signature, etc. For this Metals Ltd has to have a well-documented security plan which should be subjected to periodic review. The security guidelines must contain written statement for users of what constitutes secure and unsecured in terms of data, information and accounts. There must be an internal IS security committee headed by a Chief Security officer and consisting of IT as well as functional personnel, and this team is responsible for implementing and assuring enterprisewide IS (Information System) security.

At the same time the organisation must also have a robust backup planning and disaster recovery scheme in order to cope up with any Information System disaster that can originate from a physical calamity or manmade error.

IT Infrastructure Requirements

The entire IT infrastructure requirements has been divided broadly into the following major categories (for cost of ownership see Table 7.4).

- Servers
- Software
- Workstations/PCs/Printers
- Local Area Network (LAN)
- IT Skilled Manpower
- Training

Table 7.4. Total Cost of Ownership

Value in Rs Lakhs

Components	Quantity	Estimated Expenditure
I. Server		
- ERP Server	1 No.	15.00
- Non-ERP Server	1 No.	10.00
II. Software		
- ERP package with Database	25 license	40.00
- RDBMS and OS	10 LIC.	5.00
- Application Development tool/Packages	10.0	
- Web Tools and Security Tools		15.00
III. Workstations/PCs/printers		90.00
IV. LAN		60.00
V. IT Training		05.00
Total expenditure		**250.00**

Server

In addition to general features like hard disk, processor, RAM, the server should have the following features to meet the rigorous requirement of the system:

- robustness for supporting 24×7 schedule;
- N+1 power supply, Hardware RAID, LAN connectivity;
- sufficient expandability for CPU and RAM;
- centralised backup support; and
- support for clustering, NAS/SAN, etc.

The server requirement can be divided under the following heads:

- ERP Server
- Non-ERP Server

ERP component of the IT System should have the following three types of servers:

- development server;

- test server; and
- production server.

All these servers can be accommodated in the same physical server depending upon the users/database sizes.

The specification of non-ERP server should be decided keeping in mind the following:
- types of applications proposed;
- total expected number of users;
- architecture, i.e., two-tier/three-tier/web based; and
- proposed database.

The following set of non-ERP servers may be required:
- development server,
- production server, and
- Intranet server.

Softwares

The complete software requirement for the given IT plan can be summed up as below.
- ERP Package (SAP/Baan/RamcoSuite/PeopleSoft/JdEdwards, etc.,) with specified number of licenses.
- Operating System on ERP/non-ERP Server—Unix/Windows/Linux/Solaris.
- Relational Database Management System (RDMBS) like Oracle/SQL Server/Sybase, etc.
- Web Tools—Email s/w, Web Server, Web development tools, JAVA, FrontPage, Internet Explorer, etc.
- Security Software—Anti-Virus, Firewall, Proxy-server, Intrusion Detection system, etc.
- Office Automation and DTP Software.

Network

Metals Ltd require an enterprisewide high speed LAN with the following features:
- support up to 300 nodes;
- speed of 10/100 Mbps and scalable to gigabytes;
- low response time or delay;
- fiber-optic backbone;
- multi-layered with scope for enhancement; and
- provide high availability with redundancy features.

LAN should be based on industry standard TCP/IP suite and provide localised as well as centralised management of resources in a client–server environment.

Additionally some leased line/ISDN (Integrated Service Digital Network) based connection is required for hosting the website and corporatewide e-mail.

Workstations/Printers

There is an estimated total requirement of
- 200 Pentium based personnel computers,
- 40–50 thin clients,
- 2 network printers/line printers,
- 100 dotmatrix printer,
- 50 inkjet colour printers,
- 10 laser colour printers,
- scanners/modems/CD writers, and
- 5 notebooks/laptops.

Manpower

In terms of IT skilled manpower the requirement can be summarised as below:
- server administrator including Basis Administration for ERP package—1 no.
- Database administrator—1no.
- Network administrator—1no.
- Software Developer including ERP support—5 nos.
- Technical Assistants—2 nos.

Training

To be able to use the proposed IT solution effectively, the employees in Metals Ltd need to be imparted with some basic training in IT environment. There should be basically four types of IT training.
- User Level—users of IT at all levels should know the effective use of the under-mentioned topics: computer concepts, Windows, Ms Office, e-mail usage, Internet browsing and awareness about do's and don'ts of information security.
- Power User Level training is designed for the users who have been in the field of IT and have been extensive users of the same for a long time. This includes employees who wish to draw more power out of the IT system. They should be trained in the following topics: Windows, Unix, networking features, Ms Office, Multimedia, RDBMS (Relational Database Management System) usage and database applications; advanced programming and use of the Internet.
- Skilled User Level specialised training should be undertaken by IT people whom Metals Ltd is planning to depute for the administration

and management of the ERP project in system and database administration and network management.

- ERP User/Administration level training is required for those employees both from IT stream as well as function people who are to be put on the ERP implementation team. Few of them have to be given intensive training in ERP administration like Basis admin/ABAP. The rest of them have to be given training specific to the various ERP modules so that they can implement, configure and run the particular module successfully.

Appendices

Appendix - I

Sources of Secondary Data

1. Annual Reports of Metals Ltd and Department of Defence Production Annual Reports.
2. Periodic Performance Reviews and D.O. Letters of Metals Ltd.
3. Corporate Plan of Metals Ltd.
4. Internet/websites of Metal Industry.
5. Metal industry journals/publications.

Appendix - II

Questions for Users

1. State objectives of the shop/department.
2. Furnish the functions currently being carried out.
3. Suggest any function that might be required to be done by the section in future.
4. Give the day-to-day input/output information required within the department as well as with respect to other departments for carrying out above activities.
5. Frequency and time of information required.
6. What information the department is required to furnish to the management?
7. Give the input format and output format presently being used.
8. What do you expect from computerisation?
9. What according to you are the major areas to be computerised?
10. How the activities of your department controlled?
11. Any other information relevant for the computerisation in your area.
12. With full computerisation of department/shop, how much productivity improvement or saving can be achieved?
13. Time frame required for implementation.
14. Any problem envisaged in implementation.

Section C

Outsourcing

8
Outsourcing

S. Venkataramanaiah

*The early years were more about learning than about acting.
I had to carry on my father's work, which was a big challenge.*

Azim Premji

Introduction

There is an increasing pressure on organisations to compete more effectively to survive in the changing global trading markets. Devaluation of currency of many nations demands cost cutting, revenue expansion and innovation of world exporters. Western economies and firms ravaged by a decade of recession and mild growth seek to compete on an equal footing with the Japanese. Organisational change typically involves information technology (IT), organisation structure and strategy and human resource (HR) initiatives. Recently, organisation structures and management styles have undergone major changes featuring a core of permanent staff with a periphery of temporary staff who build up portfolio careers and may use IT to facilitate collaborative teleworking. A range of new organisational designs such as virtual corporations, hollow organisations, network structures, modular organisations, hybrid, quasi firm, spider web and hamrock organisations have emerged. Apart from these structures, many organisations have adopted the trends like outsourcing, vertical and horizontal integration, lean firms, decentralised and network firms and global enterprises (Wright and Burns 1997).

The traditional way of performing different value chain activities internally is being replaced by the idea of a network organisation or even a virtual organisation, in which fewer operations are performed within the firm. Only those functions, which generate added value and represent the firm's competitive advantage must be performed internally and the rest are outsourced. Some of the activities in which firms most often opt for outsourcing includes information management, manufacturing, support activities such as pay-roll processing, logistics, security, distribution, etc. Outsourcing means that the physical and/or human resources related to an organisation are going to be provided and/or managed by an external specialised supplier. The situation can be temporary or indefinite and can affect the client firm's whole activity, or only a part of it. This type of services became popular in the 1990s, after the spread of the success by Eastman Kodak's information systems (IS) outsourcing (Loh and Venkatraman 1992). Although the industry had not previously used the term outsourcing explicitly, such services date back to the early years of introduction of technologies such as information technology (IT), logistics, etc., into the business world under the format of facilities management and shared time services.

The most popular strategy in business today is outsourcing. Outsourcing is a strategically important activity that enables an enterprise to achieve both short-term and long-term benefits. All forms of public and private sector businesses, governments, medical and educational institutions are increasingly outsourcing various activities due to the perceived advantages of outsourcing. Businesses around the world are committed to outsourcing strategies despite the fact that outsourcing failure rates as high as 50 per cent. Outsourcing has changed the organisation way of doing business and is a mega-trend across many industries. General Motor's chief information officer (CIO) Szygenda defined outsourcing as the act of moving a firm's internal activities and decision responsibility to outside providers. Organisations are increasingly turning to outsourcing in an attempt to enhance their competitiveness. Chrysler outsourced the manufacture of half of its minicompact and subcompact cars. Furthermore, Chrysler and Ford produces less than one-half of the value of all their vehicles in-house. Similarly, Boeing has begun to rely more heavily on outsourcing partners to manufacture its aircraft, for example, the manufacture of a large portion of the Boeing 767. Boeing, the third largest commercial aircraft, is outsourced to a consortium of Japanese manufacturers including Fuji, Kawasaki and Mitsubishi. As a result, only 10 per cent of the value of the Boeing 767 is produced in-house. Due to high levels of competition many organisations are adopting outsourcing as one of the alternatives in their business.

Outsourcing is simply the transferring of an internal service function to an outside vendor. Although outsourcing of the information systems (IS) function has been the subject of much discussion recently, it is not new. Outsourcing can be traced back to the 1960s, when computers were expensive and physically large. Computers then required considerable space and needed controlled environmental conditions in which to operate, thus increasing the necessary investment. To eliminate or avoid the capital intensive investment in computer hardware, many organisations contracted for data processing function. This became known as facilities or operations management. Various definitions pertaining to outsourcing have been given in the following section.

This chapter highlights various basic concepts, definitions, and challenges faced by organisations, the reasons for outsourcing, practical tips for outsourcing, framework and problems related to outsourcing along with some empirical evidence on various issues. Other issues associated with outsourcing are also presented.

Definitions of Outsourcing

There seems to be confusion in the management literature about what is meant by the term outsourcing. Definitions given by different researchers in the literature are presented in Box 8.1. Lonsdale and Cox (1998) defined outsourcing as the process of transferring an existing business activity, including the relevant assets to a third party. This practice has been undertaken as part of a re-evaluation of attitudes towards vertical integration. Generally, the definition of outsourcing used in studies of the subject is so broad that it includes virtually any good or service that an organisation procures from outside firms. However, defining outsourcing simply in terms of procurement activities does not capture the true strategic nature of the issue. Outsourcing is not simply a purchasing decision; all firms purchase elements of their operations. Outsourcing is less common and represents the fundamental decision to reject the internalisation of an activity. Outsourcing is a highly strategic decision that has the potential to cause ripple effects throughout the organisation.

Box 8.1

Definitions of Outsourcing

Sl No	Reference	Definition/explanation
1	Loh and Venkatraman (1992)	The significant contribution by external vendors in the physical and/or human resources associated with the entire or specific components of infrastructure in the user organisation.
2	Kotabe (1992)	'Products supplied to the multinational firm by independent suppliers from around the world' and 'the extent of components and finished products supplied to the firm by independent suppliers.'
3	Lei and Hitt (1995)	The reliance on external sources for manufacturing components and other value-adding activities.
4	Lonsdale and Cox (1998)	The process of transferring an existing business activity, including the relevant assets to a third party.
5	Gilley and Rasheed (2000)	*Substitution* of external purchases for internal activities (i.e., discontinuation of internal production, whether it be production of goods or services) vertical disintegration; *Abstention* is not limited to those activities that are shifted to external suppliers; it rejects internalisation.
6	Schultze (2004)	A company decides to hire-out jobs traditionally done in-house. For example, a large bank holding corporation contracts with an outside firm located in the US/UK to carry out its cheque processing operation.

According to Gilley and Rasheed (2000), outsourcing may arise in two ways, viz., substitution and abstention. Under substitution, outsourcing may arise through the substitution of external purchases for internal activities (i.e., discontinuation of internal production, whether it be production of goods or services) and an initiation of procurement from outside suppliers. This seems to be the most commonly understood type of outsourcing. This type of outsourcing reduces a firm's involvement in successive stages of production. Substitution-based outsourcing may be viewed as vertical disintegration. However, outsourcing may also occur through *abstention*. Outsourcing need not be limited to those activities that are shifted to external suppliers. On the contrary, outsourcing may also arise when a firm purchases goods or services from outside the organisations even when those goods or services have not been completed in-house in the past. However, abstention-based outsourcing is unique from basic procurement because the former only occurs when the internalisation of the good or service outsourced was within the acquiring firm's managerial and/or financial capabilities.

In other words, as with substitution-based outsourcing, abstention-based outsourcing also reflects a decision to reject internalisation. Organisations having no choice but to acquire a particular good or service from an external source (because of lack of capital or expertise) are not outsourcing, because the internalisation of the activity in question is not an option. In other words, rejecting the internalisation of the focal activity was never a choice, and the firm is simply engaging in procurement. Certain virtual or network organisations, as well as other types of firms which have been founded from inception with the intention of performing only a narrow range of activities in-house consider outsourcing practical alternative and must be determined on a firm-by-firm (or even activity-by-activity) basis. Indeed, this definition of outsourcing may exclude many types of activities that have been considered outsourced. Although some consensus is beginning to emerge regarding the terms outsourcing and offshoring, early studies often used the term outsourcing, even when truly focused on the phenomena of jobs being shifted overseas or offshoring. Recent studies such as Schultze (2004) have given clear definition of outsourcing and offshoring and are given below.

Offshoring: A company moves existing jobs to one of its own branches or subsidiaries in another country. Example, Dell Computer moves help-desk jobs to its own offices in Mexico or Google opens its first engineering R&D centre in Bangalore, India, but continues to manage the operation.

Outsourcing: A company decides to hire-out jobs traditionally done in-house. For example, a large bank holding corporation contracts with an outside firm located in the same country to carry out its cheque processing operation.

Offshore Outsourcing: A company decides to hire-out jobs traditionally done in-house to a firm in another country in which the hiring company has no direct ownership and over which the company has no direct authority or control. Examples include Dell Computer contracts with a firm based in China to carry out a part/all of its help-desk support operations.

Offshoring occurs when firms transfer jobs abroad for work that has traditionally been done in their home country. For example, when US/UK company sends manufacturing operations to Mexico or a call centre to India, it is offshoring work. In this scenario, the company is sending jobs typically done in US/UK to another of its own branches in another country. However, outsourcing refers to steps taken by US/UK companies to hire out to other US/UK firms work that had previously been handled internally. For example, an US/UK software firm might determine that it would be more efficient to contract with a US/UK based market research firm, rather than continue to perform such work internally. This is part of the make or buy decision, with which all firms grapple as they determine how they were vertically integrated. Although the term only lately seems to be generating a lot of public discourse, firms have always been engaged in some form of outsourcing, since it is never clear exactly where the vertical integration line should be drawn. As regulations, technologies and competitors change, the optimal vertical boundaries for individual firms will naturally evolve. This process allows firms to become more efficient and concentrate on what they do best; also, the net number of jobs in the overall economy may actually grow.

Why Outsourcing?

Due to technological developments and cost differentials, many organisations are moving its operations from higher wage parts of the world to lower cost areas. However, moving jobs out of the country was more complicated and depended on several additional developments. The offshoring of manufacturing jobs did not emerge as a large-scale issue until low wage rates in countries such as Mexico and China were combined with a number of other variables such as:

- decreasing transportation costs driven in part by dramatic improvements in containerisation and supply chain management;
- falling international trade barriers that facilitated the exporting of products to the US and other countries;
- declining barriers to foreign direct investment (FDI) that encouraged multinationals from the US, UK and other Western countries to invest in production and distribution facilities in foreign nations; and
- improving worker and production standards, which, over time, raised the quality of the goods produced in foreign nations to global standards.

Outsourcing was primarily used when restructuring firms that were in bad financial shape. Outsourcing pervades the management of most companies. It has also become increasingly clear that outsourcing is more than a passing fad. According to a report from the Economist Intelligence Unit (EIU), 34 per cent of firms outsourced all or part of their IT in 1997 and is expected to reach 58 per cent by 2010. Similar increases are expected for activities such as telecommunications, accounting and human resources.

Empirical evidence suggests that carefully crafted outsourcing strategies increase the overall performance of the firm. As the CEO of a medium-sized firm that had outsourced activities as diverse as IT, logistics, financial services and facilities management had observed that outsourcing enabled the organisations to double operating income before tax while revenues remained stable. Outsourcing is generally considered as a very powerful tool to cut costs and improve performance. Through outsourcing, firms can take advantage of the best outside vendors and restructure entrenched departments that are reluctant to change. Outsourcing can also help focus on the core business. Since building core competencies and serving customer needs is critical to firm success, anything that detracts from this focus may be considered for outsourcing. Historically, many activities were performed internally because there were no outside suppliers. The continuing growth of supply markets has provided the opportunity to reassess which activities should remain in-house and which should be outsourced. Outsourcing has become a major player in the business game and despite the anti-outsourcing rhetoric, businesses must remain profitable in today's highly competitive global economic environment. Companies outsource for the following reasons:

- outsourcing is an economic saviour for many corporations;
- corporate policy and boardroom debate supports outsourcing; and
- students overseas are highly skilled and technologically literate.

Those firms that expand their line-ups into other countries are reaping rewards and meeting the bottom-line goals. Outsourcing allows the other companies to streamline and remain profitable. CNN's Lou Dobbs identified over 300 American corporations that outsource to remain profitable in today's global economies. Forrester Research predicts that 3.3 million jobs will be outsourced in the next 15 years. The number of outsourced jobs increased from 6.5 million in 1983 to over 10 million total jobs in 2005.

There are many reasons for outsourcing, the main one being the ability to purchase components, sub-assemblies, finished products or services from outside suppliers when internal production capacity is limited. An enterprise will also outsource its business when it does not possess the crucial technology, but still wants to seize the business opportunities presented. A survey by Heizer and Render (2006) on outsourcing practices found that it is around 54 per cent, while on the lowest and highest side for industries it was 27 per cent and 83 per cent respectively. The study concludes that industries spend about 50 per cent of their revenue on outsourcing activity. Quinn and Hilmer (1994) made the same observation, which suggests that outsourcing contributes a significant part of an enterprise's value chain activities. Effective use of outsourcing will, therefore, allow an organisation to focus on a limited set of strategically important tasks and will in turn lead to continuous enhancement of its core competencies (Dess et al. 1995, Kotabe 1992, Quinn 1992, Venkatraman 1989).

Moreover, advances in global logistics and information technology have encouraged companies to increase the outsourcing of non-core operations. This has led companies to develop new business strategies to manage goal-oriented activities that depend heavily on outsourcing. Outsourcing has also resulted in a significant altering of organisation configuration and boundaries, the economic restructuring of manufacturing in the UK being a good example (McCarthy and Anagnostou 2004). Outsourcing can obviously help an enterprise achieve considerable benefits, but employing outsourcing without proper consideration of long-term performance may also jeopardise competitiveness. Wu et al. (2005) has observed that excessive outsourcing leads to over-dependence on suppliers, which can in turn undermine an enterprise's R&D activities and capabilities. There is also a possibility that some core technologies will fall prey to potential technology predators because of inadequate protection, leading to a loss of competitive advantage and even to a loss of market share. Further, Chowdhry (2006), who is Chairman and CEO of HCL Infosystems Ltd, highlighted the salient features of hardware outsourcing and competitive advantage associated with India. Large-scale manufacturing is possible when all parts of the value chain are drawn to India.

Major Challenges Faced by Organisations

Organisations are facing many challenges from different competitors due to liberalisation, privatisation and globalisation (LPG) of business. Organisations across the world are facing many challenges in terms of cost, time to market, consolidation, globalisation, regulations, competition, data integration, safety, etc. According to Azim Premji, CEO of Wipro Technologies, Bangalore, India, there are five major challenges faced by organisations (see Figure 8.1). These challenges are generic to many organisations and can be addressed by outsourcing different functions.

People Challenge

This is one of the most serious challenges and can be addressed by building appropriate processes to hire, train, deploy and motivate people. One of the best examples is Infosys Technologies, which focus more on training and retraining people.

Figure 8.1: Five Major Challenges Faced by Organisations

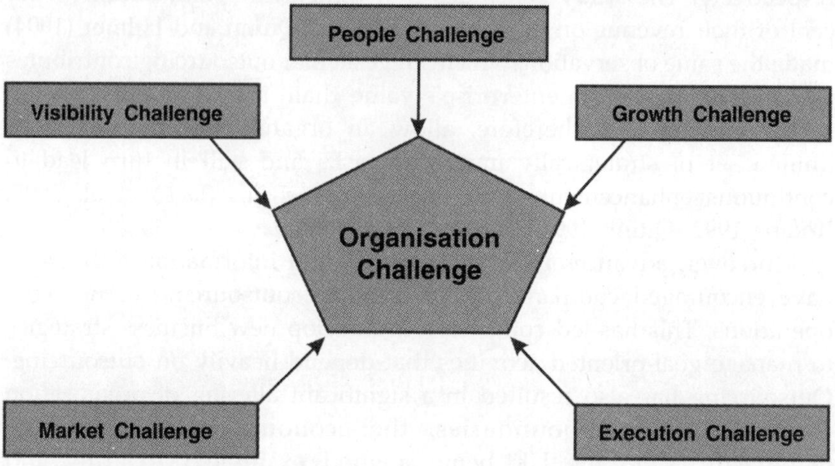

[Diagram: A pentagon labeled "Organisation Challenge" in the centre, with five boxes around it connected by arrows pointing inward: "People Challenge" (top), "Growth Challenge" (upper right), "Execution Challenge" (lower right), "Market Challenge" (lower left), "Visibility Challenge" (upper left).]

Source: Venkatesha Babu (2005)

Growth Challenge

Due to competition from many small and medium organisations both from domestic and international market growing at a steady rate is becoming very difficult. It may be easy to grow at the rate of 25 per cent for the first five years and very difficult beyond the five years.

Execution Challenge

Projects are becoming more complex and need to be implemented across geographies and requires local talent, cultural issues and language which poses severe execution problems.

Market Challenge

Many big players from India and outside are competing on several dimensions like quality, price, delivery and flexibility. Examples include auto industry, software and construction.

Visibility Challenge

Change/relocation of prominent personalities in the organisations lead to this challenge. Examples include the change of Mr Paul of Wipro Technologies and Mr Sumantran of Tata Motors.

Challenges Faced by OEMs

With the growth of the Internet, the rise of mass customisation and a renewed focus on core competencies, original equipment manufacturers (OEMs) must contract out part or all of manufacturing, assembly, distribution and support operations. Outsourcing, once a mere option, has not only become imperative but also competitive. The idea behind outsourcing is a blessing to many OEMs worldwide. Many manufacturing companies today believe that success is assured by outsourcing work in manufacturing and fulfilment operations, as they get to focus on their core competencies. The reason is that the decentralisation of manufacturing, fulfilment and support operations creates a myriad of challenges in the OEMs. Companies that fail to meet these challenges actually lose day-to-day control over their business processes and their outsourcing initiatives. There are a number of outsourcing challenges that can bog the enterprises. According to Ashuthosh Pandey of Bharouka Steel, some of the important challenges faced by OEMs are:

- outsourcing partner's ignorance of supply chain dynamics
- the risk of choosing a wrong partner
- ultimate onus of responsibility
- conflict of interests
- shortcomings of outsourcing partner
- the potential danger in outsourcing manufacturing and fulfilment work

Outsourcing Partner's Ignorance of Supply Chain Dynamics

The best partner in the world will do a great job of building perfectly to specifications and delivering on time but the product might never work. The current specifications might have changed after outsourcing deal was signed. So if there is no real-time, web-based access to their work in progress and bills of materials, the entire outsourcing exercise can end up futile. Organisations need to look at the capability of suppliers in terms of network connectivity, etc.

The Risk of Choosing a Wrong Partner

Organisations may assume that the outsourcing provider has a fully automated system and end-to-end electronic data interchange or web-based links with its suppliers. This assumption may not be grounded in reality. The reason is that most outsourcers have net profit margins in 2 to 4 per cent range, and any cost centre that does not directly relate to product quality becomes a candidate for the 'budget axe'. Consequently, new investments in IT infrastructures may not be possible. Instead, legacy systems that predate the Internet and that lack supply, chain-specific functionality are common. This could have a tremendous impact on their performance and in turn the outsource relationship.

Ultimate Onus of Responsibility

You're only responsible for the ultimate execution of your project and delivery of your products. Outsourcing is a means to an end, and your ends are necessarily different from those to whom you outsource. Consider that multiple subsets of unfinished goods generally comprise finished goods. Each unfinished good has a particular process, timetable, set of inefficiencies and potential obstacles. The result is that the acceptance of an order can be followed by missteps and missed deadlines by a variety of third parties, and any of these problems can cause serious problems with manufacturing and fulfilment.

Conflict of Interests

Your outsourcing partners are not your employees. They may get the job done, but they'll do it their way, with their own processes, and without an interest in integrating their data with yours. You must recognise that your outsourcing partners wouldn't be in business unless they had many other customers' demands to satisfy, many other deadlines to meet, and a high attention to cost containment. Further, one should understand that the partners will be, by the nature of their businesses, paying attention only to that small portion of the manufacturing/fulfilment process with which they are concerned—not to the entire supply chain. Ultimately, outsourcing and retaining control of supply chain network can turn in to an antagonistic activity.

Shortcomings of Outsourcing Partner

A little carelessness in supervising the relevant projects might give the advantage to competitors. The reason being, contract manufacturers' processes and systems have been designed for mass production, not for mass customisation. Further, they may not be in a position to respond to changes in the market conditions.

The Potential Danger in Outsourcing Manufacturing and Fulfilment Work

Vertically integrated companies has to scale linearly, not exponentially. Real estate and labour pools inherently grow in a linear fashion. Exponential growth, on the other hand, arises only from leveraging the efforts of multiple contractors/service providers, who in turn leverage other contractors/vendors. Outsourcing is then, in principle, a direct application of the network effect. But if one loses control of supply chain network, outsourcing may introduce interminable delays instead of exponential growth.

Though outsourcing is not without inherent dangers, it can bring some real benefits to both manufacturing and non-manufacturing, as well as small and large organisations. This is possible by founding outsourcing on the reality of contractors' businesses and not on hopes. Of late, organisations are addressing many of the challenges described earlier by adopting suitable outsourcing strategies. Some of the major reasons for outsourcing are described in the following section.

Major Reasons for Outsourcing

There are very many good reasons for organisations to go in favour of outsourcing different business activities. Lonsdale and Cox (1998) proposed five areas covering 20 major reasons which are listed in Box 8.2.

Box 8.2

Major Reasons for Outsourcing of Business Activities

A. Organisation Related Reasons

1. Enhance effectiveness by focusing on what you do best (core competencies).
2. Increase flexibility to meet changing business conditions, demand for products and services and technologies.
3. Transform the organisation by focusing on set targets in terms of products/services and revenue.
4. Increase products and services value, customer satisfaction and shareholder value.

B. Improvement Related Reasons

5. Improve operating performance in terms of cost, time and others (increase quality and productivity, shorten cycle times, and so on).
6. Obtain expertise, skills and technologies that are not otherwise available.
7. Improve management decision processes and control.
8. Improve risk management by using appropriate risk mitigation and management tools.
9. Encourage and acquire innovative ideas.
10. Improve credibility and image by associating with superior providers/leaders in the area.

C. Finance Related Reasons

11. Reduce investments in assets (overheads) and free up these resources for other purposes.
12. Generate cash by transferring assets to the provider.

D. Cost and Revenue Related Reasons

13. Reduce costs through superior provider performance and the provider's lower cost structure.
14. Turn fixed costs into variable costs.
15. Gain market access and business opportunities through the provider's network.
16. Accelerate expansion by tapping into the provider's developed capacity, processes and systems.
17. Expand sales and production capacity during periods when such expansion cannot be financed.
18. Commercially exploit existing skills.

E. Employee Related Reasons

19. Give employees a stronger career path.
20. Increase commitment and energy in non-core areas.

Source: Lonsdale and Cox (1998)

Reasons for Outsourcing Some empirical evidence

Gonzalez et al. (2005) proposed a framework and validated the reasons in respect of large Spanish firms. The findings from the study are also in agreement with many of the reasons listed in Box 8.2. Table 8.1 shows the reasons leading to the outsourcing of Information System (IS) services where N represents the number of responses obtained. The most important reasons are, in order of priority, the possibility that outsourcing offers to focus on IS strategic matters, the potentially increased IS department flexibility, and the chance to improve quality and to get rid of monotonous, problematic tasks that are precisely the ones firms try to outsource. The reasons based on staff or technology cost savings does not appear among the ones most often mentioned by interviewees (they are ranked 5th and 7th). Having access to new technologies does not appear either as one of the most relevant reasons, as it is ranked 6th. In general, reasons for IS outsourcing spin around the improvement of the IS department and of the services it supplies, reasons related to costs or the correction of technological deficiencies being less important.

Table 8.1. Reasons for Information Systems Outsourcing

Reason	Name	N	Valid (%)	Rank
1	Focus on IS strategic issues	176	49.3	1st
2	Increased IS department flexibility	144	47.1	2nd
3	Improved IS quality	122	39.9	3rd
4	Elimination of troublesome, everyday problems	118	38.6	4th
5	Staff cost saving	106	34.6	5th
6	Increased access to new technologies	94	30.7	6th
7	Technology cost saving	62	20.3	7th
8	Providing alternatives to in-house IS	39	12.7	8th
9	Joining the fashion	3	0.8	9th

Source: Gonzalez et al. (2005)

Gonzalez et al. (2005) analysed firms using cluster analysis with an objective to group firms according to the different reasons that led them to outsourcing. From the analysis it was found that more than 40 per cent (125 out of 306) of the firms are resort to outsourcing mainly to improve their IS, without paying so much attention to the costs. This shows the significant improvement outsourcing can bring to the firm's information system. However, about 38 per cent (116 out of 306) of the firms seeking staff cost saving without worrying about IS improvement. This reminds that many firms do not seek outsourcing in order to improve their service, but mainly to save staff costs.

The third cluster includes firms, which justify outsourcing as a way not only to save on technology, but also to improve information system; however, they do not see in outsourcing an opportunity to focus on the strategic problems of the service. Outsourcing reasons to other features of the firms such as outsourcing level and the size and characteristics of its IS department and the firm's profile. In the first place, firms with the highest outsourcing level are the ones which choose outsourcing mostly to reduce staff costs and to make easier access to new technologies; however, this does not mean that they want to find alternatives to in-house IS, as these are the firms that least mention this reason.

On the other hand, firms with the lowest number of workers are the ones that most often claim that outsourcing can be a way to have access to new technologies and those that least resort to outsourcing are able to focus on the strategic aspects of the corresponding department. Regarding the possible relationships between the reasons to outsource mentioned by the different firms, depending on their sales level, the following are observed:

- firms with the lowest sales are the ones that most often seek outsourcing as a way to save on technology;
- these firms are also the ones that most often view outsourcing as a way to facilitate access to new technologies; and
- besides, these firms see in outsourcing a possibility to improve quality. On the contrary, firms with a higher sales level are the ones that most often resort to outsourcing to be able to focus on the most strategic problems, while firms with less sales level are the ones that least mention this reason.

It can be deduced that smaller firms in terms of sales and number of workers seek outsourcing basically as a way to gain access to new technologies, not with the aim of focusing on strategic aspects, unlike what happens in larger firms. However, industrial firms are the ones that resort the most to outsourcing in order to improve quality, while service firms seek access to new technologies, which reveals possible shortages in the field of IT in these sectors. There is also an important dependence relationship between outsourcing reasons and the sector the firm belongs to. On the one hand, insurance and financial institutions are the ones that have least resorted to outsourcing in order to have access to new technologies. On the other hand, financial and insurance institutions have not resorted to outsourcing in order to improve the quality either, a strategy that is more commonly adopted by industrial firms though.

From the empirical studies it was found that the size of the department staff is somehow related to the most often mentioned outsourcing reasons. Thus, firms with fewer staff than required in their departments are the ones that most often resort to outsourcing in order to save costs on technology, to facilitate access to new technologies and to improve the quality of the service supplied (i.e., to correct deficiencies), these being reasons that were less often mentioned by firms with more staff. The latter resort more to outsourcing with the aim of focusing on strategic issues.

An increased focus on an organisation's core competencies is one of the important benefits of outsourcing. Outsourcing non-core activities allows the firm to increase managerial attention and better resource allocation to those tasks that it does best and to rely on management teams in other organisations to oversee tasks at which the outsourcing firm is at a relative disadvantage. The importance of defining and developing the core competence of the firm has attained great popularity among management researchers and practitioners (Prahalad and Hamel 1990). This has increasingly led to a move away from market-based definitions of businesses towards more competence-based definitions. For example, Honda's core competence is in small engine production and, therefore, the domain of Honda's activities can be seen as any business in which this core competence finds an application. Nike's core competencies are in the design and marketing of shoes rather than in their manufacture. Therefore, Nike has focused on these aspects of the athletic shoe industry and has relied on outside firms for all manufacturing activities. Quinn et al. (1990) and Quinn (1992) also make a strong case for outsourcing activities in which a firm cannot excel to provide the firm with heightened focus on its core competencies.

Other non-financial benefits of outsourcing have received less attention. One additional advantage is that it tends to promote competition among outside suppliers, thereby ensuring availability of higher-quality goods and services. Outsourcers may also realise quality improvements, because they can often choose suppliers whose products or services are considered to be among the best in the world (Dess et al. 1995; Quinn 1992). Gilley and Rasheed (2000) have attempted to determine the performance implications of outsourcing strategies. It was found that although no direct effect of outsourcing on performance was detected, outsourcing interacted with firm strategy and environmental dynamism to predict performance. Many studies suggest that the benefits of outsourcing may be more fully realised by firms pursuing cost leadership and innovative strategies. Furthermore, firms operating in relatively stable environments may also achieve performance increase through outsourcing.

Advantages of Outsourcing

Although the definition of outsourcing has been somewhat uncertain, many potential benefits of outsourcing have been identified in the literature. Those most often discussed are improved financial performance which is attributable to cost improvements and various non-financial performance effects, such as a heightened focus on core competencies. Outsourcing firms often achieve cost advantages relative to vertically integrated firms (Kotabe 1989, Lei and Hitt 1995, Quinn 1992). Through outsourcing, manufacturing costs decline and investment in plant and equipment can be reduced (Bettis et al. 1992). This reduced investment in manufacturing capacity lowers fixed costs and leads to a lower break-even point. The short-run cost improvement swiftly reinforces the outsourcing decision. Thus, outsourcing may be an attractive method of improving a firm's financial performance, especially in the short run. Outsourcing may contribute to other advantages as well. In-house production increases organisational commitment to a specific type of technology and may constrain flexibility in the long run. However, firms focusing on outsourcing can switch suppliers as new; more cost-effective technologies become available. In addition, outsourcing allows for quick response to changes in the environment.

Thus, firms that outsource may achieve long-run advantages compared to firms relying on internal production. An increased focus on an organisation's core competencies is another important benefit associated with outsourcing (Quinn 1992, Venkatraman 1989). Outsourcing non-core activities allows the firm to increase managerial attention and resource allocation to those tasks that it does best and to rely on management teams in other organisations to oversee tasks at which the outsourcing firm is at a relative disadvantage. One additional advantage is that it tends to promote competition among outside suppliers, thereby ensuring availability of higher-quality goods and services in the future. Outsourcers may also realise quality improvements, because they can often choose suppliers whose products or services are considered to be among the best in the world (Dess et al. 1995 Quinn 1992). By using outside suppliers for products or services, an outsourcer is able to take advantage of the emerging technology without investing significant amounts of capital in that technology. Thus, the outsourcer is able to switch suppliers when market conditions demand.

Disadvantages of Outsourcing

Although outsourcing's potential benefits are many, some argue that reliance on outside suppliers is likely to lead to a loss of overall market performance (Bettis et al. 1992, Kotabe, 1992). One of the most serious threats resulting from a reliance on outsourcing is declining innovation by the outsourcer. Outsourcing can lead to a loss of long-run research and development (R&D) competitiveness (Teece et al. 1987) because it is often used as a substitute for innovation. As a result, firms that outsource are likely to lose touch with new technological breakthroughs that offer opportunities for product and process innovations (Kotabe 1992). In addition, as suppliers gain knowledge of the product being manufactured, they may use that knowledge to begin marketing the product on their own (Prahalad and Hamel 1990). In fact, firms from the Pacific Rim have a well-established pattern of market entry based on outsourcing partnerships. Many Asian firms have made their initial entrance into US markets by first entering supplier arrangements with US manufacturers and subsequently marketing their own brands aggressively. In this way, many Asian firms have achieved market dominance.

There are several other dangers associated with outsourcing. First, the cost savings associated with outsourcing may not be as great as they seem, especially with respect to foreign suppliers. The transaction costs associated with repeated market-based transactions, especially overseas, can be significant. In addition, as long as foreign wages remain relatively low and the dollar remains relatively strong, foreign outsourcing is attractive. However, success attributable to low foreign wages and a strong dollar is a fleeting advantage. Also, outsourcing requires a shift in overhead allocation to those products or activities that remain in-house. This reallocation of overheads degrade the apparent financial performance of the remaining products or activities and raises their vulnerability to subsequent outsourcing, perhaps leading to an outsourcing spiral. Thus, those remaining products or activities that were performing satisfactorily before the onset of outsourcing may erroneously be targets for future outsourcing. In addition, longer lead times resulting from spatial dispersion cause several problems, such as larger inventories, communication and coordination difficulties, lower demand fulfilment, and unexpected transportation and expediting costs. Tariffs are another danger associated with outsourcing, as are increases in the difficulty of bringing back into the firm activities that may now add value because of market shifts. Reliance on outsourcing is not necessarily a viable competitive strategy always. On the contrary, continuously switching from one supplier to another may merely postpone the 'day of reckoning' when firms must fix what is wrong with their organisations (Prahalad and Hamel 1990).

Practical Tips for Successful Outsourcing

Horror stories about vendors keep many organisations from capitalising on the benefits of outsourcing. Knowing how to prepare for contract negotiations can help you optimise those relationships. Past studies show that in many cases, the vendors are not able to deliver what they promise. In most cases, the answer comes down to a bad experience with a vendor, whether experienced first hand, or passed on in gory detail by another organisation. Add to this the complex legal web that overlays outsourcing contracts and an organisation has reason to pause. Callahan (2005) proposed ten useful tips for successful outsourcing. These are not intended as a substitute for specific, competent legal advice but provide practical help in navigating the difficulties organisations are likely to encounter when negotiating an outsourcing arrangement. These are briefly described below.

- Compare Apples to Apples
- Pay Attention to the Agreements
- Hire a Professional
- Hold Them Accountable
- Watch Out for Hidden Costs
- Don't Forget Acts
- Remember Your Employees
- Leave Yourself an Out
- Don't Rush It
- Keep Uncle Sam Happy

Compare Apples to Apples

One of the most common mistakes that organisations make is requesting bids from vendors without fully specifying the products/services they want to outsource and award the contract to the least expensive vendor. When it turns out that the vendor has a very different idea about the scope of these products/services, trouble ensues. Organisations can avoid this predicament by developing a request for proposal (RFP) that specifies the following aspects—

(a) the location where the products/services are to be provided/delivered;

(b) the number of in-house employees who are currently involved; and

(c) the number of products/services required per shift/day/week.

Such a detailed document ensures that the vendor and the organisations are in agreement on the scope of the products/services to be outsourced; thus heading off additional charges for products/services not included in the original quote.

Pay Attention to the Agreements

Major outsourcing companies spend millions of dollars annually to market their products. They hire some of the best sales people in the industry and compensate them by commission. Consequently, it is common for a salesperson to promise an organisation the world, while urging it to close the deal as quickly as possible. The outsourcing agreement, he or she assures the organisation is just a formality. This sales pitch is far from the truth. Outsourcing agreements typically are voluminous, extremely complex, and deserving of a detailed review. Such as agreement

- removes any obligation on the part of the vendor to provide services in accordance with accepted standards;
- requires the organisation to hear responsibility for the vendor's negligent actions; and
- prohibits the organisation from terminating the contract in case it is not satisfied with the services it is receiving.

Hire a Professional

Given the complexity of vendor contracts, it makes sense to hire legal advisers who have experience with contractual agreements with outsourcing vendors. As an added plus, lawyers who specialise in specific functions of outsourcing usually have developed positive working relationships with vendors' attorneys, which reduces the time and effort needed to negotiate agreements without sacrificing attention to detail.

Hold Them Accountable

Some of the most important provisions an organisation can include in its outsourcing contracts are those designed to ensure that the vendor is living up to reasonable performance standards. For example, a contract should make clear that the vendor must provide the services in accordance with applicable law and the standards of the organisation's accreditation agencies.

Watch Out for Hidden Costs

In many cases, the decision to outsource is driven by an organisation's desire to cap or reduce the cost of providing the product/service. At first glance, the base fee in an outsourcing contract may be less than the cost of providing the service internally. But add-on fees can quickly add up. For example, many contracts include start-up charges associated with the transition of the service to the vendor. In some instances, the vendor will charge for carrying inventories, interviewing staff or bringing equipment or facilities into regulatory compliance, equipment maintenance. Either negotiate these hidden charges out of the contract or include them in the calculations of the costs the organisation is likely to incur by outsourcing.

Don't Forget Acts

Various acts tightly restrict the ways in which information can be used, transmitted and disclosed. It addresses this restriction by requiring the organisation and outsourcing the vendor to enter into a business associate agreement or privacy and security addendum. In some cases, regulators have stated that certain kinds of vendors (e.g., those that provide only housekeeping or laundry services) are not required to enter into business associate agreements under certain circumstances. Unless the vendor can point specifically to such an exemption, you should insist that they sign the agreement.

Remember Your Employees

While outsourcing can be a financial boon to an organisation, the prospect of outsourcing any service can make some employees apprehensive. It is important for the organisation to develop an effective employee communication plan that articulates the organisation's goals and candidly explains how an outsourcing transaction will affect specific jobs. Typically, the organisation and the outsourcing vendor work together on developing the communication plan. In some situations, the organisation and vendor may agree that the organisation will terminate certain employees, who then will be hired immediately by the vendor. In such cases, the organisation can make certain demands on the employees' behalf. These can include the following.

- that the transitioned employees be paid salary and benefits consistent with those paid by the organisation;
- that the transitioned employees be given credit, for seniority purposes, for the time they worked for the organisation; and
- that the vendor continues to employ the transitioned employees for a limited time.

Leave Yourself an Out

Many outsourcing contracts used by vendors tightly constrain the circumstances under which an organisation can terminate the agreement for poor performance. For example, if the vendor fails to meet the performance standards under the agreement, many contracts state that the organisation's exclusive remedy is to require the vendor to attempt to perform the service a second time. Under such provisions, even if the organisation remains unsatisfied, it cannot terminate the contract. Outsourcing contracts also often limit the organisation's termination rights to those portions of a contract applicable to the service that was not provided properly, even if it does not make financial sense to maintain the other portions of the agreement. To avoid getting stuck if a vendor fails to perform as agreed, make sure that all agreements allow the organisation to terminate a contract by considering the following aspects.

- Breach of contract provisions—if the vendor fails to correct a problem after being notified and given a reasonable period of time to fix it.
- The vendor files for bankruptcy.
- Change of law provisions—the law changes in a way that calls into question the legality of the organisation–vendor relationship, a situation that most commonly arises when the outsourced service is one that could affect the organisation's status.
- If the vendor is causing problems or rising concerns, the organisation should have an absolute right to request the removal of individual employees.

Don't Rush It

It is next to impossible to negotiate a sound agreement, complete a regulatory analysis of a relationship, or ensure that organisation employees will be treated fairly when the process of negotiating an outsourcing contract is rushed. The pressure to close a deal may not always come from the vendor. Organisations should also be prepared to stand firm against internal pressures to speed things up. The key here is to plan ahead as much as possible to allow sufficient time to distribute and collect an RFP. Evaluate bids from various vendors, and negotiate a carefully crafted legal document that fully protects the organisation's interests.

Keep Uncle Sam Happy

Before negotiating any outsourcing transaction, you should carefully analyse the legal and regulatory implications, which will vary according to the type of services and the vendor involved. If the buildings in which the outsourced services are performed are financed with the proceeds of tax-exempt bonds, relevant regulations may restrict the allowable length of the contract and/or the manner in which fees may be structured. In most instances, the laws do not forbid an organisation from outsourcing, but they may require the organisation to demonstrate that the purpose of the transaction is legitimate. As an example, the organisation may need to obtain an independent valuation that the vendor's fee are consistent with fair market value. In other situations, procedural safeguards must be put in place to ensure that the structures of the organisation–vendor relationship comply with the law. There is no excuse for an organisation to sign any agreement before carefully examining these issues.

Apart from the above ten tips for successful outsourcing, the following are useful tips that organisations can use for successful offshoring in respect of IT/ITES outsourcing.

- Never outsource your core value.
- Get boardroom ownership.
- Forge international competencies.
- Fix your processes before offshoring it.
- Demand domain expertise.
- Require evidence of best practices.
- Write talent into the contract.
- Investigate pricing model.
- Acclimate to central differences.
- Get your feet wet.

The Seven Sins of Outsourcing

While outsourcing is a powerful tool to cut costs, improve performance and refocus on the core business, outsourcing initiatives often fall short of management's expectations. Barthelemy (2003) conducted a survey of nearly a hundred outsourcing efforts in Europe and the US and it was found that one or more of the seven sins underlie the most failed outsourcing efforts and these include:

- outsourcing activities that should not be outsourced;
- selecting the wrong vendor;
- writing a poor contract;
- overlooking personnel issues;
- losing control over the outsourced activity;
- overlooking the hidden costs of outsourcing; and
- failing to plan an exit strategy.

While firms may now have the opportunity to outsource, outsourcing initiatives do not necessarily fulfill all their expectations. For instance, three quarters of the US managers surveyed by the American Management Association (AMA) reported that outsourcing outcomes had failed to meet expectations. Literature on outsourcing has often sought to draw lessons from highly visible companies that have been successful in outsourcing. Barthelemy (2003) has reported on failed efforts. Failed outsourcing endeavours are rarely reported because firms are reluctant to publicise them. Firms do not like to report their failures because such information can damage their reputation. However, valuable 'best practices' can be inferred from outsourcing failures (Barthelemy 2003), especially when such failures are compared with successful outsourcing efforts. A few such experiences are listed in this section.

First Sin: Outsourcing Activities That Should Not Be Outsourced

Outsourcing is often associated with automatic cost reduction and performance improvement. Determining which activities can be best performed by outside vendors requires a good understanding of where the firm's competitive advantage comes from. Resources and capabilities are valuable and are difficult to imitate as well as difficult to substitute for superior performance. Activities that are based on such resources and capabilities (i.e., core activities) should not be outsourced because firms risk losing competitive advantage and becoming hollow corporations. On the other hand, non-core activities may be outsourced for two reasons. First, outsourcing non-core activities allows firms to focus on the activities they do best and improve their overall performance. Second, transferring non-core activities to specialised vendors can help reduce the costs and improve the performance of such activities.

An Example

In the early 1990s, the newly appointed top managers of a car rental company decided to outsource information technology (IT) to reduce costs. At that time, IT costs stood at 5 per cent of revenue, which was higher than the industry average (3 to 4 per cent). Three years into the outsourcing contract, IT costs stood at 10 per cent of revenue and the car rental firm could not get out of the contract. The entire IT department has been outsourced, but application development and maintenance should have been kept in-house. These activities are too close to core business, and it's hard not to have total control over them.

Second Sin: Selecting the Wrong Vendor

Selecting a good vendor is crucial for successful outsourcing. For instance, the third-party logistics provider selected a vendor who offered the lowest bid and whose main business was transportation. It did not have the capabilities to manage a full logistics function, let alone implement a just-in-time organisation. The client's requirements had been made clear from the outset, and the failure of this outsourcing effort could essentially be attributed to a lack of expertise of the third-party logistics provider. While one important argument for outsourcing is that specialist vendors have lower costs than their clients, it is important to note that firms do not necessarily outsource to cut costs. According to the VP of supply chain management of a US consumer goods firms, outsourcing logistics to a third party provider is more expensive than keeping logistics in-house. Yet, the cost increase is more than offset by an increase in revenues and a reduction in opportunity costs. Revenues increase due to the ability to implement innovative logistics practices, and economic value-added (EVA) measures improve because outsourcing avoids keeping fixed assets.

An Example

A European equipment manufacturer outsourced its entire logistics activity. The logic underlying this decision was that most customers wanted increasingly small and frequent deliveries, the US top management was not sure that the internal logistics department of their European subsidiary had a sufficient level of expertise to implement a just-in-time organisation. They also knew that a badly implemented just-in-time organisation results in tremendous costs. As the headquarters asked for the move to be made very quickly, the managers of the subsidiary had to find a third-party logistics provider, sign a contract, transfer the activity, and handover the management, all only within six months. Shortly after the contract was signed, things started going sour as the third-party provider did not live up to expectations. Goods were either delivered too late or not delivered at all. There were large shortfalls in the inventory. A benchmark study showed that this particular subsidiary had the highest logistics costs of all European subsidiaries.

Third Sin: Writing a Poor Contract

A landmark IT outsourcing deal popularised the notion that outsourcing vendors are partners and that contracts play a minor role. In 1989, Eastman Kodak outsourced a large part of its IT operations to IBM, Digital Equipment, and Businessland. As the relationships between Eastman Kodak and its vendors were both cooperative and based on loose contracts, it has been wrongly inferred that tight contracts were not necessary to be successful with outsourcing. A good contract is essential to outsourcing success because the contract helps to establish a balance of power between the client and the vendor. Drafting a good contract is always important because it allows partners to set expectations and to commit themselves to short-term goals. Moreover, it provides a safety net in case the relationship fails. The following are some of the essential features of good contracts.

- *Precise.* Ill-defined contracts often result in high costs and poor service levels. Cost and performance requirements should be established.
- *Complete.* Contracts should be as complete as possible and simple and straightforward. Such contracts will have smaller risk and negotiations will also be easy.
- *Incentive based.* The contract should be written to encourage the right behaviour from the vendor. The contract could call for a

change to a gain-sharing arrangement so that the client and the vendor have a joint stake in the outcome.
- *Balanced.* In general, one-sided contracts do not last long. Even a contract that is weighed against the vendor is not necessarily beneficial for the client: service levels quickly drop, and the vendor tries to win back some value by imposing extra fees.
- *Flexible.* Due to evolving technology and changing business conditions, medium and long-term outsourcing contracts should not be written in an inflexible way. Flexibility clauses can help both parties accommodate to environmental changes.

Spend as much time as possible while developing the contract. A contract is an investment whose value really becomes apparent if the relationship with the supplier becomes sour.

An Example

A European bank outsourced its entire telecommunications network to cut costs and refocus on its core business. This endeavour turned out to be a complete failure with increasing costs and decreasing service quality. The main reason for the failure was that the management had rushed to enter into relationship with the vendor. Too little time was spent on developing a good contract and several mistakes were made. The contract, though very long, was not precise. For instance, the bank had to pay extra fee even for basic services. There were no objective performance measurement clauses either. Fixed fee had been set when the client's business was booming. As turnover shrunk, the ratio of telecommunications fixed fee to the total revenue became increasingly large. Moreover, the contract made it impossible to switch vendors even after the relationship with the incumbent vendor had become increasingly sour. The failure experienced by the European bank can essentially be attributed to a badly drafted contract that lacked preciseness (i.e., extra fees had to be paid even for basic services), flexibility (i.e., fixed fee had been set when the business was booming) and completeness (i.e., it was impossible to switch vendors because extremely huge penalties would have been incurred). The bank learned the hard way.

Fourth Sin: Overlooking Personnel Issues

The efficient management of personnel issues is crucial because employees generally view outsourcing as an underestimation of their skills. This may result in a massive exodus even before an actual outsourcing decision has been made. Secrecy in outsourcing feasibility and decision-making are very difficult, and open communication is the key to managing personnel issues in outsourcing. When attempts at secrecy fail, rumours start spreading. As soon as employees know that outsourcing is under consideration, counterproductive anxiety arises and employees begin handing in their notice in anticipation of outsourcing.

Firms that contemplate outsourcing must face two interrelated personnel issues. First, key employees must be retained and motivated. For most activities, outsourcing does not mean transferring all the employees to the vendor. When an activity has been performed in-house for a long period of time, firm-specific knowledge about how to run the activity smoothly has accumulated. Employees who possess this firm-specific knowledge must be identified. To keep them in-house, the management must be prepared to offer them higher salaries and benefits. Outsourcing has a negative impact on employees' sense of job security and loyalty even when they keep their positions within the firms. This may lead to decreased productivity or even dysfunctional actions such as strikes. New responsibilities may be offered to secure the commitment of retained employees. Generally, their role tends to shift from service delivery to interface with the vendor and end users. This important shift requires new skills that can only be acquired through considerable training and ongoing support. A second personnel issue is that the commitment of employees transferred to the vendor must also be secured.

An Example

A utilities firm paid very careful attention to its employees when the decision was made to outsource 85 per cent of its IT budget to an outside vendor. In the deal, the vendor was contractually asked to offer the same pay and benefits to the 160 employees transferred to the vendor. The vendor also promised to neither fire outsourced employees nor to transfer them to other accounts without their approval. The outsourcing deal was endorsed by the works council, and finally turned out to be quite successful. At first glance, it seems surprising that firms may gain something from outsourcing if they merely transfer their employees to the third party and ask that they maintain the same pay and benefits. However, there is more to outsourcing than transferring people and renegotiating their pay and benefits. Multiple clients enable specialised vendors to operate at a scale unattainable by their individual clients. Because of the variety of their clients, specialised vendors also have a depth and range of experience that an individual client cannot match.

Fifth Sin: Losing Control over the Outsourced Activity

When the performance quality of an activity is low, managers are often tempted to outsource it. If poor performance is attributable to factors such as insufficient scale economies or a lack of expertise, outsourcing makes sense. If poor performance is attributable to poor management, outsourcing is not necessarily the right solution. On the one hand, it is often easier to manage an outside vendor than an in-house department. On the other hand, outsourcing entails great changes regarding the management of an activity. With outsourcing, control through direct ownership of assets and employment of staff is replaced by control through a contract. Instead of issuing orders, managers in charge of outsourced activities must negotiate results with vendors. They must also ensure the effective use of the outsourced service by internal users who are often reluctant to work with external vendors. For an outsourcing client, it is particularly important to avoid losing control over an outsourced activity. Such a loss of control has two distinct origins. First, the client may not have the capabilities to manage the vendor. Second, the client may not actively manage the vendor.

An Example

A computer manufacturer outsourced a large part of its after-sales service activity. Though the rationale for outsourcing was essentially cost reduction, a high standard of performance from the vendor was also important. In the computer industry, after-sales service is crucial, and the computer manufacturer did not want to lose business due to its outsourcing vendor. The first way to deal with this important issue was to devise a contractual clause stating that the vendor had to fix 85 per cent of the problems encountered by end-users within a day. However, the interviewee made clear that such a clause is useless if it is not correctly implemented. Low performance cannot be accepted because it would result in a loss of business. While a good contract is necessary, good enforcement is also essential.

Sixth Sin: Overlooking the Hidden Costs of Outsourcing

Outsourcing clients are generally confident that they can assess whether or not outsourcing results in cost savings. However, they often overlook costs that can seriously threaten the viability of outsourcing efforts. Transaction Cost Economics (TCE) suggests two main types of outsourcing costs, namely, outsourcing vendor search and contracting costs and outsourcing vendor management costs. Outsourcing vendor search and contracting costs include the costs of gathering information to identify and assess suitable vendors. Contracting costs are the costs of negotiating and writing the outsourcing contract. Both search and contracting costs are incurred before the outsourcing operation actually takes place. Outsourcing vendor management costs consist of three different costs, viz., *(a)* monitoring the agreement to ensure that vendors fulfill their contractual obligations, *(b)* bargaining with vendors and sanctioning them when they do not perform according to the contract and *(c)* negotiating changes to the contract when unforeseen circumstances arise. Outsourcing vendor management costs are incurred while the outsourcing operation actually takes place.

Transaction Cost Economics suggests that the hidden costs of outsourcing are essentially influenced by the idiosyncrasy of the resources underlying outsourced activities. Specific physical resources refer to specialised equipment tailored to a firm's requirements. Specific human resources refer to expertise that employees have acquired through years of training and that is useful only in the context of a single firm. When idiosyncratic resources have been transferred to an outside vendor, switching vendors or reintegrating the outsourced activity is quite difficult. As vendors know they cannot easily be replaced, they may act opportunistically. While such commoditisation enables vendors to reap greater economies of scale, it also means that the unique needs of their clients are no longer met. Firms that select the right vendor and write up a good contract are less likely to suffer from the potential opportunism of their vendor. A good vendor must be proficient and trustworthy. A good contract must be simultaneously precise, complete, incentive based, balanced and flexible. However, searching for a reliable vendor and drafting a good contract is expensive.

An Example

Table 8.2 highlights two cases of hidden costs in outsourcing. The first case is a manufacturing firm, which outsourced a subset of its logistics activity (warehousing). The second case is a manufacturing firm, which outsourced its entire logistics function. Search and contracting costs were nearly ten times higher for the entire logistics activity than for the warehousing outsourcing contract (6.2 per cent versus 0.7 per cent). Vendor management costs were more than twice as high for the entire logistics activity as for warehousing (15 per cent vs. 6.7 per cent). The figures for the second case were high enough to nullify cost savings from outsourcing.

Table 8.2. The Hidden Costs of Outsourcing in Two Logistics Cases

	Low level of idiosyncrasy (i.e., warehousing)	High level of idiosyncrasy (i.e., entire logistics function)
Contract amount	$1.5 million	$4 million
Contract duration	1 year	3 years
Search and contracting costs		
Number of internal employees	4	5
Outside consultants and lawyers	0	4
Total search and contracting cost	$10,000	$250,000
Ratio of total search and contracting cost amount	0.7%	6.2%
Vendor management costs		
Number of employees	2	2
Number of formal meetings per year	1	12
Number of informal meetings per year	4	12
Annual vendor management costs	$100,000	$200,000
Ratio of annual vendor management costs to total contract amount	6.7%	15%

The hidden costs of outsourcing are an important topic for managers because they can challenge the rationale for outsourcing. It is also paradoxical that these costs are both necessary and detrimental to the outcome of outsourcing efforts. While successful outsourcing requires substantial spending on vendor searching, contracting and management costs, these costs can also turn potentially successful outsourcing efforts into a complete failure. While carefully selecting the vendor and crafting contracts with well-articulated expectations and clearly set performance measures is expensive, such expenses are necessary to keep vendor management cost at a decent level. Considering the potential impact of the hidden costs of outsourcing, it may be worth the additional cost of hiring outside experts. Legal experts are useful when it comes to writing the outsourcing contract and negotiating with the vendor. Technical experts can help develop precise measures such as service-performance level.

Seventh Sin: Failing to Plan an Exit Strategy

Many managers are reluctant to anticipate the end of an outsourcing contract. Therefore, they often fail to plan an exit strategy (i.e., vendor switch or reintegration of an outsourced activity). Shrinking the vendor base and establishing long-term relationships with a few selected vendors is not always the best solution. Actually, outsourcing relationships can be viewed on a continuum. At one end are long-term relationships where one or both partners have made investments specific to the relationship. There is a considerable advantage in recontracting with the same vendor because switching vendors or reintegrating the outsourced activity is very difficult. At the other end are market relationships where the client has a choice of many vendors and the ability to switch vendors with little cost and inconvenience. In this case, there is no real advantage in recontracting with the same vendor. For instance, a firm in the computer industry successfully outsourced telemarketing. The duration of the contract was only one year. Every year, the incumbent vendor's price and performance were benchmarked against other vendors. If the incumbent vendor had not made the best offer, its contract would never have been renewed.

Managers who do not want to anticipate the end of an outsourcing relationship also have a tendency not to include material reversibility clauses (i.e., option to buy back promises and equipment from the vendor) and human reversibility clauses (i.e., option to hire back employees from the vendor) in the contract. The absence of such clauses leads to weak power bases for any negotiation with the vendor and makes it very difficult to back out of an outsourcing agreement.

An Example

One retail company outsourced several IT activities that senior management considered to be commodities (data centres, applications maintenance and user support). However, outsourcing failed due to

Table 8.3. The Seven Sins of Outsourcing and Lessons Learned

Deadly Sin	Lesson Learned
Outsourcing activities that should not be outsourced	Only activities that do not belong to the core business can be safely outsourced. The core versus non-core approach can be implemented both at the firm and activity level.
Selecting the wrong vendor	Outsourcing clients should look for vendors that are able to provide state-of-the-art solutions and are trustworthy.
Writing a poor contract	The contract is the main tool to establish a balance of power in outsourcing relationships. Good contracts have four characteristics. They must be precise, complete, balanced and flexible.
Overlooking personnel issues	Loss of key employees and lack of commitment can seriously threaten the viability of outsourcing efforts. However, good communication and ethical behaviour towards employees can help avoid such problems.
Losing control over the outsourced activity	In order to keep control over outsourced activities, clients must retain a small group of qualified managers. An active management of the vendor is also crucial.
Overlooking the hidden costs of outsourcing	The hidden costs (i.e., search, contracting and managing costs) can threaten the viability of outsourcing efforts. Hidden costs are likely to be lower when commodities are outsourced.
Failing to plan an exit strategy	The end of the outsourcing contract must be planned from the outset. Building reversibility clauses into the contract is crucial.

Source: Barthelemy (2003)

high costs and low performance. Though the vice president of information services wanted to get out of the contract, he was reluctant to cancel it. Indeed, he knew that a vendor switch would take over six months while reintegrating the activities would require as much as ten months. All he could do was to renegotiate the contract, implementing a 15 per cent reduction in services due to poor performance.

Table 8.4 summarises the experiences of both successful and failed cases. From this it is to be noted that there are more failures than successes. Among the seven sins, the most significant one is a poor contract followed by outsourcing of wrong activities and the least is hidden cost. Hence importance should be given to contract preparation over cost aspects of outsourcing. On the other hand, from successful cases, organisations should plan appropriate exit strategies followed by activities suitable for outsourcing.

Table 8.4. Summary of Seven Sins

Name of the Sin	Number (and percentage) of failed efforts that committed the sin	Number (and percentage) of successful efforts that committed the sin
Outsourcing activities that should not be outsourced	50 (55%)	26 (28%)
Selecting the wrong vendor	27 (30%)	8 (9%)
Writing a poor contract	63 (69%)	21 (23%)
Overlooking personnel issues	35 (38%)	19 (20%)
Losing control over the outsourced activity	34 (37%)	5 (6%)
Overlooking the hidden costs of Outsourcing	13 (14%)	4 (4%)
Failure to plan an exit strategy	41 (46%)	33 (36%)

Source: Barthelemy (2003)

Risks in Outsourcing

Outsourcing performed well can have tremendous payback. However, with great opportunity comes great risk. Companies that take advantage of the hard-won lessons learned about outsourcing will minimise the chance of failure; and they will maximise the organisation's ability to free up the time that managers can devote to core business functions (Tompkins 2006).

Primary incentive of outsourcing is believed to be cost reduction. Moreover, intelligently combining core competencies and extensive outsourcing strategies can improve returns on capital, cut risk, provide greater flexibility and make companies more responsive to the needs of their customers. Most important problem is how to identify and manage risks involved in outsourcing. If the expected benefits are not realised owing to certain risks, then the whole outsourcing initiative is jeopardised. However, with an objective to optimise and reap the maximum benefit from domain specialists, firms started outsourcing some core functions to third party experts. The major outsourcing contracts today typically involve the transfer of jobs, assets, information systems, functional processes and process management. From the past research and empirical studies it is to note that over half the number of outsourcing deals signed every year do not deliver the expected value. Sometimes, the expected value itself is mistaken. If one gets to the root cause of 'why outsourcing arrangement did not deliver what it should deliver', the reasons are mostly attributed to lack of contract planning, flawed vendor selection, poorly articulated SLA, not clearly articulated goal setting and inability to pre-empt, identify and mitigate the risks involved. Study conducted by a leading consulting firm substantiated that only near half of the total number of outsourcing contracts signed globally were successful. Out of all other unsuccessful contracts majority

were completely failed and remaining were only partially successful. Karprekar (2006), highlighted the following six major risks associated with outsourcing:
- pre-empt, identify and mitigate risks;
- infrastructure related risks;
- information security related risks;
- people related risks;
- technology related risks; and
- schedule and cost related risks.

These are briefly explained below.

Pre-empt, Identify and Mitigate Risks

Risk is an inherent factor of any outsourcing project. Risk in the outsourcing project can be defined as any event that might push the performance of the outsourcing arrangement below expectations. It is imperative to manage the risks both for the outsourcing firm and the vendor. The measure of risk could be linked to information, schedules, revenue, cost/cash flow, etc. In view of mitigating the risks involved in the outsourcing arrangement it is important first to pre-empt the risks and be proactive in planning to mitigate them. A well-thought risk mitigation approach right at the time of commencement of the contract can be very helpful. While planning for the risk mitigation, the following points need to be considered:
- expected value creation;
- expertise available to oversee and manage the outsourcing project and relationship;
- adequacy of infrastructure and technology;
- scope of the project and criticality of functions;
- continuity of most critical functions; and
- timeframes and cycles at which risks may come into existence

Infrastructure Related Risks

Infrastructure related risks are largely addressed in a business planning and disaster recovery planning. All involved functions in this planning are usually classified based on their criticality as real time, critical, essential and necessary functions. The damage prevention and protection strategy, the strategies for response to disaster, damage assessment, resumption and recovery must be addressed in detail as part of this plan.

Information Security Related Risks

It is imperative that necessary measures are taken to protect the information assets of the firm. Leakage of certain information can cause the firm massive losses. Firms should not just look for vendors to have robust regulatory and policy framework but also should expect them to have several security checks in place.

People Related Risks

Most severe risks come from the organisation's own employees. A high rate of turnover threatens the loss of knowledge asset. Firms need to ensure that recruitment, training, internal transfer processes are built around acquiring and retention of the knowledge in specific areas. An automated knowledge repository can be created and referred whenever needed. Moreover, risks owing to people are also attributed to planning a right team to steer the outsourcing project, proper training and involvement of the senior management. Usually, people from IT department are appointed in project steering team by default. Today's complex arrangements, however, require a deal-making team with a wide range of skills that go well beyond those of most IT experts.

Technology Related Risks

Technology related risks arise from reliability, security and scalability of the technology being used. Transition of processes from the firm to the outsourcing partner sometimes involves using customer-defined technology. In such cases, it is important to allocate adequate time for the outsourcing partner to understand and inherit the customer's technology. In other cases, the outsourcing partner may have his own technology. In any case, the outsourcing partner must have well-defined processes to validate any technology solution; include reliability checks, functional accuracy checks, volume testing to ensure scalability and security validation.

Schedule and Cost Related Risks

There are two parameters to this risk, i.e., *(a)* inadequate definition of requirement and *(b)* ineffective operational control. A contract requirement sets the platform for all outsourcing actions and forms the basis for subsequent management of the outsourced activity. If the contract requirements are not understood correctly then it will upset the schedules and lead to higher cost. Ineffective operational control happens when companies accept vendor's target prices or risky promises at face value. If the vendor is unable to fulfill the service levels and transition plan, schedules will be at risk. To mitigate schedules and cost related risks, the steering team of the outsourcing project should involve pricing experts, change management specialists, experienced negotiators, technology experts, human resources experts, domain experts and finance experts. A third party consultant may be required on a case-to-case basis. It is also required that a proper communication plan and transition plan is brainstormed and agreed.

The organisations should take necessary precautions and use appropriate tools while outsourcing so that some of the above risks can be minimised, if not eliminated completely.

The following are the top ten outsourcing strategy risks given by Tompkins (2006):
- outsourcing undesirable functions versus the ones that provide the greatest competitive advantage;
- not clearly defining goals and objectives before starting the outsourcing process;
- not establishing an effective internal baseline against which providers are measured—including costs, service and value adds;
- outsourcing in the international market without international operations experience;
- inadequate business case development for the outsourcing decision;
- making the decision to outsource without complete information on internal costs and processes;
- not considering the impact of outsourcing on other functions, and ignoring areas of risk such as environmental and regulatory factors;
- failure to understand human relations and employment law requirements for an outsourcing initiative;
- announcing outsourcing before sufficient details have been finalised, creating morale issues; and
- lack of risk analysis and risk assessment planning.

Outsourcing Framework

Outsourcing is a dynamic process in the sense that the related decisions and actions must continuously be adapted to changes in the strategic direction of the company. In addition, outsourcing is a recurring process (cycle) because the company at the end of the contract period faces the decision on whether to prolong the relationship, find an alternative supplier or take back the functional area (insourcing). Considering this dynamic and recurring nature of outsourcing, the process must be supported by feedback and throughput mechanisms to ensure that continuous measures on both company and supplier performance are converted into corrective and preventive actions. This puts heavy demands on the company's strategic preparedness, development resources, employee skills and adaptability, technology base, etc.

In the outsourcing literature, lot of work has been done and reported for the past five decades. Review on existing framework is not the objective of this section. However, for the benefit of the user few selected models and related information has been given in this section. Table 8.5 summarises the major ideas of the three classical outsourcing decision models proposed by Venkatesan (1992), Quinn and Hilmer (1994) and Olsen and Ellram (1997). Venkatesan (1992), suggests that manufacturing industry should distinguish between strategic operations and commodity operations of producing components and outsourcing the commodity operations. The outsourcing model proposed by Venkatesan uses a single variable to describe the make-or-buy decision for outsourcing. Essentially, a core component here is one that is critical to the functioning of the product; a non-core component denotes otherwise. For core components, their manufacture should be performed in-house, and simple purchasing can be made for the non-core. Venkatesan's model is simple but the full spectrum of outsourcing scenarios between simple make-in and purchasing has not been sufficiently addressed. In practice, it may be difficult to judge with certainty whether a product or process should be categorised as core or non-core. Strategically, this should not be seen as a simple matter of internal or external manufacturing; other situations exist that are between simple make-in and simple purchasing.

Table 8.5. A Comparison of Outsourcing Models

Outsourcing approach	Venkatesan (1992)	Quinn and Hilmer (1994)	Olsen (1997)
In-house manufacture	Critical effect on feature of final product (core component)	High potential competitive edge; high strategic vulnerability (high control component)	Nil
Collaboration	Nil	Medium potential competitive edge; medium strategic vulnerability (medium control component)	1. High strategic importance of purchasing—difficult to manage the purchasing (strategic component); 2. Low strategic importance of purchasing—difficult to manage purchasing (bottleneck component) 3. High strategic importance of purchasing—low difficulty of managing purchasing (leverage component)
Arm's length purchasing	Non-critical effect on feature of final product (no core component)	Low potential competitive edge; Low strategic vulnerability (low control component)	Non-critical component: low strategic importance of purchasing, low difficulty of managing purchasing situation

Quinn and Hilmer (1994) model focuses on the importance of control of component knowledge. Two indices are defined based on the properties of the components including the potential competitive advantage and strategic vulnerability. The first index measures the potential competitive advantage that an enterprise can derive from that particular component. The other index, the vulnerability index, denotes the degree to which the technological content of a particular component can be deciphered and captured by the competitor. In addition, the following three types of outsourcing are presented.

- For components with a high potential competitiveness and vulnerability, a strict control strategy will need to be adopted and they will be produced in-house.
- For components whose two indices are on the low side, a loose control strategy can be adopted; the corresponding outsourcing decision is to adopt a simple purchasing relation with supplier.
- When the two indices are both in the medium range, the control policy can be one of collaborative outsourcing.

In contrast to the above two models, Olsen's model does not address situations involving in-house manufacture, and is entirely concerned with outsourcing. In particular, it addresses the grey area between make-in and simple purchasing that is ignored in the above two models. The model employs two indices: one to indicate the difficulty of sourcing a component and the other the criticality or relative importance of that component. The index of significance of purchased components are used to describe the component's properties including functional importance, economic factors, image aspects such as brand name and safety. The indices can be high and low creating four different scenarios. Of these, three relate to the domain of collaboration, which is for significant, bottleneck and leverage components, while the other relates to simple purchasing. He assumes a significant component is one that is difficult to purchase, or has a relatively high importance to the product. Olsen's model seems to place emphasis on the effect of outsourcing on production with the aim to avoid disruption.

Nellore and Söderquist (2000) extended Quinn and Hilmer's model by introducing the concept of specification, and by attempting to quantify such specifications as indices. For example a bracket used in motorcars has a low degree of strategic vulnerability and high competitive advantage. However, it seems that these indices still need further refinements.

In outsourcing one needs to find out the factors that affect the benefits of the firm. Several factors were used before such as transaction cost economics, strategy or commodity. Some researchers suggested that the factors like economics and technology, and project management, business focus of the organisation need to be considered. Others argued that firms could enhance the productivity and improve quality by outsourcing. Different organisations should have different considerations. Firms should include all factors, which can affect the organisation's benefit as possible as they can. Yang and Huang (2000) suggested five major factors viz., management, strategy, technology, economics and quality and are shown in Table 8.6. Firms should increase or decrease the attributes that are suitable for them while they make decisions.

Table 8.6. The Factors and Attributes of Outsourcing

#	Factor / Attributes
1	**Management**
	Stimulate IS department to improve their performance and enhance morale.
	Improve communication problems and selfishness between IS department and operational department.
	Solve the floating and scarcity of employee.
	Increase the ability of management and control of IS department.
	Keep the flexibility to adjust department, including consolidation or decentralisation.
2	**Strategy**
	Focus on core competence.
	Make strategic alliance with vendor to make up the shortage of resources or technology.
	Form a new company by focusing on core competencies of these strategic alliances to develop new products and sell.
	Share the risks.
	Time to market.
3	**Technology**
	Get new technology.
	Learn new technology of software management and development from vendors.
4	**Economics**
	Reduce the developing and maintaining cost of information systems.
	Make the fixed costs to become variable costs.
	Increase the flexibility in finance.
5	**Quality**
	Procure higher reliability and performance of IS.
	Reach higher service level.

Source: Yang and Huang (2000)

Figure 8.2 shows the framework proposed by Wu et al. (2005) considering manufacturing specification (MS), which depends on degree of specification (DoS) and risk of discloser (RoD) and their interaction. In order to assess the level of MS transfer/sharing during outsourcing, it is necessary to obtain an understanding of the interaction in the model between manufacturer and supplier. To measure the degree of interaction in the outsourcing processes an analysis of the complexity of manufacture is required and, in turn, requires the product to be decomposed into subsystems, modules and components.

For example, the manufacture of a motor car involves the coordinated manufacture of engine, chassis, transmission, electronic control, upholstery and car body. The model shown in Figure 8.2 helps to delineate the various possibilities of collaboration and the necessary interactions between manufacturer and suppliers. The model shown in Figure 8.2 describes the flow of product knowledge (subsystem, module and component) between manufacturer and suppliers at different product levels. In this context, outsourcing is divided into three levels: between manufacturer and first level (subsystem) supplier; manufacturer and second level (module) supplier; and between manufacturer and third level (component) supplier.

Figure 8.2: Interaction between manufacturer/buyer and supplier

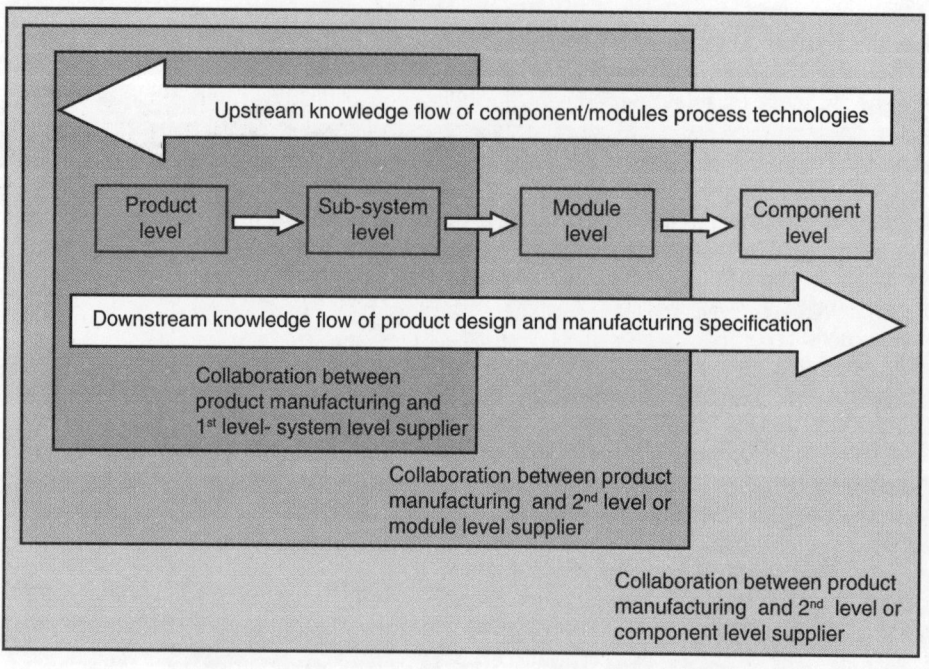

Source: Wu et al. (2005)

In the car manufacturing industry, many large car manufacturers have now evolved into assembly manufacturers on a global scale, and the supply of the various subsystems (control electronics, engine, chassis, audio system, etc.) is now achieved through various outsourcing approaches. The suppliers occupy different positions and play different roles in the global supply chains. Some of the subsystems are not directly outsourced to individual suppliers, but are performed in a layer-by-layer manner in the context of competence. However, some modules and components are directly outsourced to suppliers for manufacturing, with the core company performing the final leg of manufacturing by collecting and assembling all these product modules. A subsystem supplier is also called system-level supplier, who, generally speaking, always maintains a close partnership with the manufacturer. Such a system-level supplier will further outsource manufacturing activities to a lower second-level supplier as it sees.

There are two types of knowledge flow in this type of outsourcing process. The first involves the flow of complete product design from manufacturer to subsystem-level supplier, module supplier or component supplier. In contrast, knowledge flow in the latter case has the opposite direction, i.e., from component supplier to module and subsystem supplier, and finally to the manufacturer, who is responsible for the final assembly. In manufacturing environments exercising vertical integration, the boundaries between competing agents are often clear-cut. Manufacturers exercise tight control measures to protect their core competencies against possible disclosure to competitors. Also, within the enterprise boundary, strict measures are adopted to protect relevant technological know-how (for example, against commercial espionage). Subsystem and module assembly are kept within the firewall management system of a manufacturer, making the value chain of technology clear and controllable. Non-alliance partnership and multi-faceted collaborations can increase the complexity of knowledge control considerably, and the basis for collaboration/partnership can shift significantly, involving more in-depth knowledge of transfer/sharing. Good manufacturing practice nowadays requires that a manufacturing enterprise share with external agents its basic technological knowledge.

For example, the MS of an entire car may need to be transferred from manufacturer to the first-level or system-level supplier, or even to other, lower-level suppliers. If collaborative partnerships are to be created and developed in obtaining design solutions, some knowledge of technologies and know-how needs to flow from supplier to manufacturer. For products with a high degree of complexity, the major competitive factors consist of design fashion, uniqueness and fundamental technologies. A variety of know-how is critical in achieving the various forms of market differentiation. The disclosure of such critical know-how to competitors will in effect undermine the enterprise's competitiveness. The establishment of a close partnership therefore involves the making of difficult trade-off decisions. The attributes of interactivity define the process of transfer/sharing of knowledge during collaboration, which need not only depend on the frequency of interaction, but also on the scope and depth of interaction in the particular outsourcing context.

Momme (2002) proposed a comprehensive framework for outsourcing considering the following six generic phases and is shown in Figure 8.3—

- competence analysis;
- assessment and approval;
- contract negotiation;
- project execution and transfer;
- managing relationship; and
- contract termination.

The proposed framework has been validated by applying to an outsourcing project associated with land-based pressure vessels organisation. The above framework could comply with twofold objectives; it would provide the organisation with a better understanding of incentives and pitfalls (i.e., reduce the main risks of outsourcing and augment the potential benefits).

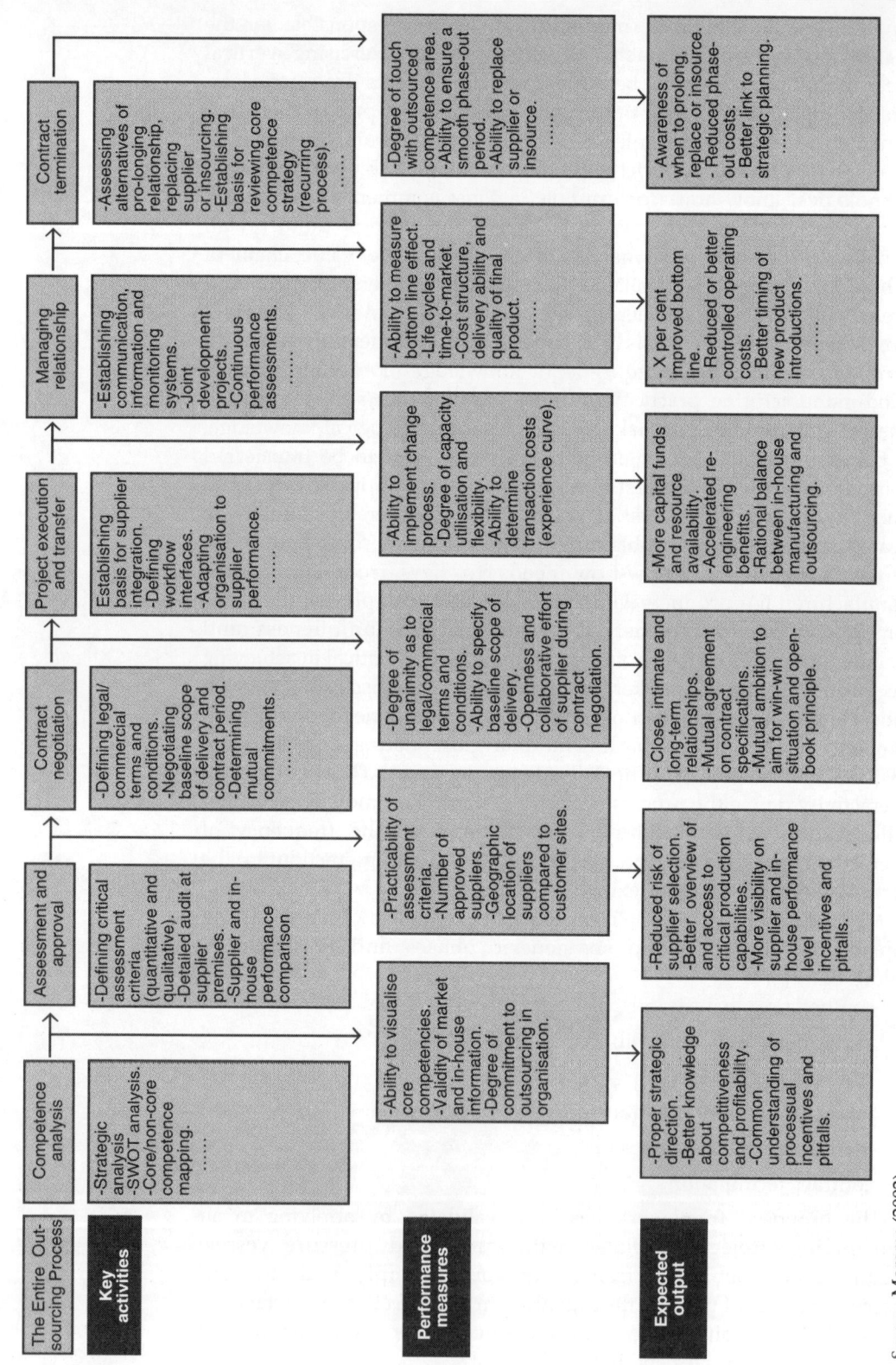

Figure 8.3: Outsourcing Framework (Built-in Key Activities, Performance Measures and Expected Output).

Source: Momme (2002)

For each of these phases, a varying number of key activities with related performance measures and expected output are identified (i.e., decision variables). The six phases and the decision variables are mainly synthesised from the four strategic phases of SOP and the model integrates six steps that links core competence thinking of outsourcing and the operational ideas. The framework was adopted from open systems modelling research on order management process at Proctor and Gamble where the order management process is divided into concrete steps or activities and their core processes. The framework depicts the processual correlation between the phases and the decision variables, giving three examples for each set of decision variables. Hence, it shows an extract, and is not exhaustive. It is emphasised that the decision variables depend on the context and scope of the individual company. This means that they must be thoroughly reviewed and adapted by the responsible outsourcing team based on situational factors. As indicated, an interdisciplinary group of people should be assigned to the outsourcing projects as this will add a wide range of synergistic perspectives to the decision variables, hence, facilitating identification and prioritisation. The system model supports the establishment of a capable outsourcing team due to the key support functions identified.

The framework implicitly contains feedback and throughput mechanisms insofar as the output from one phase provides input to one or more of the other phases. Part of the process involves re-engineering where the company adapts its organisation to the supplier performance. During this transformation, the company has a strong incentive to rethink its vision and strategy and assess the quality of its knowledge bases and operating procedures relative to suppliers and competitors. This is likely to result in certain spin-offs as to strategic direction and human/technical assets. In addition, the access to the supplier's complementary competencies is expected to produce a number of benefits like shared resource base for organisational learning and product/technology development, greater flexibility, reduced operating costs and improved cycle times. However, the company must also be aware that it can lose critical competencies or develop the wrong competencies, which can be fatal due to the risk of expropriation. Collectively, the outsourcing framework aims to facilitate proper planning, control and continuous improvement of the buyer–supplier relationship. This makes allowance for establishing a rational balance between in-house production and outsourcing.

Problems Related to Outsourcing

Outsourcing is a complex decision-making problem and needs to consider several key variables such as proximity, the regulatory environment, firm-level security and intellectual property rights, and the socio-political context within which the outsourcing phenomenon is unfolding. On the other hand, the decision to outsource (versus insourcing) involves several issues such as planning process, the implementation of an outsourcing project, the measurement and benchmarking of the project's performance, and continuous monitoring and decision processes. The complexity of these problems demand the use of tools based on operations research methodologies. Some of the major problems that need to be addressed as part of outsourcing exercise include the following:

- outsourcing decision-making;
- outsourcing vendor selection;
- proportioning outsourcing with insourcing;
- international country selection of outsourcing services;
- outsourcing project planning;
- supply–chain considerations in outsourcing;
- quantitative methods in benchmarking outsourcing performance; and
- implementing issues in outsourcing.

Approaches for Solving Outsourcing Related Problems

Outsourcing is multi-criteria decision-making problem and needs sophisticated tools and approaches to address. There are a number of tools available for addressing outsourcing problems. These include:

- mathematical models-lp, transportation, assignment models;
- goal programming and dynamic programming approaches;
- heuristics approaches;
- non-traditional approaches-genetic algorithms, simulated annealing, neural networks, agent-based models, etc;
- artificial intelligence;
- analytical hierarchical approach;
- game theoretic approaches;
- Activity-Based Cost (ABC) models;
- Transaction Cost Economics (TCE) models;
- auction theoretic methods;
- yield management models;
- utility theory based models;
- statistical methods, regression analysis;
- data warehousing and data mining techniques; and
- simulation, etc.

Apart from these, the following are some of the approaches in use
- SWOT Analysis;
- QFD approach for selection of outsourcing partner;
- SERVQUAL model;
- Spider chart, etc.

Conclusion

Outsourcing is a strategically important activity that enables an enterprise to achieve both short-and long-term benefits. Most companies are either considering outsourcing or have already decided to pursue it. There is an increasing interest in outsourcing among firms in a wide range of industries. Outsourcing is an increasingly important initiative being pursued by corporations all over the world in pursuit of improved efficiency. All forms of public and private sector businesses, governments, medical and educational institutions are increasingly outsourcing various activities due to the perceived advantages of outsourcing. There is no doubt that outsourcing can be a critical business solution; however, it is not something that happens magically. Outsourcing must be a core competency, just like any other important business process. There is no evidence that the factors that made outsourcing a viable option are about to fade any time soon. A strong, vibrant industry has developed to help manufacturing and logistics operations reduce costs by focusing on core functions.

All the business challenges that have pushed companies toward outsourcing relationships still exist, as do all the benefits to be gained from a successful initiative. Moreover, the outsourcing partners available to help you pursue your own initiative are thriving. But if an organisation does not view outsourcing as a core competency, it becomes vulnerable to setbacks. In fact, outsourcing performed poorly can bring a business to its knees. On the other hand, outsourcing performed well can have tremendous payback. The opportunity and the risk are both great.

Based on the experiences of both successful and failed cases, it is to be noted that there are more failures than successes. Among many parameters of outsourcing, the most significant one is poor contract preparation followed by wrong outsourcing activities and the least is hidden cost. Hence importance should be given to contract preparation over cost aspects of outsourcing. On the other hand from successful cases, organisations should plan appropriate exit strategies followed by activities suitable for outsourcing.

References

Barthelemy, J. 2003, 'The Seven Deadly Sins of Outsourcing, *Academy of Management Executive*, vol. 17, pp: 87–98.

Bettis, R., S. Bradley and G. Hamel. 1992, Outsourcing and Industrial Decline, *The Academy of Management Executive*, vol. 6, pp: 7–22.

Callahan, J. M. 2005, '10 Practical Tips for Successful Outsourcing', *Healthcare Financial Management*, pp: 110–16.

Chowdhry, A. 2006, 'Extend Outsourcing to the Hardware Sector', *The Financial Express*, 16 January 2006.

Dess, G. G., A. Rasheed, K. McLaughlin and R. Priem. 1995, 'The New Corporate Architecture', *The Academy of Management Executive*, vol. 5, pp: 7–20.

Gilley, K. M. and A. Rasheed. 2000, 'Making More by Doing Less: An Analysis of Outsourcing and its Effects on Firm Performance', *Journal of Management*, vol. 26, pp: 763–90.

Gonzalez, R., J. Gasco and J. Llopis. 2005, 'Information Systems Outsourcing Reasons in the Largest Spanish Firms', *International Journal of Information Management*, vol. 25, pp: 117–36.

Heizer, J. and B. Render. 2006, *Production and Operations Management*, Pearson, Prentice Hall.

Kaprekar, M. 2006, 'Ensuring Risk Free Outsourcing', *Financial Express Investor*, 15 January, http://www.financialexpress.com/fearchive_frame.php

Kotabe, M. 1992, *Global Sourcing Strategy: R&D, Manufacturing, and Marketing Interfaces*, New York: Quorum.

Lei, D. and M. Hitt. 1995, 'Strategic Restructuring and Outsourcing: The effect of Mergers and Acquisitions and LBOs on Building Firm Skills and Capabilities', *Journal of Management*, vol. 21, pp: 835–59.

Loh, L. and N. Venkatraman. 1992, 'Diffusion of Information Technology Outsourcing: Influence Sources and the Kodak Effect', *Information Systems Research*, vol. 3, pp: 334–58.

Lonsdale, C. and A. Cox. 1998, *Outsourcing: A Business Guide to Risk Management Tools and Techniques*, UK: Earlsgate Press.

McCarthy, I. and A. Anagnostou. 2004, 'The Impact of Outsourcing on the Transaction Costs and Boundaries of Manufacturing', *International Journal of Production Economics*, vol. 88, pp: 61–71.

Momme, J. 2002, 'Framework for Outsourcing Manufacturing: Strategic and Operational Implications', *Computers in Industry*, vol. 49, pp: 59–75.

Nellore, R and K. Söderquist. 2000, 'Strategic Outsourcing through Specifications', *Omega*, vol. 28, pp: 525–40.

Olsen, R.F. and L.M. Ellram. 1997, 'A Portfolio to Supplier Relationships', *Industrial Marketing Management*, vol. 26, pp: 101–13.

Prahalad, C.K. and G. Hamel. 1990, 'The Core Competence of the Corporation', *Harvard Business Review*, vol. 68, pp: 79–93.

Quinn, J.B. 1992, *Intelligent Enterprise: A Knowledge and Service Based Paradigm for Industry*, New York: Free Press.

Quinn, J.B., T.L. Doorley and P.C. Paquette. 1990, 'Technology in Services: Rethinking Strategic Focus', *Sloan Management Review*, vol. 31, pp: 79–87.

Quinn, J. B. and F. Hilmer. 1994, 'Strategic Outsourcing', *Sloan Management Review*, Summer, vol. 35, pp: 43–55.

Schultze, C. 2004, 'Offshoring, Import Competition and the Jobless Recovery', *Brooking Institution Policy Brief No. 136*.

Teece, D., G. Pisano and A. Shuen. 1997, 'Dynamic Capabilities and Strategic Management', *Strategic Management Journal*, vol. 18, pp: 509–33.

Tompkins, J. A. 2006, 'The Business Imperative of Outsourcing', *Industrial Management*, January–February, pp: 8–12.

Venkatesha Babu. 2005. Azim Premiji, CEO, Wipro Technologies Speaks on Exit of Vivek Paul, Vice Chairman of Wipro, *Business Today*, 31 July 2005.

Venkatesan, R. 1992, 'Strategy Sourcing: To Make or Not to Make', *Harvard Business Review*, November/December, pp: 98 –108.

Venkatraman, N. 1989, 'Beyond Outsourcing: Managing IT Resource as a Value Centre', *Sloan Management Review*, vol. 38, pp: 51–64.

Wright, D.T. and N.D. Burns. 1997, 'Cellular Green-Teams in Global Network Organisations', *International Journal of Production Economics*, vol. 52, pp: 291–303.

Wu, F., H.Z. Li, L. K. Chu and D. Sculli. 2005, 'An Outsourcing Decision Model for Sustaining Long-Term Performance', *International Journal of Production Research*, vol. 43, pp: 2513–35.

Yang, C. and J. B. Huang. 2000, 'A Decision Model for IS Outsourcing', *International Journal of Information Management*, vol. 20, pp: 225–39.

9
Operational Issues in Outsourcing

S. Venkataramanaiah

Introduction

In order to enjoy the benefits of outsourcing, the firms must have appropriate business decision-making models with appropriate tools and techniques. One of the reasons why many firms failed to achieve business success is that they do not have a clear understanding of which operational practices are appropriate to the different circumstances they face. Firms are often unaware of the full range of tools and techniques which are available to them, and as a result, over-utilise practices which are currently fashionable. The firms must have appropriate business decision-making model that is built on sound tools and techniques. For example, partnership sourcing would appear to have been used by many firms in an inappropriate manner. There is considerable merit to the idea of developing closer links with suppliers and it can assist the firm in capturing the innovation and improved quality it requires, but it cannot afford to develop in-house. The problem with the application of the concept, in many firms, is that it has not been understood when it is appropriate to be used. Firms need to align their operational tools and techniques to the outsourcing/business plan. Tools and techniques must complement the strategy, not contradict it. The two elements, viz., *(a)* awareness of managers of the full range of tools and techniques, which are available to manage external relationships; and *(b)* an understanding of the circumstances when it is appropriate to use these tools and techniques, are necessary to effectively manage supply in outsourcing situations. The terms supplier and vendor are used interchangeably.

In this chapter a range of operational tools and techniques are presented based on past research and empirical studies. The key operational areas for effective outsourcing are:
- vendor selection;
- vendor development; and
- vendor performance measurement.

Vendor Selection

During recent years the questions of vendor selection and performance evaluation have become key issues. Most firms spend 50–65 per cent of their sales revenue on parts and material supplies. The material costs represent a larger portion of total costs. The percentage of sales revenues spent on materials varies from more than 80 per cent in the petroleum refining industry to only 25 per cent in pharmaceutical industry (Krajewski and Ritzman 1999). Hence, the requirement to increase a worldwide competitive edge on the deliver from vendor has increased significantly. Mohanty (1990) has identified that almost all materials managers from Indian industries view the selection of vendors as the most important decision problem. Vendors decide the vital determinant to ensure the profitability and survival of a firm in the dynamic business environment. Therefore, vendor selection in the firm appears to have foremost cost reducing opportunities. Many firms attempt to rationalise the number of vendors from which they procure the material. Goffin et al. (1997) found that in a variety of industries in the UK between 1991 and 1996, the number of suppliers went down as much as 36 per cent. Vendors are evaluated on different criteria such as pricing structure, delivery (timeliness and costs), product quality, and service quality and facilities capability, research and development, etc. Vendor Selection Problem (VSP) deals with the selection of right vendors and their quota allocation. It poses high degree of uncertainty due to several reasons such as:

* selected vendors are to be evaluated on more than one criterion;
* vendors may have different performances for different criteria, etc. It is extremely difficult for any one vendor to do extremely well in all dimensions of performance. For example, a high quality vendor might not be the one with the lowest cost;
* the emphasis on quality and timely delivery in today's globally competitive market adds a new level of complexity; and
* the dynamics of the market driven by customer needs affect the relative importance that the various criteria have for VSP.

Many researchers and practitioners have stressed the importance of firms developing robust tools and models for both selecting activities for outsourcing and selecting supplier relationship types. However, this guidance will be of no avail if the firm selects suppliers, who are unable or unwilling to provide the firm with the goods or services it requires. Consequently, in outsourcing firms need to be advised in making the right decision.

One of the problems with most of the firms is that they are organised into functional silos, even when it is clear that many of the important issues facing them cut across such boundaries. This tendency is, of course, further legitimised by the way business is taught in most of the academic community. A number of most prominent writers in the area of purchasing and supply raise this issue when discussing the selection of suppliers. According to Burt and Doyle (1993), the selection of suppliers was too often the responsibility of well-intentioned engineers and others who were not sensitive to the strategic or commercial implications of their decisions, or equally well-intentioned buyers with little sensitivity to important technical, quality and service considerations. Hence, the supplier selection teams must be cross-functional, tapping the expertise of professionals from across the entire firm. In a manufacturing firm those involved should include personnel from purchasing, design engineering, marketing, operations, manufacturing and quality, finance, etc.

The extra dimension for the outsourcing decision, as against other external sourcing decisions, is that employees from the firm will often be transferred to the supplier as part of the agreement. Consequently, many others have suggested that people who are likely to be transferred under the agreement should not be involved in the selection process. They argue that this helps to ensure decision-making integrity and means that there are employees left within the customer organisation, with knowledge of the selection and negotiation process, to help manage the ongoing relationship with the supplier.

The Vendor Selection Process

Once the team is in place, the process by which supplier selection is to be made can be formulated. For most firms this will be an already well-established set of procedures, especially in the case of those firms governed by the EU Procurement Directives. The beginning of the process will involve the issuing of requests for proposals (RFPs), or, for those governed by the EU rules, an invitation to tender (ITT). These documents will include the following:

- a statement on the scope of the work being offered;
- the current costs; and
- the contract terms and conditions.

This fits in with the call from Lacity and Hirschheim (1993) to reject the standard contract of the supplier. Generally, the firms would be interested to have a short list of sufficient suppliers to allow a genuine competition to take place. The competition will encourage the suppliers to reduce their prices and increase their offerings. This basic rule has two important caveats.

First, taking the lowest-cost bid, or forcing down all of the bids to a very low cost, can be a shortsighted policy. If the bid is too low the winning supplier may simply reduce its level of service after the contract has been won. Further, if there are high switching costs, and this can lead to a poor level of service. Alternatively, if the supplier has a high dependency on the business of the firm it may be that some months into the contract they get into financial difficulties.

Second, it is often said by those involved in outsourcing, to beware of the suspiciously low-cost bid. Suppliers which present very low-cost bids are often presenting a loss-leader and hope to increase the price later on, either during the contract or at the recontracting stage. The discussion on asset specificity has shown the circumstances, which can accommodate the latter.

Vendor Selection Criteria

In order to choose between the short-listed suppliers the firm must have a set of criteria against which to judge them. Clearly, given that firms will be looking for different attributes from suppliers in different situations, there is not a single set of criteria, which can be applied on all occasions. One exception to this is the need for the firm to be certain that, whatever be the capabilities of the supplier, there are grounds for believing that it will act in a cooperative manner. A key indicator for ensuring this is the degree to which the firm's business is of significance to the turnover or growth plans of the supplier. Many firms contract with a supplier which has an excellent track record, without understanding that the circumstances of their exchange relationship with the supplier are not such that will precipitate the same level of performance as it offers other firms. Traditionally, firms had adversarial relationships with suppliers, and so the focus was on simple quality, price and delivery. But, as Saunders et al. (1997) comments, standard criteria are appropriate for short-term, transactional purchasing, but they are inadequate when searching for partners. For the latter purpose, factors that determine long-term future performance and the potential for innovation and improvement need to be identified. Table 9.1 shows various criterion proposed by Dickson (1966) for selection of vendors. These are categorised into four major categories depending on the level of importance. Apart from these, the CBI/DTI body, Partnership Sourcing Ltd, has compiled the following nine selection criteria for the relationship type they are promoting.

- Possession of a total quality management policy.
- Possession of ISO 9000 certification.
- Capability in the latest purchasing and supply techniques, for example, JIT and EDI.
- Possession of an in-house design capability.
- Capabilities to supply all round the world.
- Evidence of consistency in delivery, service and product quality.
- Attitude on total acquisition cost.
- Possession of a change culture and flexible workforce.
- Innovative supplier of services.

Baily and Farmer (1990) have observed that one manufacturing firm selected its supplier based on the supplier's capability to contribute in production process. This would enable to participate in the early phases of product design and development as a full partner in the process and would openly share information on the functional, assembly and in-services requirements of the parts, including cost and quality targets and would be orientated towards taking cost out of product and improving total system performance to mutual benefit.

Table 9.1. Dickson's Vendor Selection Criteria

Rank	Factor	Mean	Evaluation Rating
1	Quality	3.508	Extreme importance
2	Delivery	3.417	
3	Performance history	2.998	
4	Warranties and claim policies	2.849	
5	Production facilities and capacity	2.775	Considerable importance
6	Price	2.758	
7	Technical capability	2.545	
8	Financial position	2.514	
9	Procedural compliance	2.488	
10	Communication system	2.426	
11	Reputation and position in industry	2.412	
12	Desire for business	2.256	
13	Management and organisation	2.216	
14	Operating controls	2.211	Average importance
15	Repair service	2.187	
16	Attitude	2.120	
17	Impression	2.054	
18	Packaging ability	2.009	
19	Labour relations record	2.003	
20	Geographical location	1.872	
21	Amount of past business	1.597	
22	Training aids	1.537	
23	Reciprocal arrangements	0.610	Slight importance

Source: Dickson (1966)

That many of those advocating closer buyer–supplier relationships are in favour of openness and honest dealings between the two parties is reflected in the advice on supplier selection. The key ingredients for any successful American Keiretsu-type (AKT) relationship are strategic fitness and trust. Obviously, a potential supplier must demonstrate or be willing and able to develop the required engineering, quality, capacity, responsiveness, flexibility, cost and dependability. But if it is not possible after a reasonable period of time to develop an open, trusting relationship, then this is not the right supplier. Partnerships can be used as a tool of leverage, and the language, which is commonly associated with them, can be used to conceal true intentions.

Managing vendors for a meaningful time period is very difficulty due to many reasons. This can be managed better by considering one or more of the pitfalls as suggested by Richards-Peidl (2003).

Pitfalls in Vendor Relationships

- Lack of commitment, accountability.
- Unknown vendor relationships.
- Over selling.
- Contracts not scrutinised.
- Vague service level agreements.
- Vendors not held accountable.
- Assumed knowledge.

Vendor risks cannot be adequately identified and managed without a commitment of resources. Senior management must formally recognise the need to dedicate resources and allow appropriate staff time to manage vendor relationships. It is the senior management's responsibility to set expectations for meaningful due diligence analysis, contract review, financial and internal control assessments, and continuing vendor management. Each vendor should be assigned a relationship manager. This is the person who engaged the vendor and/or is responsible for its performance and adherence to contract terms. While the vendor-relationship manager may be a senior manager or department manager, the key is to formally establish clear lines of accountability and include these duties as part of the job description.

The vendor-management programme is a shared responsibility that should involve all departments or business lines relying on vendors. However, this distributed accountability is part of the problem. It often means a lack of oversight and inconsistency in key processes, such as due diligence, contract review and relationship management. Distributed accountability without a coordinated programme results in an inability to understand the risks, new or current, that vendors may present. While one individual shouldn't be responsible for all the contracts, one person should oversee programme coordination, effectiveness, regulatory compliance and programme improvement. This individual should be a good project manager, and should have the authority to implement policy procedures and monitor compliance. Many of these pitfalls and problems can be avoided by following service level agreements.

The relationship model given in Figure 9.1, establishes those factors internal to the two parties, which are relevant to the relationship, and the various facets of the relationship itself. Of particular importance is that both parties understand the competitive pressure they are each under, so that they can both respond to such pressures in an ordered way, which does not destroy the relationship. Many relationships have a great potential for breakdown because of poor communication, which in turn, breeds suspicion. Lamming et al. (1996), argued that organisations have their own perspectives of a relationship's actual performance and their own desired (or expected) levels of relationship performance. The

RAP (Relationship Assessment Programme) tool enables the two parties to gain a common perspective on what is actually happening between them and provides a clearer picture of the relationship's performance. Without a clear picture of what is happening in a relationship no meaningful relationship management process can be developed. Of course, whether it is possible or desirable for buyers or suppliers to involve themselves in such equity is an open question. In some circumstances it may be appropriate, but that in many it will not. The task for managers using the tool will be to recognise the situations when it is appropriate.

Managing vendor relations includes:

- identifying outsourcing opportunities;
- components of effective contractual agreements;
- legal issues surrounding contractual relationships;
- qualifying vendors and writing the request for proposal;
- principles of effective negotiation;
- developing service level agreements;
- maintaining effective outsourcing partnerships; and
- training and development.

Figure 9.1: The Relationship Assessment Programme (RAP) Model

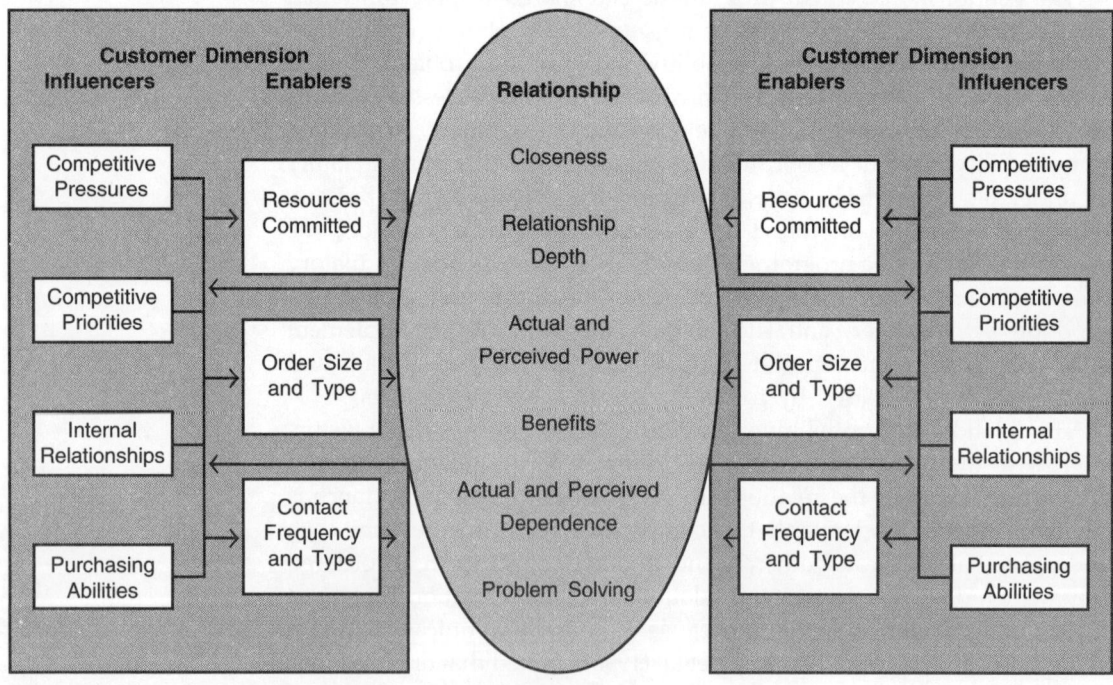

Source: Lamming et al. (1996)

The importance of each category varies with the clients. The first category experience, includes issues such as the vendor's track record in outsourcing. Knowledge of the client's industry is another variable that should be explored. The vendor should also show evidence of long range planning. Security, backups and disaster planning should be analysed. In addition, the vendor should have a global perspective. The ability to support the potential client's applications and languages with the needed technology and personnel is essential. Not only should the vendor have state-of-the-art equipment, but also adequate plans to upgrade technology in the future. The analysis should also include the willingness to negotiate the contract issues of price, service, ownership and control. Communication and the working relationship with prospective vendors during negotiations should be analysed. Continued communication between vendor and client is essential throughout the duration of the contract. The final category of vendor characteristics includes the financial status of the vendor. Is the vendor financially stable and likely to remain in business for the duration of the contract?

The vendor does have advantages in the negotiating processes. While the vendor has negotiated numerous outsourcing contracts, the client is generally entering an outsourcing contract for the first time. However, the vendor does have unique concerns. For example, the vendor may desire to hire part or all of the IS staff of the client. These employees are knowledgeable in the client's procedures and are a valuable asset to the vendor. However, transferring individuals from the client's firm to the vendor is not always successful. There is a 20 to 30 per cent attrition rate during the first year. What is most harmful for the outsourcing vendor is that the most qualified individuals leave first. Other employees may not accept a transfer to the vendor because of a previous relationship. Table 9.2 summarises the vendor and contract issues in the outsourcing.

Table 9.2. Vendor and Contract Issues

Attribute	Related issues
Experience	1. Prior success in outsourcing 2. Knowledge of client's industry
Planning	1. Evidence of long range planning 2. International perspective
Technology/personnel	1. State of the art technology 2. Trained personnel in appropriate areas 3. Plans for technology improvements
Contract issues	1. Flexibility in entering/existing contract 2. Willingness to negotiate—price, service, ownership
Communication	1. Working relationship between vendor and client 2. Importance of client's input/communication

Source: Ketler and Walstrom (1993)

Service Level Agreements (SLAs)

Service level agreements (SLAs) are explicit statements that describe service or product expectations. While SLAs may or may not accompany the contract, they should be requested and negotiated prior to contract signing. The concern with most SLAs is that they should establish general performance without measurable standards. SLAs must be specific to department and must allow identifying breach of contract or deterioration in service quality. When feasible, the SLA should include a measurable attribute with the service commitment, e.g., suppose a vendor agrees to provide telephone or onsite support and all software upgrades and patches and notify the department if a security breach occurs. One may want to add additional conditions like response through telephone within 24 hrs and define the timelines of software maintenance, particularly when there is a risk of vulnerability. Also make sure special fee and costs are defined for service that exceeds contractual service levels such as supplemental training, custom maintenance and extended support.

Components of Effective Contractual Agreements

A contractual agreement establishes a mutual exchange of rights among parties. Components of effective contractual agreements include the following:

Describe the Desired Partnership

Create a statement that outlines the essential details of the desired relationship. If you are planning on outsourcing your entire call centre operation, for instance, the type of relationship will differ from the partnership you expect from a more limited engagement. For example, a description of a full-service arrangement could be expressed as 'to engage with a full-service outsourcer to handle all aspects of our current operations.' (Ketler and Walstrom 1993) A description of a more limited arrangement may be to find an outsourcer well versed to manage.

Identify the 'Must Haves' of a Contract

You will save time during the selection process by quickly eliminating vendors that do not meet the organisation's essential requirements. For example, if you must have a vendor who is able to visit your location on short notice, the contractual criteria should include a requirement that the vendor be located nearby. If you require a vendor who can provide you with multilingual candidates, this should be included in the 'must haves'.

Develop Clear Cost Expectations

It may be difficult to determine the comparative value of vendor pricing and cost structures. For instance, one call centre outsourcer may charge per transaction fee and include management, training and recruiting in those costs. Another vendor may charge per hour cost for each agent, manager, trainer and recruiter. It is important to determine your budget for the entire project and your pricing preferences prior to agreeing to a vendor's pricing structure.

Vendor Development

Baily and Farmer (1990) has defined supplier development activities as a planned process of getting suppliers to produce the things the purchaser wants, to the purchaser's quality standards, in the quantities and to the delivery schedules required, by providing technical assistance and advice, commercial help with procurement and perhaps transport, and possibly also financial assistance in the form of loans and equity investment to pay for new equipment and tooling. Some features of supplier development as suggested by Hahn et al. (1990) are given in Table 9.3. Hahn et al. (1990) have developed not a dissimilar range, and also link in some of the specific activities, which are associated with the broad categories.

Table 9.3. Supplier Development Activities

	Product Related	Process Related	Operating Sys Related
Cost	e.g., Value analysis	e.g., Process efficiency	e.g., Work efficiency
Delivery	e.g., Materials lead time	e.g., Capacity level	e.g., Inventory system
Quality	e.g., Incoming materials control	e.g., Testing equipment	e.g., Quality assurance system
Technical	e.g., Design	e.g., Process capability	e.g., JIT

Source: Hahn et al. (1990)

In 1995, the UK government published its view of what a broad framework should be for supplier development by central government departments. The advice was part of best practices on procurement and is given below.

UK Government Supplier Development Guidelines

The development of suppliers will be critical to increasing the efficiency and competitiveness. Treasury (1995) suggested following ways in which it will be encouraged.

- Informing the market about the Department's likely needs, in general terms, before the procurement process starts.
- Keeping the market informed about emerging thinking during the crucial development stage of the specification of requirements.
- Being as open and informative as possible to all potential suppliers throughout the procurement process.
- Publishing tendering evaluation criteria.
- Debriefing suppliers after the procurement decision has been made.

- Working with suppliers after award of contract to overcome problems and weaknesses and to resolve technical issues, so that they can provide a better service.

Departments will ensure that these activities are carried out in ways, which do not restrict or distort competition or give one supplier an unfair advantage over another.

Vendor development is another important operational area concerning the need for firms to develop their suppliers. This has also been an area where long-standing attitudes have been questioned in the 1990s. Traditionally, the term supplier development has usually referred to attempts to broaden the firm's supply base. Hahn et al. (1990) defined the supplier development programme as any systematic organisational effort to create and maintain a network of competent suppliers. In a narrow sense, it involves the creation of new sources of supply when there are no adequate suppliers to meet the firm's requirements. In a broader perspective, it also involves activities designed to upgrade existing suppliers' capabilities to meet the changing competitive requirements.

Supplier development programmes aim to develop the kind and quantity of suppliers the business needs. Different situations will warrant different approaches, and it is no coincidence that the recent, broader interpretations of supplier development are broadly located within the school of thought, which favour the development of long-term and collaborative relationships. Some of the characteristics of good supply partners are given in Table 9.4.

Table 9.4. Characteristics of Good Supply Partners

Flexible	Has bonded warehouse
Reliable	Quick response to reordering
Long-term relationship	Ready to accept feedback
Proactive	Supply market information, new technology
Responsible	Free technical support and consulting service
Responsive	Have cooperative spirit
Dependable	Meet urgent orders
Straight to the point	Understand and satisfy needs
Communicate effectively	Win–win situation
Handle complaints quickly	Systematic operation
Producing samples quickly and timely	Innovative
Professional	Setting up plants next to us
Dedication	Good after-sales service
Change with environment	Technical support
Lean structure	Flexibility in logistic arrangement
Efficient and direct	Easy to get problems solved
Good connections and relationship	Problem solving
Competitive pricing	Good Quality

Source: Hahn et al. (1990)

Supplier development programmes will usually come about after one of the two measurement activities: either the evaluation of the performance of existing suppliers or the preliminary assessment of new suppliers. During these measurement exercises a gap will often be identified between the requirements of the firm and the capabilities of the supplier or potential supplier in question. The nature of this gap will largely determine the type of supplier development activity, which should be adopted by the firm—there should be no hard and fast rules about what activities form the programme. Nevertheless, there are certain broad areas of activity, which can be identified, specific activities that can be put forward as means of illustration of these broad areas, and real-life case examples, which show the potential of supplier development to provide actual business gain.

Vendor Development Programmes—Examples

Many well-known and effective vendor development programmes have been recorded in the literature. One of the best known is the policy used by Marks and Spencer. It has been noted that the firm has been developing suppliers for 60 years or more, since in 1928 they first cut out the middleman and dealt direct with the manufacturer. Marks and Spencer has no financial stake in their suppliers, but does invest very substantially in them in terms of technical support, management advice, and a thorough educational process to bring the manufacturer's outlook and operating policy close to that of Marks and Spencer. These are seen as long-term investments.

Lamming et al. (1996) notes that, in contrast to most Western firms, Japanese manufacturers have a much better focus on supplier development. Such firms have set up in other economic regions in the world despite the fact that the local supply base does not contain all the skills, capabilities and capacities they need. The firms are comfortable with this situation, as they have practised techniques for improving supplier performance.

In 1991, Nissan in the UK began holding purchasing seminars for its first-tier suppliers, to help them in selecting their own suppliers. Nissan also helps to develop its non-first-tier suppliers. Due to this support over 30 firms got benefited from the second-tier suppliers.

Honda also provides an example, with its development programme designed for its relationship with Parker Hannifin Corporation, a supplier of hydraulic valves and hoses, filters and pumps. Honda engineers worked with this supplier's engineering team at a number of its plants. At one, the joint initiative, which resulted and precipitated a change in the production system, increased its efficiency to such an extent that a process, which previously took 19 days, only took five minutes after the change. Overall, Honda managed to save Parker Hannifin about £1.6 million through increased efficiency.

Benefits of Effective Vendor Development— an Evidence

In a survey by Watts and Hahn (1993), the benefits firms were obtaining from their efforts at supplier development were recorded and some of the selected items are given below where 1 indicates no improvement and 7 denotes significant improvement. These are adopted based on likert scale (Watts and Hahn 1993).

Top Three:	
Percentage of orders meeting design specification	5.58
Percentage of on-time deliveries	5.47
Percentage of orders meeting quantity requirements	5.42
Bottom Three:	
Average investment in purchased parts inventory	4.60
No. of product improvements initiated by suppliers	4.43
No. of cost reduction programmes initiated by suppliers	4.40

Managing Vendor Relationships

The organisations can achieve competitiveness and avoid vulnerability by focusing on flexibility and control issues. Further, the firms should consider the trade-off between these two activities. The issue is less whether to make or buy an activity than it is how to structure internal versus external sourcing on an optimal basis. Quinn and Hilmer (1994) proposed a relation between flexibility and control (given in Figure 9.2) illustrates how best certain trade-offs can be managed by certain relationship types. Quinn and Hilmer suggested the organisations to follow their own decision-making model, which may be built on the basis of competitive edge. If there exists high potential for competitive edge and high potential for strategic vulnerability the firm should

Figure 9.2: Flexibility and Control Relationships in Contracts

Source: Quinn and Hilmer (1994)

retain activities in-house. At the other end of the spectrum, where both are low, the response is to outsource, making spot market transactions. For those activities, which fall into the very broad category of medium importance to competitive edge and strategic vulnerability, there is a range of sourcing options.

Quinn and Hilmer (1994) stated that the practice and law of strategic alliances are rapidly developing new ways to deal with common control issues by establishing specified procedures that permit direct involvement in limited stages of a partner's activities without incurring the costs of ownership arrangements or the loss of control inherent in arm's-length transactions. The make–buy model of Probert (1997) also contains instructions on which relationship types should be adopted with again partnership-style relationships being deemed appropriate for activities which are of medium importance to the business. Probert identifies a range of non-adversarial supplier relationship forms

- co-makership;
- partnership sourcing; and
- preferred suppliers.

Co-makership is deemed to be the closest type of such relationships, and is characterised by openness including open book accounting and shared risk. There is also cooperation in the development of new product and improved methods. Partnership sourcing is similar in terms of product development, but with lesser-cost transparency. Preferred suppliers are those, which the firm can select to pursue problem solving and cost reduction targets.

Asset specificity is on one of the important aspects of outsourcing. Recurrent transactions, which are of high asset specificity, should be undertaken within the boundary of the firm (through vertical integration). Other transactions, those characterised by medium and low asset specificity, are conducted on an inter firm basis, but the type of supplier relationships or governance structures employed are different. For transactions of low asset specificity, the firm is able to source from the market. The low switching costs mean that the number of alternative suppliers in the market is what protects each party from opportunism by each other. The transactions with a medium asset specificity require a different response. Although problems arising from a fundamental transformation during the contract are not as serious as is the case with highly specific transactions, there is still, for reasons of efficiency, a desire on the part of the two parties to ensure continuity in the relationship. Williamson (1985) suggests that organisations should go for bilateral governance structures. These are intended to assist firms in achieving the still available scale economies, while relieving the firm of the costs of legal ownership. The goal of outsourcing can be accomplished partly by (a) recognising that the hazards of opportunism vary with the type of adoption proposed and (b) restricting adjustments to those where the hazards are least. Table 9.5 shows the range of sourcing options based upon asset specificity suggested by Williamson (1985). This concept is very different to those, which are born-out of the core competence concept. An activity can be non-core but of high or low asset specificity.

Table 9.5. The Effect of Asset Specificity on the Choice of Sourcing Options

Boundary of the Firm

High Asset Specificity	Medium Asset Specificity	Low Asset Specificity
Vertical Integration	Bilateral Governance	Market Governance

Source: Williamson (1985)

Due to high asset specificity of many IT services, and the high degree of uncertainty, it is difficult, even with a high degree of competence, to contract tightly over a long period. This may appear to be obvious, yet the marketing of the IT vendors has proved to be very effective, and firms are still entering into strategic partnerships in a sub-optimal manner. Outsourcing is no longer an all-or-nothing decision, outsourcing options offer many benefits. One of the important issues is how to manage outsourcing contractual arrangements. Many organisations jump into the vendor selection process without taking the necessary steps to arm themselves with a clear definition of the desired relationship. This haphazard approach will result in wasted time and energy, reviewing proposals and interviewing vendors that do not meet the minimum criteria. The more effort an organisation puts into identifying their specific requirements, the more efficient and effective the selection process will be. A comprehensive list of appropriate criteria allows the organisation to focus their efforts on the right pool of prospective vendors.

The difference between successful outsourcing and a disaster may simply be determined by the selection of the vendor and the terms of the contract. Vendors vary in size and in niche. At one end of the vendor spectrum are the large hardware manufacturers. They offer complete (and partial) outsourcing to a wide range of clients. Other small vendors position themselves in a niche, such as banking and financial systems. Various checklists for vendor selection have been developed and the key variables include:

- experience;
- planning;
- technology and personnel;
- contract negotiations;
- working relationship including communications; and
- financial status.

Determining Outsourcing Contractual Relationship

Lacity and Hirschheim (1993) quote an example of a petroleum company being charged about $500,000 in excess fees in the first month of the contract. Therefore, even in situations where close contact with the vendor is necessary for the service to be properly provided, the contract should always reflect this. In order to assist firms in developing appropriate IT contracts, Lacity and Hirschheim (1993) have suggested the following guidelines for contracting and negotiation.

- Discard the vendor's standard contract.
- Do not sign incomplete contracts.
- Develop service-level measures.
- Include cash payments for non-performance.
- Determine growth rates.
- Adjust charges to changes in business.
- Include a termination clause.

The following steps can help in determining the ideal contractual relationship.

- Conduct internal interviews. Gather input from managers who will interact with the vendor and/or be affected by the scope of the contractual relationship. Ask questions such as: should we contract with a vendor to develop a proprietary application or customise an existing tool? do we want to hire new employees on a permanent basis or consider temporary options?
- Create a profile. Construct a generic profile of your ideal supplier based on the information gathered from the internal interviews and management's consensus. The best way to ensure you identify the right vendor is to base your decision on the right criteria.
- List qualifying criteria. Make a list of criteria vendors must meet to qualify as a candidate for your business. For instance, you may require that a technology vendor have experience with a certain vertical industry, that a staffing agency be able to interview candidates at your location or that an outsourcer have experience handling e-mail contacts. This list will serve as the basis for your initial research and qualifying interviews.

Supplier Performance Measurement

Various surveys, which have been undertaken into outsourcing in recent years, have shown that for a large proportion of firms there is a gap between what suppliers are promised and what they have delivered. Part of the reason for this is that it has been found that firms have not been monitoring the performance of their suppliers properly. Perhaps due to the nature of some of the services, which are outsourced, or possibly because of the non-purchasing personnel that sometimes take responsibility for outsourcing, some firms virtually ignore the provision of certain services once they have been passed to a third party.

Performance measurement is essential, however, as suppliers will often seek to cut the costs of service provision as much as they can, usually by reducing the quality of the service they are offering. The following are the two main elements to the measurement of performance:
- setting of standards against which the supplier is expected to conform; and
- enforcement regime, the mechanism that allows the judgements to be made.

The criteria against which a supplier should be judged are, of course, dependent on the service or product it provides (although, as was stated earlier, firms should always monitor the extent to which suppliers have tried to leverage them). This is true both in terms of the nature of the product and service, and the importance of it to the customer firm. For certain products and services the important criteria will simply be cost, whereas for others there will be a need to judge their contribution to quality and innovation (criteria for performance measurement will, of course, be linked to the criteria used for supplier selection). Nevertheless, in business literature a number of models have been developed which attempt to provide a framework, which can be adapted by firms to suit their particular circumstances.

At a very general level, Burt and Doyle (1993) presented a universally applicable measurement philosophy. This provides what they believe are the broad rules of the measurement challenge and are listed below.
- There should only be a small number of measures.
- The measures must be straightforward.
- The focus of a measure must have a significant impact on the business.
- Measures must be assigned to a named individual or individuals.
- Measurement report distribution must be agreed and formalised.
- Responses to various levels of performance must be agreed in advance.

A more detailed framework has been provided by Kaplan and Norton (1992). They have noted that senior executives understand that their organisation's measurement system strongly affects the behaviour of managers and employees. They also contend that traditional accounting measures, for example, return on investment, are unable to recognise the importance of innovation. As a consequence, they have developed a measurement tool, 'the balanced scorecard'. This tool involves four perspectives: financial, internal business, customer, and innovation and learning. The scorecard brings together, in a single management report, many of the seemingly disparate elements of a company's competitive agenda: becoming customer oriented, shortening response time, improving quality, emphasising teamwork, reducing new product launch times, and managing for the long-term. The breadth of the model also allows the Board to assess whether improvements in one aspect of the business's performance is causing lower performance elsewhere. Some of the widely used measures proposed by Mummalaneni et al. (1996) have been listed in Table 9.6.

Table 9.6. Six Attributes and Levels of Supplier Performance

Attribute	Levels
On-time delivery	1. Seldom/few times 2. Most times 3. Almost always
Quality	1. Poor (more than 5% defective) 2. Good (2X-5% defective) 3. Excellent (less than 2% defective)
Price/cost	1. 5 % above target price 2. Approximately at target price 3. 5% below target price
Professionalism of Salesperson	1. Not highly professional 2. Highly professional
Responsiveness to Customer	1. Low level of responsiveness (Late, Needs not satisfactory) 2. Moderate level of responsiveness (Average) 3. High level of responsiveness (Quick and satisfactory)
Quality of Relationship with Supplier	1. Poor 2. Good 3. Excellent

Source: Mummalaneni et al. (1996)

Quantitative Approaches to Vendor Selection and Evaluation

Measuring the performance of vendors and the analysis of criteria for Vendor Selection Procedure (VSP) is the focus of research since 1960 (Dickson 1966, Weber et al., 1991). Linear weighting method proposed by Wind and Robinson (1968) for VSP was the most common way of rating different vendors and this approach was linked to a matrix representation of data. It then rated the different vendors for their quota allocations. Monozka and Trecha (1988) proposed multiple criteria vendor service factor ratings and an overall vendor performance index. A survey by Weber et al. (1991) reveals that very limited number of studies have focused on applied mathematical programming models to VSP such as linear programming (LP), mixed integer programming (MIP), goal programming (GP), etc. Anthony and Buffa (1977) formulated the VSP and LP problem to minimise the total purchasing and storage costs. Pan (1989) developed a single item LP model to minimise the aggregate price under constraints of quality service level and lead-time. Moore and Fearon (1973) and Kingsman (1986) also suggested applying LP. Bendor et al. (1985) proposed a MIP approach with the objective of minimising purchasing; inventory and transportation related costs without any specific mathematical formulation and demonstrated it through selecting the vendors at IBM. Others include Turner (1988), Narasimhan and Stoynoff (1986), and Chaudhry et al. (1993). Rosenthal et al. (1995) also proposed a MIP approach. Sharma et al. (1989) proposed a GP formulation for attaining goals pertaining to price, quality and lead-time under demand and budget constraints. Buffa and Jackson (1983) also proposed the use of GP for price, quality and delivery objectives. Benton (1991) and Hong and Hayya (1992) structured the VSP as non-linear programming. Webber et al. (2000) presented a data envelopment analysis method for VSP. Narasimhan (1983) and Handfield et al. (2002) used the analytical hierarchical process to generate weights for VSP. Ghodsypour and O'Brien (1998) developed a decision support system by integrating the analytical hierarchy process with linear programming. The deterministic approach for solving VSP suffer from the drawbacks in practical situations due to the fact that a purchasing manager does not have sufficient information related to the different criteria. Few literatures are available in the existing literature, which incorporate information uncertainty in the VSP.

Some of the quantitative approaches to vendor selection that were used and reported in the literature are given below.

- Linear weighting models.
- Mathematical programming models.
- Statistical/probabilistic approaches.

The most utilised approach has been linear weighting models. Linear weighting models place a weight on each criteria (typically subjectively determined) and provide a total score for each vendor by summing up the vendor's performance on the criteria multiplied by these weights.

A simple hybrid approach for vendor selection decision must be established that will handle its multi-criteria nature and uncertainty of practical situations. For the benefit of the readers, three different models covering various aspects of vendor selection and evaluation are presented in this section. These include (a) DSS (Decision Support System) model developed by Akinc (1993), as a decision support system for selection of vendors in a manufacturing environment, (b) Activity Based Costing (ABC) approach of Roodhooft and Koning (1996) followed by a hybrid approach of Kumar (2006) are presented below. These cases cover US, UK and India based organisations.

A Decision Support System (DSS) Approach for Vendor Selection and Evaluation

Decision Support System (DSS) is a computer-based system that help decision makers confront ill-structured problems through direct interaction with data analysis and models. A typical decision support system consists of three interrelated components.

(a) Model base for analysis of the structured aspects of the problem;

(b) a database containing relevant data needed by the models and any other data that the user can directly query on; and

(c) a user-friendly interface to facilitate the use of the previous two components.

The annual material costs and the number of suppliers constitute the structured aspects of this ill-structured problem, while the quality and delivery performance levels of the vendors are the unstructured elements. In order to capture as much of the structured aspects of this problem as possible, the unit quoted costs are adjusted to reflect the quantifiable aspects of quality and delivery performance. Accordingly, c_{ij} are calculated using the cost ratio method. This method is based on the tools of standard cost analysis and three categories of cost associated with the vendor (quality, delivery and service) are estimated and expressed as a percentage of the expected dollar volume for part i. The relevant unit cost c_{ij} ish then the sum of the quoted price plus the adjustments based on the percentage for each category.

Although the direct cost consequences of quality and delivery performance of the vendors are captured by the cost ratio method, in general, quality and delivery performance imply other aspects that cannot be converted into cost figures. The costs associated with returns due to poor quality, for instance, can be incorporated into c_{ij} using the cost ratio method, but the quality of design, specifications and the ability of the vendor to quickly implement required design changes cannot be incorporated. A common means of incorporating such subjective criteria into a systematic evaluative method is a categorical scoring technique. In this method, an ordinal grade, such as 1= acceptable, 2= good and 3= excellent, is assigned to each vendor on these criteria reflecting vendor's perceived ability to meet the critical quality and delivery factors. The model details are given below.

Model Notations

- i   number of parts, i=1,2,......n;
- j   number of potential vendors, j=1.....m;
- d_i annual forecast requirements for part i;
- c_{ij} unit cost of part i from vendor j;
- Q_{ij} quality level of part i from vendor j
- D_{ij} delivery performance level from vendor j in supplying i;
- S_i set of feasible vendors for part i;
- T_j set of parts that vendor j can feasibly supply;
- Y_{ij} 1 if vendor j is selected to supply part i, 0 otherwise;
- Z_j 1 if vendor is used at all, 0 otherwise.

Provided that the trade-offs among conflicting objectives can be resolved a priori in an all encompassing utility function, U, the VSP can be formulated as a mathematical problem—

$$\text{Max } U\left(\sum_i z_i, \sum_i \sum_j c_{ij} d_j Y_{ij}, Q_{ll}, \ldots, Q_{nm}, D_{ll}, \ldots, D_{nm}\right) \qquad (1)$$

Subject to

$$\sum_j Y_{ij} = 1 \quad \forall i, \quad (2)$$

$$\sum_i Y_{ij} \leq |T_j| z_j \quad \forall j, \quad (3)$$

$$Z_i, Y_{ij} = 0 \text{ or } 1 \quad \forall i, j \quad (4)$$

The objective function is associate with a cardinal utility index with the different values of the individual criteria; constraints (2) require that all parts be supplied, (3) require parts to be supplied only from the selected vendors. Constraint set (4) represents the integrality restriction on Y_{ij}. There are several practical difficulties with this formulation, which includes:

(a) the difficulty of quantifying quality and delivery performance of potential vendors;
(b) the lack of obvious decision rules for trade-off resolution implicit in U; and even if these are overcome; and
(c) the size of the problem and the form of the objective function, which would rule out a practical solution method.

Due to the above limitations in estimating the value of utility function and trying to solve the problem to optimality, a trade-off among a number of suppliers, total material cost, quality and delivery performance of suppliers has been considered through a suitable model that form the DSS. The DSS is intended to help the decision maker to answer questions such as—

(a) what is the increased short-run cost due to reducing the vendor base?
(b) what price are we going to pay to limit out candidate supplier base only to those who can supply the most important items at excellent quality levels and excellent delivery performance for all the items?

Since the unstructured elements of quality and delivery performance are often multi-dimensional (for example, quality may mean quality of design and defective rate from a supplier), representing them by a single ordinal grade may be too aggregate in some cases. Suppliers may have to be graded on these dimensions separately. For instance, a vendor receiving a grade of three and two would imply excellent design and good defective rate. One can either use his tuple as is to represent this vendor's quality to compare with others, or calculate a single average grade, as commonly done in point rating methods, provided there is some basis of associating relative weights with these directions. Variables (or tuple) Q_{ij} and D_{ij} are thus intended to capture aspects of quality and delivery performance criteria, which cannot be incorporated into cost calculations.

The existence of a large number of parts, which may vary greatly in their importance, volume and cost renders it impractical to deal with each part individually. Therefore, it will be useful to categorise the parts into relatively homogeneous groups. Furthermore, different criteria may be important for different classes for parts. For example, for some items, quality (or some specific dimension thereof) may have higher priority than delivery performance. This way, different minimal levels of quality and delivery performance may be specified for different category items. For instance, the decision maker may insist on excellent quality for certain critical items while being content with an acceptable level for some others. For the purpose of illustration, the well-known ABC inventory classification system was used. However, one can, without altering the basic analysis, define as many categories as needed to adequately reflect the important differences.

Let P_A, P_B and P_C be defined as the set of A, B and C type parts, and quality and delivery aspects of these part types are given as six-tuple in relation (5). To be the minimal acceptable performance levels for quality and delivery performance for A, B and C items. Any specific selection for these levels defines a scenario of the vendor selection problem. For instance (3,3,3,2,2,1) would represent a situation where the decision maker wants excellent quality level for A and B items, good quality level for C items, and excellent, good and acceptable delivery performance levels of A, B and C items respectively, where 1, 2 and 3 represents acceptable, good and excellent performance. The set of feasible vendors are given by relation (6).

$$I = (Q_A^*, D_A^*, Q_B^*, D_B^*, Q_C^*, D_C^*) \qquad (5)$$

$$S_i = \{j \mid Q_{ij} \geq Q_A^* \text{ and } D_{ij} \geq D_A^*\} \; \forall i \in P_A$$

$$S_i = \{j \mid Q_{ij} \geq Q_B^* \text{ and } D_{ij} \geq D_B^*\} \; \forall i \in P_B \qquad (6)$$

$$S_i = \{j \mid Q_{ij} \geq Q_C^* \text{ and } D_{ij} \geq D_C^*\} \; \forall i \in P_C$$

Database and Model base

To support the models and to allow the user to do ad hoc queries, the relevant data are arranged in a relational database consisting of two tables for parts and vendors which contain part and vendor specific data, such as part classification, annual usage, vendor's geographical distance, its JIT (just-in-time) implementation status, etc. A third table, the part/vendor table, contains crucial data for the models at a minimum for each feasible part–vendor combination, the adjusted unit costs, cost and predicted delivery and quality performance level of the vendor in supplying the part in question. In order to provide the user with the trade-off information between the two structured elements of the problem, namely, annual adjusted material cost and number of suppliers, the following three models are used.

Model 1: Vendor Selection Model

This model is associated with selection of vendors such that the total cost is minimised. Given a problem instance i and associated sets S_i, this model selects the vendor to minimise the total cost. Since no consideration is given to the other objective, i.e., the number of vendors, this amounts to selecting the cheapest source for each part with regards to z variables as:

$$Y_{ij}^* = 1 \quad \text{if } c_{ij} = \underset{k}{\text{Min}}\, c_{ik} = c_i^* \qquad (7)$$
$$= 0, \quad \text{Otherwise}$$

Given Y_{ij}^* and the definition of z_j we can set:

$$Y_j^* = \sum_i Y_{ij} > 0, \qquad (8)$$
$$= 0 \quad \text{Otherwise}$$

with the minimum cost $S\, c_i^* d_i$ and the largest rational number of vendors $K_{max} = S_j\, z_j$.

Model 2

The minimum number of vendors, K_{min}, that can supply all parts at desired minimal performance levels specified by a scenario i, is found from the solution of (9) to (12).

$$\text{Min} \sum_j z_j \qquad (9)$$

$$\sum_{i \in T_j} Y_{ij} \leq T_j\, z_j \quad \forall\, j, \qquad (10)$$

$$\sum_{i \in S_i} Y_{ij} \geq 1 \quad \forall\, j, \qquad (11)$$

$$Y_{ij}, Z_j = 0 \text{ or } 1 \quad \forall\, i, j \qquad (12)$$

This is a well known set covering problem for which greedy heuristic procedures based on sequentially selecting the best z_j variable have been shown to be effective. At every iteration of the greedy heuristic procedure one chooses k such that $|T_k| = \text{Max}|T_j|$ and lets $z_k = 1$; deletes all $i \hat{I} T_k$ from the T_j sets of the remaining potential vendors; recalculates the $|T_j|$ and repeats until all parts are assigned.

If we define $V = \{j\,|\,z_j = 1\}$, then $K_{min} = \sum z_j$ and

$$Y_{ij} = 1 \quad if \quad c_{ij} = \underset{K \in V}{Min}\, c_{ik} = 0, \text{ Otherwise} \qquad (13)$$

Notice that apart from rule (13), which assigns parts to vendors in V, the heuristic procedure is essentially insensitive to resultant costs. No attempt is made to obtain, among alternative solutions with K_{min} vendors, the one with the minimum cost.

Model 3

The solutions obtained from model 1 and model 2 determines the range of feasible and rational size of the supplier base, K_{min} and K_{max}. Model 3 is used to explore the magnitude of the trade-off between the number of suppliers and annual material costs within this range. Given minimally acceptable performance levels specified by some i and the associated Si sets, model 3 determines a set of no more than some pre-specified K vendors (between K_{min} and K_{max}) who can supply all parts at the minimum cost and is given in (14) to (18).

$$Min \sum_i \sum_{j \in S_i} c_{ij} d_j Y_{ij} \qquad (14)$$

$$\text{Subject to} \sum_{j \in S_i} Y_{ij} \geq 1 \qquad \forall i \qquad (15)$$

$$\sum_{i \in T_j} Y_{ij} \leq T_j z_j \qquad \forall j \qquad (16)$$

$$\sum_j Z_j \geq K \qquad (17)$$

$$Z_j Y_{ij} = 0 \quad or \quad 1 \qquad (18)$$

The objective is to find the solution for the above K-median problem for a wide range of values of K, the greedy heuristics are quite attractive. Using the add heuristic to solve (14) - (18) for some value of K, say p, one obtains solutions for the cases K= P-1, K=P-2, etc. Likewise while using the drop heuristic to solve for K = P, one obtains the solutions for values of K = P+1, P+2, etc. Therefore these heuristic methods need not be applied afresh for each value of K but rather the solution for K = P is obtained from that of K = P-1 by applying only one iteration of add, or from that of K = P+1 by one iteration of the drop heuristic.

From the past studies on the worst-case behaviour of the add and drop heuristics, it was proved that the add heuristic has the best error bound. However, for the drop heuristic no theoretical error bound exists which is short of the worst possible solution to the problem. Despite these theoretical results, the drop heuristic was not dropped for several reasons. First, the drop heuristic is the more natural one since it more closely models the actual implementation of vendor reduction programmes of many companies. Second, it can be implemented at a very modest computational cost. And finally, since the number of parts that any vendor can typically supply is quite limited related to the entire list of parts, there is a minimum number of vendors that can be added. Although the solution of model 2 can be used for this purpose, it may give the add heuristic a poor start as this model simply minimises the number of suppliers. The solution obtained may not be the least-

Table 9.7. Cost versus Number of Suppliers for Various Scenarios

Number of Suppliers	Scenario				
	333333	233333	332222	332333	222212
12	Not feasible	Not feasible	Not feasible	Not feasible	$16,357,059
13	Not feasible	Not feasible	$17,418,060	Not feasible	$15,448,961
14	Not feasible	Not feasible	$15,963,601	Not feasible	$14,767,962
15	Not feasible	Not feasible	$14,828,602	Not feasible	$13,913,632
16	Not feasible	Not feasible	$13,994,811	Not feasible	$13,189,113
17	Not feasible	$17,399,968	$13,236,753	$16,756,901	$12,622,366
18	Not feasible	$16,326,359	$12,725,903	$15,946,743	$12,191,407
19	Not feasible	$15,412,843	$12,316,772	$15,330,391	$11,793,256
20	$15,306,798	$14,709,340	$11,982,907	$14,817,252	$11,399,239
21	$14,764,314	$14,081,882	$11,654,882	$14,359,780	$11,136,726
22	$14,270,994	$13,587,687	$11,362,809	$14,083,023	$10,986,433
23	$13,830,938	$13,377,023	$11,213,605	$13,817,048	$10,844,208
24	$13,635,711	$13,191,796	$11,089,499	$13,564,987	$10,716,740
25	$13,452,257	$13,022,904	$10,967,206	$13,334,589	$10,594,472
26	$13,278,730	$12,877,960	$10,847,756	$13,191,971	$10,474,987
27	$13,136,112	$12,735,342	$10,745,269	$13,053,284	$10,356,138
28	$12,994,713	$12,594,448	$10,646,446	$12,936,545	$10,238,314
29	$12,878,575	$12,478,310	$10,573,534	$12,820,407	$10,195,541
30	$12,816,372	$12,412,187	$10,518,641	$12,758,204	$10,153,613
31	$12,766,937	$12,348,747	$10,469,547	$12,708,769	$10,117,036
32	$12,725,675	$12,286,544	$10,424,901	$12,667,507	$10,090,667
33	$12,694,021	$12,237,109	$10,398,532	$12,635,853	$10,067,392
34	$12,665,879	$12,200,509	$10,373,016	$12,607,711	$10,050,308
35	$12,648,024	$12,172,367	$10,349,549	$12,580,991	$10,034,630
36	$12,634,086	$12,148,015	$10,326,274	$12,563,136	$10,023,043
37	$12,630,053	$12,130,155	$10,312,816	$12,550,008	$10,017,036
38	$12,626,107	$12,117,027	$10,309,198	$12,545,165	$10,013,654
39	$12,622,273	$12,112,184	$10,308,052	$12,541,219	$10,010,608
40	$12,619,554	$12,108,238	$10,308,867	$12,537,385	$10,008,226
41	$12,617,170	$12,104,404	$10,308,967	$12,534,666	$10,008,141
42	$12,617,170	$12,102,020	$10,308,967	$12,532,282	$10,008,106

Source: Akinc (1993)

cost solution among those with the same smallest number of suppliers. However, the drop heuristic starts with the proven least-cost solution among those with the same smallest number of suppliers. However, the drop heuristic starts with the proven least-cost solution of model 3. The add heuristic did not dominate in generating the better of the two solutions (see Table 9.8 below).

Table 9.8. Performance of Drop and Add Heuristics and the Langrangean Lower Bound for Scenario 222212

Number of Suppliers	Drop	Add	UB[a]	LB[b]	Gap(%)
12	$18,404,154	$16,357,057	$16,357,059A	$15,870,370	2.9754
15	$13,913,632	$14,128,606	$13,913,632D	$13,489,321	3.0496
20	$11,399,239	$11,797,941	$11,399,239D	$11,321,244	0.6842
25	$10,594,472	$10,713,318	$10,594,472D	$10,575,985	0.1745
30	$10,153,613	$10,205,522	$10,153,613D	$10,148,363	0.0517
35	$10,034,631	$10,034,630	$10,034,630A	$10,032,168	0.0245
40	$10,008,227	$10,008,227	$10,010,226A	$10,008,225	0.0000
41	$10,008,142	$10,008,141	$10,008,141A	$10,008,141	0.0000
42	$10,008,107	$10,008,106	$10,008,106A	$10,008,106	0.0000

Source: Akinc (1993)

While analysing the case the following solution strategy is used. First models 1 and 2 were solved to obtain the least-cost (LC) and smallest-number-of-vendors (SV) solution, respectively. The drop heuristic is then applied to LC solution to generate candidate solutions for all K between K_{min} and K_{max}. In order to have a good start for the add heuristic is then applied to this, to generate a second set of solutions for all possible values of K. The smaller of the add or drop heuristic solution is taken to be the heuristic solution. Information on the quality of the solutions that a heuristic procedure typically generates is often employed to justify its use. Others have amply established excellent general performance of the add and the drop heuristics to solve the K-median problem. However, in the context of the proposed decision support system, it is also possible to make a direct judgement on the quality of a specific solution in reference to a tight lower bound by identifying a narrow interval within which the true optimal lies. The computational complexity of both the drop heuristics are non-iterative and require a number of operations bounded from above by n (to calculate cost change of adding or dropping a supplier) and hence has computational complexity of $O(n)$.

Application of DSS

An example described in Akinc (1993) is adopted to illustrate the DSS approach. The case under consideration consisting of 100 parts and 50 potential vendors who can supply some of these parts is used for illustration. Parts are 20 per cent A items, 40 per cent C items and the remaining 40 per cent are B items. The price data were generated so that (a) average price (from various sources) varied across products to simulate parts with different values; and (b) for a given part, prices from various sources varied around this average. This is done using the relation (19).

$$C_{ij} = \alpha_i + \beta_i \cdot \Upsilon_j \tag{19}$$

Where $\alpha_i + \beta_i$ and Υ_j were uniform in (0, 3.2768), (0, 2.184533) and (0, 32.768). (These values are adopted from Akinc 1993). Usage for part i is assumed as d_i, and was uniform in (0, 32768). Values for Q_{ij} and D_{ij} were generated so that they equaled to 1, 2 and 3 in roughly 10 per cent, 27 per cent and 63 per cent of the cases respectively.

The scenario (1,1,1,1,1,1) represents base case where a vendor must be able to supply at least at acceptable quality and delivery performance levels. The database for any other scenario can be extracted from this by filtering it to restrict the vendors for each part only to those, which conform to the minimal requirements of the desired scenario. In doing this however, it is possible to have one or more parts with empty lists. When such a case is encountered, i.e., for a part no vendor exists meeting the minimal quality and delivery levels, the filtering routine lists on the screen all the vendors for this part regardless of the desired minimal levels. At this point, in order to avoid an infeasible situation, the user must override the automatic selection process by subjectively selecting at least one vendor for the part. These are called 'forced inclusions' and must be considered by the user in judging different scenarios. Table 9.7 contains the expected annual material costs for various numbers under a sampling of quality and delivery performance scenarios obtained from the application of the add, drop and the exchange heuristics. Such a table gives a clear picture of the range of available alternatives for scenarios under examination. In order to illustrate the sort of useful information that the decision maker can glean from this table consider the following: the minimum number of suppliers that can be considered with the most restrictive scenario (3,3,3,3,3,3) is 20 (with several forced inclusions); relaxing the quality level for A items, i.e., the scenario (2,3,3,3,3,3), will allow a feasible solution with as few as 17 suppliers. With this scenario, a 20-supplier solution will cost about $600,000 less per year compared to (3,3,3,3,3,3). Relaxing the quality level for B items instead of A items, i.e., (3,3,2,3,3,3), results in a slightly more expensive.

From the numerical analysis (Table 9.8) for scenario (2,2,2,2,1,2) it was observed that the quality of the heuristics is extremely good across the range of K values. The gap between the lower bound and the heuristic solution is quite narrow, not exceeding 3 to 4 per cent, mostly less than 1 per cent. Furthermore, the gaps do tend to increase as K decreases. From the above results it is to be noted that the gaps remain quite narrow around the values of K, which is most likely to be of interest to the user. For very small values K will probably be of only marginal interest to the user. Finally, the decision maker can use various types of information and resolve the trade-off between cost and the number of suppliers for any given scenario.

This DSS approach could be exploited to take better advantage of JIT purchasing by achieving its primary objective: selecting a few reliable and high-quality suppliers without undermining the other essential competitive factor, the material costs. This system is conceived of as an extension of the decision maker as there are many relevant but subjective aspects of this problem, which can best be dealt with by intuition. A human decision maker 'drives' this system to sharpen his/her insights, intuition and enhance his/her personal decision-making style. As a further step, one can conceive of a rule-based expert which would provide the decision maker not only with reliable information but would also guide him in making choices among alternatives with their measurable as well as subjective consequences.

Activity Based Costing (ABC) Approach for Vendor Selection and Evaluation

There are several advantages to use the ABC system for vendor selection and evaluation, not only for the purchasing company but also for the vendor as well as for the relationship between the purchasing company and the vendor. For the purchasing company the ABC system allows to quantify the internal production problems caused by a vendor and therefore gives an objective measure for the criteria that traditionally were considered as non-financial. Second, it offers an alternative approach to a multi-objective optimisation problem (minimising invoice cost, delivery time, maximising quality, service after sales, etc.) by comparing absolute cost figures (S/B). Third, the system allows identifying the relative importance of the different cost components, which allows the company to design strategies to reduce the different cost driver rates (C_j), thereby increasing efficiency. Similarly, the purchasing company may attempt to influence estimated units of cost drivers Do. by reducing or eliminating some of the activities.

The vendor benefits from the ABC system for it provides an objective indication of customer's satisfaction and the importance of the different criteria involved in the purchasing process. By evaluating the customer's feedback the vendor may be forced to review its strategy. A final advantage is the improvement of the relationship between vendor and purchaser. Modern production philosophies emphasise the importance of a close relationship between the purchaser and a few reliable suppliers. Knowledge of the several criteria and their relative importance gives the vendor an incentive to reduce his score. Since both parties have the same incentive, there is scope for developing inter-organisational cost management systems.

Vendor selection and evaluation by Activity Based Costing (ABC) approach proposed by Roodhooft and Koning (1996) is presented in this section. The ABC approach consists of several steps.

(a) Identification of company's most significant activities.

(b) Determination of overhead costs associated with each of these activities.

(c) Determining the cost factors of an activity and are referred to as cost drivers, which is used to describe the events or forces that are significant determinants of the cost of these activities.

(d) Overhead costs per unit cost driver (cost driver rate) are applied to cost objects.

Most applications of the ABC system are associated with the hierarchical structure of activities and cost drivers and consist usually of the following five levels (Kaplan 1990):

(a) unit level;

(b) batch level;

(c) product level;

(d) facility level; and

(e) customer level activities and cost drivers.

ABC for vendor selection and evaluation is given below. Relation (20) gives the total vendor cost, which is the sum of all shortcomings that cause extra costs.

$$S_i^B = (p_i - p_{min})q + \sum_j C_j^B D_{ij}^B \tag{20}$$

Where,

S_i^B = Estimated score of vendor i,

P_i = Selling price per unit of vendor i

P_{min} = Selling price per unit of the cheapest vendor

q = Units purchased

C_j^B = Estimated cost per cost driver j in the purchasing company,

D_{ij}^B = Estimated units of cost driver j in the purchasing company caused by vendor i.

The objective is to minimise the total cost. A first important component of relation (20) is the difference between the total selling price of supplier i and that of the price of the cheapest supplier (Pi - Pmin). A second part of the total cost ($\sum (C_j^B \times D_{ij}^B)$) is due to vendor i. Thus besides least invoice costs supplementary costs caused by for instance quality, delivery and service problems are taken into account for supplier selection.

An ABC approach developed by Roodhooft and Koning (1996) to evaluate ex-post performance of the selected supplier(s) is presented here. Actual cost relation (21) is obtained by using relation (20) (denoted by superscript A).

$$S_i^A = (p_i - p_{min})q + \sum_j C_j^A D_{ij}^A \qquad (21)$$

Subtracting (20) from (21) gives the difference between the budgeted and actual score, or

$$S_i^A - S_i^B = \sum_j C_j^A D_{ij}^A - \sum_j C_j^B D_{ij}^B \qquad (22)$$

Relation (23) can be obtained by manipulating relation (22)

$$S_i^A - S_i^B = \sum_j (C_j^A - C_j^B) D_{ij}^B + \sum_j (D_{ij}^A - D_{ij}^B) * C_j^B + \sum_j (C_j^A - C_j^B)(D_{ij}^A - D_{ij}^B) \qquad (23)$$

The first term in (23) is a purchaser effect, the second term is a supplier effect and the final term is a combined effect. These are described below.

The purchaser effect $(PE) = \sum_j (C_j^A - C_j^B) D_{ij}^B$, refers to factors which allow the purchasing company to improve its efficiency by reducing its cost driver rates C_j. In doing so, the vendor's score will improve without necessarily improving vendor performance. The difference between actual and budgeted cost should be eliminated for vendor evaluation purposes.

The supplier effect $(SE) = \sum_j (D_{ij}^A - D_{ij}^B) * C_j^B$ refers to the difference between actual and budgeted use of cost drivers for which the supplier is responsible since he can potentially affect the cost drivers. Actions related to just-in-time delivery, delivered quantity and quality of the products can seriously affect the supplier effect and hence vendor performance.

Finally, the combined effect $(CE) = \sum_j (C_j^A - C_j^B)(D_{ij}^A - D_{ij}^B)$ refers to the difference in costs that cannot be uniquely attributed to either the supplier or the purchaser. Including this effect in the purchaser and/or supplier effect is not theoretically correct and hence separated.

Activity Based Costing (ABC) for Vendor Selection and Evaluation—A Case Study

This case is adopted from Roodhooft and Koning (1996). Rovapo Limited is a medium-sized company operating in a JIT environment. Purchasing contracts specify strong quality requirements. Quality control is transferred to the supplier. A delivered product that does not conform to quality standards causes a production stop. Consequently, the product is wasted and loses its sales value. The supplier when delivering the next order replaces the wasted product.

A delivery arriving too late causes extra costs and requires rescheduling to avoid complete stoppage, implying a one-day delay in the planned production. During this period another product will be manufactured. Thus a one-day delay in supplying the goods causes one extra planning activity and two set-ups. Each additional day gives rise to an extra planning activity. In addition to the timing of deliveries, the delivered quantity is an important criterion for the organisation. A breakdown may be caused by a shortage of delivered goods. The production process has to be reinstalled for every shortage in stock. A planning activity, two set-ups and a supplementary reception of delivered goods (with an additional invoice) are necessary. The relevant activities in the ABC vendor selection model include planning of a production order, reception of delivered goods, production process stop, and setting up of the machinery and administration. The cost drivers (D_j) and cost driver rates (c_j) associated with these activities come from the ABC system in place and are listed in Table 9.9.

Table 9.9. Cost Drivers and Cost Driver Rates for Rovapo

Sl. No.	Activity	Cost driver	Cost driver rate (£)
1	Planning	Production order	600 per order
2	Reception	Delivery	500 per delivery
3	Production stop	Stop	250 per stop
4	Setting up	Set-up	1,250 per set-up
5	Administration	Invoice	300 per invoice

Source: Roodhooft and Konig (1966)

After the obvious elimination of some potential suppliers for 100 orders of 50 parts each (thus 5000 units in total), three selected companies, viz., Lincon, Malsey and Tubar are studied in detail. Lincon offers a good price—£100 per unit—and has an excellent quality and delivery reputation. Malsey offers the lowest invoice price—£98 per unit—but has a poor reputation for quality and delivery requirements. Finally, Tubar is the most expensive supplier—£103 per unit—but is known for good quality and JIT delivery. Table 9.10 reports the estimated delivery and quality performances.

Table 9.10. Vendor's Estimated Delivery and Quality Performance

Performance	Lincon	Malsey	Tubar
Exceeded delivery date	5 orders	5 orders	3 orders
Quantity problems	3 orders	8 orders	6 orders
Quality problems	100 units	130 units	80 units

Source: Roodhooft and Konig (1966)

The influence of delivery and quality performances on the activities of the organisation is given in Table 9.11.

Table 9.11. Influence of Performance Criteria on Activities

Performance Criteria	Activities
Expected delivery date	2 Set-ups 1 Planning activity
Quantity Problems	1 Planning activity 2 Set-ups 1 Reception activity 1 Administrative activity
Quality problems	1 Production set-up

Table 9.12 shows the total cost and its components, based on relation (20), for the three suppliers. Total scores are obtained by substitution of cost driver rates and estimated delivery and quality performances in relation (20). For Lincon's case the total score is 2 × 5000 + 1,250 × 2 × 5 + 600 × 5 + 1,250 × 2× 3 +600× 3 +500× 3 +300× 3 + 250 X 100 = 62,200. It is clear that Lincon has the lowest total score of budgeted extra costs and hence Lincon is chosen as the preferred supplier. The purchaser effect, the supplier effect and the combined effect are described below. Table 9.12 shows the selection of best supplier for the total order. Ex-post, the actual cost driver rates for this supplier turned out to be £550 for a production order, £520 for a delivery, £230 for a stop, £1,250 for a set-up and £300 for an invoice. With respect to the actual performance of the supplier, the following information was gathered. Four deliveries arrived too late. There was a shortage of delivered goods for four other orders and 105 products did not compile with quality standards. The performance of Lincon is evaluated using relation (21) and results are given in Table 9.12.

Table 9.12. Evaluation of Supplier's Performance

Costs caused by	Lincon	Malsey	Tubar
Exceeded delivery date	15,500	15,500	9,300
Quantity problems	10,800	28,800	21,600
Quality problems	25,000	32,500	20,000
Administration	900	2,400	1,800
Price difference	10,000	0	25,000
Score	62,200	79,200	77,700

Source: Roodhooft and Konig (1996)

The second column in Table 9.13 gives the budgeted score used to select Lincon (as in Table 9.12). Actual costs, based on the actual performance of the organisation and Lincon are presented in the final column. Adjustment 1 gives the vendor's score given the actual performance of the purchasing company and the budgeted performance of the supplier. The purchaser effect can be derived by comparing the budget column with the Adjustment 1 column, implying a total purchasing effect of £ 2,340. This means that the organisation is responsible for a cost saving of £2,340. The purchaser effect for the different components can easily be derived from Table 9.13.

Table 9.13. Lincon's Performance Evaluation

Costs	Budgeted	Adjustment 1	Adjustment 2	Actual
	$C_j^B D_{ij}^B$	$C_j^A D_{ij}^B$	$C_j^B D_{ij}^A$	$C_j^A D_{ij}^A$
Exceeded delivery date	15,500	15,250	12,400	12,200
Quantity problems	10,800	10,710	14,400	14,280
Quality problems	25,000	23,000	26,250	24,150
Administration	900	900	1,200	1,200
Price difference	10,000	10,000	10,000	10,000
Score	62,200	59,860	64,250	61,830

Source: Roodhooft and Konig (1966)

The fourth column, Adjustment 2, measures the actual supplier performance for budgeted cost driver rates. The supplier effect can be obtained from comparing column two with column four and is equal to £2,050. In other words, the supplier causes an excess cost of £2,050 (due to quantity and quality problems), despite a decrease in the total score. Finally, the combined effect resulting from differences between actual and budgeted performance of both parties is equal to £-80 since the combined effect is simply the sum of the budgeted and actual score minus the sum of Adjustments 1 and 2. Thus an extra cost of £80 cannot be uniquely attributed to the supplier or the purchaser.

Vendor selection in the ABC system occurs by choosing the supplier who minimises the total additional costs associated with the purchase decision. These include price differentials and supplementary estimated internal production costs caused by the supplier. Vendor evaluation involves a companion of the budgeted and actual scores after delivery of the products. The performance measure is estimated by capturing difference in purchaser effect, vendor effect and combined effect. The combination of vendor selection and evaluation makes the ABC system a useful concept to improve the purchaser–vendor long-term relationship. The ABC approach could be used to assist a company in choosing to produce internally or to buy externally. A third application exists in revising traditional performance measures to evaluate a company's purchasing manager. Finally, the determination of transfer prices could be affected by the ABC approach. A different actual or budgeted score S_i for internal and external suppliers could influence cost based or market based transfer prices.

A Hybrid Approach for Vendor Selection Problem

In this section a hybrid approach based on utility theory and interval programming proposed by Kumar (2006) is presented. The problem is formulated as a multi-objective vendor selection problem, when some of the parameters of vendors are uncertain. Vendor selection problem (VSP) is typically a multi-criteria decision problem relating quantitative and qualitative criteria and some of which may be conflicting in nature. Utility theory is used to make trade off between multi-criteria of VSP and to formulating it to a synthesis function. The synthesis objective function of vendor selection decision incorporates three important objectives, viz., sales revenue maximisation, quality maximisation and maximisation of on time delivery performance with the realistic constraints such as buyers demand, budget amount allocated to vendors, etc. For decision makers preference the uncertain parameters of the constraints are represented between the intervals, by the left limit and the right limit. The optimal solution distributes the quota to the selected vendors against the worst case and the average case respectively. The effect of uncertainty variation is also studied that how quota allocation to the vendors change and some of the vendors loose their entire quota in an uncertain environment. A case example, of an automobile manufacturer, illustrating the approach has been presented. The following set of assumptions, index set, decision variable and parameters are considered.

Assumptions

1. Only one item is purchased from one vendor.
2. No shortage of the item is allowed for any of the vendor.
3. Quantity discounts are not taken into consideration.
4. Demand of the item is constant and known with certainty.

i - represents index for vendor, for all i=1, 2.......n and xi denote (decision variables) order quantity for the vendor i,

R_i - Net sales revenue return of the item supplied by the vendor i

q_i - Percentage of the quality level delivered by the vendor i

l_i - Percentage of the on-time delivery by the vendor i

p_i - Price of a unit item of the ordered quantity from the vendor i

b_i - Upper limit of the budget amount allocated to the vendor i

D - Number of vendors competing for selection

Model: (MIP_VSP): The mixed integer programming vendor selection problem for three objectives and constraints related to policy is given in (24–29).

Model MIP_VSP:

$$\text{Maximise} = Z1 = \sum_{i=1}^{n} R_i(x_i) \quad (24)$$

$$\text{Maximise} = Z2 = \sum_{i=1}^{n} q_i(x_i) \quad (25)$$

$$\text{Maximise} = Z3 = \sum_{i=1}^{n} l_i(x_i) \quad (26)$$

Subject to

$$\sum_{i=1}^{n} x_i = D \quad (27)$$

$$p_i(x_i) \leq b_i \text{ for all } I; I = 1, 2, .. n \quad (28)$$

$$x_i \geq 0 \text{ and integer} \quad (29)$$

Objective function (24 to 26) tries to maximise the net sales revenue, quality level and on-time delivery performance of the vendors. Constraint (27) restrict the total demand of the item. Constraint (28), puts restrictions on budget amount allocated to the vendors for supplying the items and finally relation (29) is an integrality restriction on order quantity.

Modelling with Utility Theory

Using utility method of DeWispelare and Sage (1981), multi-objective problem is converted into a single objective synthesis function. The linear transformation of the multi-objective problem into the utility function can be done as follows:

Determine the optimistic value X_1 = Optimum $f_1(x_1)$ (30)
$$x \varepsilon D$$

Determine the optimistic value Y_1 = Pessimum $f_1(x_1)$ (31)
$$x \varepsilon D$$

Determine the utilities u_1 of all the optimistic and pessimistic values as follows:

$$X_1, X_2, X_3, ..., X_1 \quad Y_1$$
$$u_1, u_2, u_3, ..., u_1 \quad u_{1+} \quad (32)$$

For transforming the objective functions $f_j(x_i)$ into utility functions, $f_j(x_i)$ the values of α_j and β_j are obtained by solving the following linear equations:

$$\alpha_j X_j + \beta_j = u_j, \text{ for all } j = 1 \quad (33)$$
$$\alpha_j Y_j + \beta_j = u_{j+1}, \text{ for all } j = 1 \quad (34)$$

The objective functions $f_j(x_i)$ are transformed into utility function $f_j(x_i)$ as follows:

$$f_j(x_i) = \alpha_j f_j(x_i) + \beta_j = \sum_{i=1}^{n} \alpha_j c_{ij} x_i + \beta_j = f_j(x_j) + \beta_j,$$

for all $j = 1, \ldots, 1$ \hfill (35)

This single objective synthesis function may be expressed as:

$$\text{Optimise } f^* = \sum_{j=1}^{l} f'_j(x_i) = \sum_{i=1}^{n}\sum_{j=1}^{l} \alpha_j c_{ij} x_i \hfill (36)$$

In practical situations of VSP, the parameter sets related to the various vendors are uncertain. For example, at the time of allocating budget amount to different vendors, value of budget amount may be uncertain such as 'budget amount allocated to a vendor X is somewhere between $ 5000000 to $ 5500000', etc. The deterministic formulation of the problem is unable to handle such type of uncertainty in decision parameters. Interval programming based on the interval analysis has been developed as a useful and easy technique to deal with this form of uncertainty. This hybrid approach helps in addressing uncertainty in the decision parameters of VSP and can be handled with conventional optimisation tools.

Modelling with Interval Parameters

The uncertainty in constraints can be represented as interval numbers. For the constraints it is desired to attain at some aspiration level and instead of strictly satisfying the constraints. Several authors, such as Ishibuchi and Tanka (1989, 1990), Nakahara et al. (1992) and Bitran (1980) have studied linear programming problems with interval coefficients. The focus is on integer linear programming problems (ILP) in which the coefficients in the constraints are intervals. The conventional ILP problem (ILP) and its corresponding uncertain integer linear programming with interval coefficients in constraints (I-ILP) form is conventionally expressed in (37) and (38).

(ILP1)
Maximise $\quad Z = C_x$
Subject to $\quad A x \leq b$ \hfill (37)
$\quad\quad\quad\quad\quad x \geq 0$ and integer

(I-ILP1)
Maximise $\quad Z = C_x$
Subject to $\quad A x \leq_* (b_1, b_2)$ \hfill (38)
$\quad\quad\quad\quad\quad x \geq 0$ and integer

The symbol '$\leq_*$' in the constraint set denotes order relation. Where b_1 and b_2 are the left limit and right limit of interval respectively.

A real interval b is defined by a closed and bounded set of real numbers as given in (39).

$$b = (b_1, b_2) = \{x: b_1 \leq x \leq b_2 ; x \in \Re\} \tag{39}$$

Where,

b_1 and b_2 is the left limit and right limits of interval b respectively.

$\Re$ is the set of all real numbers.

An interval also can be defined by its mean and width as in (40).

$$B = <b^M, b^W> = \{x: b^M - b^W \leq x \leq b^M + b^W ; x \leq \Re\} \tag{40}$$

Where,

b^M and b^W are the mean and width of interval b, respectively and are calculated using relation (41).

$$b^M = \frac{1}{2}(b_1 + b_2) \text{ and } b^W = \frac{1}{2}(b_1 - b_2) \tag{41}$$

The magnitude $|b|$ of an interval b may be given as +ve. The basic concept used to formulate the (I-ILP) is given below.

Definition 1 (Alefeld and Herberger 1983): If a and b are two intervals. Let $\otimes \in \{+, -, \times, \div\}$ be a binary operations on the set of real number, then $a \otimes b$ defines a binary operation on the set of all the closed intervals. The following operations are used

$$a + b = [a_1 + b_1, a_2 + b_2]$$
$$a - b = [a_1 - b_1, a_2 - b_2] \tag{42}$$
$$k_a = (k_{a1}, k_{a2}) \text{ for } k >= 0$$
$$= (k_a, k_{a1}) \text{ for } k < 0$$

Definition 2 (Ishibuchi and Tanaka 1990): Let $a = (a_1, a_2)$ and $b = (b_1, b_2)$ be two intervals.

The order reaction $\leq_*$ between intervals a and b, which is used to formulate the (I-ILP) is given in (43).

$$a \leq_* b \text{ if and only if } a_1 \leq b_2 \text{ and } \frac{1}{2}(a_1 + a_2) \leq \frac{1}{2}(b_1 + b_2) \tag{43}$$

$a \leq_* b$ if and only if $a \leq_* b$ and $a \neq b$

Definition 3: A feasible solution x is said to be a non-inferior solution to (I-ILP) if and only if there is no other feasible solution x' such that

$$Z(x) \leq_* Z(x') \tag{44}$$

Application of Utility Theory to the (MIP_VSP)

The multi-objective (MIP_VSP) is converted into single objective synthesis function by application of the utility theory. In analogy to formulation (30) to (36) the single objective synthesis integer linear programming problem (SLP_VSP) may be written as follows:

(SLP_VSP)

Maximise $\quad f^* = \sum_{j=1}^{l} f_j(x_i)$

Subject to $\quad \sum_{j=1}^{n} x_i = D \quad$ (45)

$p_i(x_i) \leq_* b_i$ for all i; i=1,2,...,n

$x_i \geq 0$ and integer

Application of (I-ILP1) Model to the (SLP_VSP)

The decision maker's ambiguity about the uncertainty in the budget amount allocated to vendors' is captured by applying the (I-ILP) model to the (SLP_VSP) model. The imprecise form (I-SLP_VSP) is expressed as:

(SLP_VSP)

Maximise $\quad \sum_{j=1}^{l} f_j(x_i)$

Subject to $\quad \sum_{j=1}^{n} x_i = D \quad$ (46)

$p_i(x_i) \leq_* [b_{1i}, b_{2i}]$

$x_i \geq 0$ and integer

The interval on the right hand of the constraint denotes the uncertain total budget amount allocated to the vendors for supplying the items. The constraint denote that the feasible solution to (I_ILP_VSP) is a solution such that the average costs and the costs of the item in the worst-case scenario are less than or equal to the average value and the maximal possible value of the uncertain budget allocated to the vendors respectively.

By definition 3, the non-inferior solution set o (I-ILP_VSP) is equivalent to the non-inferior solution set of the following integer linear programming (D-SLP_VSP)

Maximise $f^* = \sum_{j=1}^{l} f_j(x_i)$

Subject to $\sum_{j=1}^{n} x_i = D \quad$ (47)

$p_i(x_i) \leq b_{2i}$

$p_i(x_i) \leq (b_{1i} + b_{2i})/2$

Clearly, the centre of an interval is the expected value and the pessimistic value is denoted by its right limit. Linear programming algorithms, such as the simplex method can be used to solve this (D-SLP_VSP) problem efficiently. The steps of the computational procedure to solve (MIP_VSP) are given below.

Step 1:	Prepare the vendor source data of the company as provided in Table 9.14.
Step 2:	Transform the vendor source data into the multi-objective (MIP_VSP) form of the problem in analogy to the formulation (24) to (29).
Step 3:	Convert the multi-objective (MIP_VSP) problem into single objective synthesis integer linear programming problem (SLP_VSP) in analogy to (45).
Step 4:	Set interval numbers for the uncertain parameters and transform (SLP_VSP) form of the problem into (I-SLP_VSP) form in analogy to the formulation (46).
Step 5:	Transform the (I-SLP_VSP) form of the problem into (D-SLP_VSP) form in analogy to the formulation (47).
Step 6:	Solve the crisp integer linear programming formulation (D-SLP_VSP) of the problem.
Step 7:	Solve the (D-SLP_VSP) formulation at different degree of uncertainties to decide the vendors' quota allocation at varying degree of uncertainties.

A Case Illustration of Hybrid Approach for Vendor Selection and Evaluation

This case is adopted from Kumar (2006). The original author has obtained the data set for the formulation of (MIP_VSP) model from the purchasing manager of an automobile manufacturer company taking an example of purchase of an axle shaft. At the time of the study, the company has four potential suppliers in the market that can supply the axle shaft. In this problem, suppliers are selected and quota is allocated among them. The author approached the company's purchasing manager who was concerned with the quota allocation of purchased orders among selected suppliers. Every effort was made to involve the firm's purchasing manager early in the process and to fully work together. In consultation with the purchasing manager three objectives have been considered. This includes maximisation of sales revenue, quality and on-time delivery with few realistic constraints such as buyers' demand, and uncertain budget amount allocated to suppliers, etc. The formulation and data set are modified to maintain anonymity of selected vendors, the quota allocation scheme and sales figure. The data used for calculating the coefficients and right hand sides of the equations in the model such as sales revenue (R_i), the percentage quality level (Q_i), the percentage on time delivery (l_i), price quoted by vendors' (P_i), budget amount allocated to the vendors (b_i) are provided in Table 9.14 and the aggregate demand is considered as deterministic and is 80,000.

Table 9.14. Vendor Source Data for the Case Illustration

Vendor Number	R_i($)	q_i(%)	l_i(%)	s_i(%)	P_i($)	B_i($)
1	300	0.80	0.65	0.88	200	5000000
2	400	0.85	0.70	0.91	250	12500000
3	350	0.98	0.60	0.97	300	6000000
4	250	0.90	0.80	0.85	180	2700000

Source: Kumar (2006)

In analogy to the formulation (24) to (29), (MIP_VSP) model is formulated based on the data set given in Table 9.14. The optimistic and pessimistic values of the individual objective function of the (MIP_VSP) model are obtained by solving for maximisation and minimisation case respectively by using commercially available linear programming (LP) software lime LINDO. The optimistic of the three objectives are obtained as $ 30000000, 71,350 units and 56,445 units respectively. The pessimistic values of the three objectives are obtained as $26800000, 67,767 units and 53,000 units respectively. The utility indexes for the optimistic values of these three objectives are set in order to purchasing manager's relative preferences as 0.9, 1.0 and 0.9 respectively. Whereas, the utility indexes for the pessimistic values of the three objectives are set in order to purchasing manager's relative preferences as 0.1, 0.5 and 0.2 respectively. In analogy to the formulation (45), single objectives synthesis function is obtained. In analogy to the formulation (46), the (SLP_VSP) model is formulated. This provides the deterministic solutions with zero uncertainty level in budget amount allocated to the vendors. In analogy to the formulation (47), the (D-SLP_VSP) model is formulated in which uncertain budget is taken as interval numbers. While the value of the lower limit interval (b_i) is kept same as the deterministic formulation, the value of the upper limit of the interval (b_i) is increased in a step of 5 per cent of b_i. The limiting value of budget constraints for different vendors for deterministic case and at the increased degree of uncertainty of 5 per cent interval in interval programming model are given in Table 9.15. The (D_SLP_VSP) model was solved using LINDO. The results of the above two models (SLP_VSP) and (D_SLP_VSP) are shown in Table 9.16.

Table 9.15. Limiting Values for (SLP_VSP) and (D-SLP_VSP) Problems

(SLP_VSP) model		(D-SLP_VSP) model (5% increment in the intervals)
Budget constraints		
Vendor 1	5000000	(5000000, 5250000)
Vendor 2	12500000	(12500000, 13125000)
Vendor 3	6000000	(6000000, 6300000)
Vendor 4	2700000	(2700000, 2835000)

Source: Kumar (2006)

Table 9.16. Solutions for (SLP_VSP) Model and (D-SLP-VSP) Problems

(SLP_VSP) model		(D-SLP_VSP) model (5% increment in the intervals)
Quota allocation		
Vendor 1	0	0
Vendor 2	50000	52500
Vendor 3	15000	11750
Vendor 4	15000	15750

Source: Kumar (2006)

Computational results indicate that there are significant differences between deterministic solutions and the (D_SLP_VSP) solutions. In the deterministic solution quota of vendor 1 depleted to nil. Vendor 1 is minority. Vendor 1 lost the entire quota due to inferiormost performance on quality and delivery objectives, less net sales revenue objective, less budget allocation and reasonably poor on other criterion. Hence, vendor 1 is the inferiormost in different criteria among entire contending vendors. Even in increasing the degree of uncertainty of the (I_ILP_VSP) model the quota of vendor 1 remained nil. Hence, management recommended three vendors only. In case of (D_SLP_VSP) solutions the quota of vendor decreased by 22 per cent. Vendor 3 received least value of quota allocation. Vendor 3 has worst delivery record among all the challenging vendors. Vendor 3 has comparatively less value of rate of return of sales revenue than vendor 2. Hence vendor 3 is on the third rank and inferior than vendor 2 and 4. This increase in quota allocations of vendor 2 and vendor 4 is practical due to uncertainty that has been captured in the budget amount allocated to different vendors' constraints of the model and the trend is shown in Figure 9.3.

Figure 9.3: Relation between Vendor allocation and uncertainty

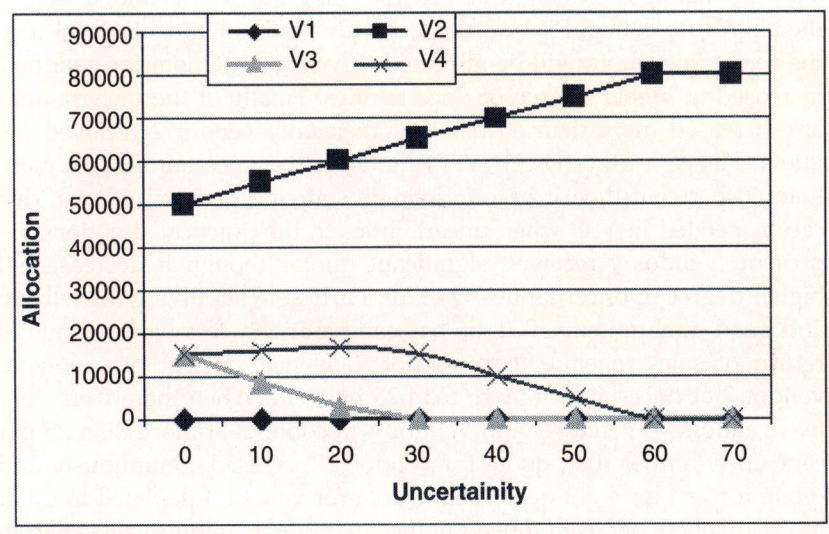

Source: Kumar (2006)

The above formulation of (I-ILP_VSP) model is solved at varying degrees of uncertainties in the budget amount allocated to different vendors. We have considered 5 per cent uncertainty as a base to understand the behaviour of the model. The solutions of the (D_SLP_VSP) model are obtained at the corresponding increase in the level of uncertainty that is modelled in interval numbers. While the value of lower limit of the interval (b_{1i}) is kept same as the deterministic formulation, the value of upper limit of the interval (b_{2i}) is increased in a step of 5 per cent of (b_{1i}) and the (D_SLP_VSP) model is solved for each step that represents increased uncertainty in knowing the budget amount allocated to vendors. In case of (D_SLP_VSP) solutions quota is allocated to the three vendors initially but as the uncertainty in the model is increased quota is distributed to two vendors at 25 per cent uncertainty. Finally, at more increased uncertainty in (D_SLP_VSP) model it becomes a single sourcing decision and quota is allocated to vendor 2 only.

The quota allocations to the different vendors depend on the coefficients of objective function, coefficients of the constraints and the degree of uncertainties captured in the budget amount allocated to the vendors. The overall demand for the item is constant. But as the uncertainties in the (I-ILP_VSP) model are increased more than 25 per cent then quota for vendor 3 also vanished to nil. Management at increased degree of uncertainties is forced to suggest two vendors — (vendor 2 and vendor 4) only. Vendor 2 received the maximum. In this formulation vendor 2 has the highest rate of return of sales revenue among the entire contending vendors. Percentage on time delivery of vendor 2 is highest among all the participating vendors. Hence vendor

2 is best among the contending vendors and received the highest quota allocate. Management suggested to allocating quota to vendor 2 first. If the aggregate demand is not fulfilled with vendor 4 and vendor 3 then the remaining quota will be allocated to vendor 1. Quota for vendor 2 increased at higher degree of uncertainties. Finally, if the uncertainties are increased more than 60 per cent then only vendor 2 received the quota. Hence, in the (D-ILP_VSP) model if the uncertainties are more than 60 per cent then it becomes single sourcing decision. Hence, due care is needed in VSP when uncertainties in the practical situations are present. Vendor 4 received significant quotas though it decreased at higher degree of uncertainties. Vendor 3 is best in supplying the reliable and good quality items. But, he has comparatively less value of rate of return of sales revenue than vendor 2. Hence, he lost his quota to vendor 2 at uncertainties more than 25 per cent. When there were only two vendors — vendor 2 and vendor 4 in contests at more than 25 per cent uncertainties then quota for vendor 2 increased continuously and quota for vendor 4 got decreased. Quota for vendor 4 depleted to nil at more than 60 per cent uncertainties in budget amount allocated to vendors. After allocating quota to vendor 2 and vendor 4 remaining quota is allocated to vendor 3. Vendor 3 received least value of quota allocation. Vendor 3 has least on-time delivery value among all the challenging vendors. Vendor 3 has comparatively less value of rate of return of sales revenue than vendor 2. Hence, vendor 3 is on the third rank and inferior than vendor 2 and vendor 4. Vendor 1 is the inferiormost in different criteria among entire contending vendors. Even in increasing the degree of uncertainty of the (I-ILP_VSP) model the quota of vendor 1 remained nil. The results indicate that the quota of different vendors may be quite different when uncertainties are captured. At the different levels of uncertainty in the assessment of budget amount allocated to the vendors, the allocation of vendors' quota changes. In some cases, few vendors as vendors 3 and 4 lost their entire quota to the other vendors who had buffer capacity but have superior performance under uncertain decision parameters.

The hybrid approach illustrates relevance of models in addressing uncertain situations. The proposed approach is a good strategy to incorporate uncertainties in vendors' parameters for VSP.

The models and cases described in this section highlight the degree of complexity involved in vendor selection and evaluation and need for different approaches. Hence, it is strongly recommended that the organisations need to adopt suitable models while selecting vendors for long-term benefits. Also care should be taken while selecting suitable models for vendor selection and evaluation.

IT Outsourcing and India

The IT industry in India has started in the late 1960s. Tata Consultancy Services (TCS) started in 1968 when there was no IT industry existing in India and since then it has grown as one of the world's largest IT companies. Some of the major services that Indian IT industry offers include consulting, IT services, engineering and industrial services, asset based solutions, BPO (Business Process Outsourcing), KPO (Knowledge Process Outsourcing), IT infrastructure, etc. According to recent Nasscom's fifth India Leadership forum 2006, Indian IT industry is expected to touch $36.3 billion in revenue in the year 2006, which is about 28 per cent increase from the year 2005. According to experts (Pascal Matzke of Forrester, Europe), the Indian IT industry is expected to touch $60 billion by 2010 with a yearly growth rate of 25 per cent. The most important issue behind Indian IT success is its continuous improvement and productivity and innovation in services. India has great potential to capture engineering services. Indian IT industry contributes around 21.3 per cent of India's total exports as on December 2005.

India has not only good opportunities but also threats from other countries like China, New Russia, Canada, Ireland, Philippines, Mexico and other Eastern Europe. This is due to global clients movement to multi-location model. Future growth of IT industry in India depends on the level of talent pool available, infrastructure, government regulations, etc. According to experts, the current eligible workforce is around 28 per cent and efforts to address these issues are in place. Table 9.17, shows the IT industry break-up. The BPO sector is on the high growth arena and hardware needs to improve significantly. A new area KPO is also emerging and market potential is huge.

Table 9.17. IT Industry Outsourcing Business Break-Up

Sl	Sector	2005 ($ bln)	2006 ($ bln)	(estimated) % Change
1	IT services	13.5	17.5	29.63
2	ITES- BPO	5.2	7.2	38.46
3	Engg service, R & D, S/w products	3.9	4.8	23.08
4	Total software and Services Revenue	22.6	29.5	30.53
5	Hardware	5.9	6.9	16.95
6	Total IT industry (including Hardware)	28.4	36.3	27.82

Source: Swami and Sekhar (2005)

Indian IT outsourcing is positioning through innovation, in this regard a Nasscom has initiated a forum on IT innovation in the year 2004 to target the next phase of growth among small companies. A telecom product made for India can be sold in 150 countries and estimates show that over one billion connections are expected to be sold in developing countries over the next 10 years and business potential is around $70 billion in telecom products and services. Established software vendors including IBM, Microsoft, Oracle and SAP, already tap Indian talent not just to develop code but also to help design and develop commercial offerings. Increasingly, Indian software entrepreneurs want to put their own companies' names on product labels, at home and abroad, by capitalising on their country's highly educated and low-cost workforce to build and sell software for everything from back-office programmes to customer-facing applications. Experience, talent and ambition are propelling the growth of the Indian software market. Like other foreign software vendors that saw big opportunities in the US—SAP among them—Indian companies increasingly want to turn their local successes into a greater US presence. China is another natural market for Indian-made software. According to Mr Vivek Paul, former Vice Chairman, Wipro technologies observed that India is almost certain to have a major role as a centre of software development. Oracle plans to spend $316 million to acquire a 41 per cent stake in i-flex Solutions Ltd., a Mumbai banking software maker owned by Citigroup Venture Capital.

It's not just the cost structure that makes Indian software companies interesting. Many of the entrepreneurs come from India's IT-services industry, and their development teams bring with them the disciplined Six Sigma and CMM-I approaches to quality management and experience with Web services and hosted applications to the products they develop. It's a mindset that fits well with the business world's slow march toward more services-oriented, web-friendly IT architectures.

Polaris Software Lab Ltd., Chennai, India, shows how Indian companies can parlay industry knowledge gained others' products and industrial examples. The 20-year-old company began as an IT-services shop supporting Citibank's global operations, giving it the bonafides to claim a world-class understanding of banking technology. Polaris software company marketing its business-process software for the financial-services industry. The company's commercial software customers now include ABN Amro, Lloyd's, UBS and Citibank.

India Outsourcing and Small Players

UNIDO has established around 60 Sub-contracting and Partnership Exchanges (SPXs) worldwide to promote outsourcing from small Third World vendors. Out of 60 SPXs seven of them are in India. According to Andre de Crombrugghe, UNIDO Programme Coordinator, SSIs have big chance and UNIDO planned to add ten more SPXs in India by 2006, covering 8,000 Small Scale Industries (SSIs). UNIDO and CII planned to set up a national SPX online network as well. On the other hand, many government organisations like DRDO, ISRO, HAL, BEML are procuring more than Rs 10,000 crore worth of equipment annually, according to Major General Chary, Director-General of Quality Assurance of Defense Production. Domestic SSIs are contributing significantly in India. Maruti Udyog, which is worth Rs 9,000 crore, and which pioneered India's vendor development initiative in 1982, today buys out components worth Rs 3,500 crore from over 350 direct small suppliers. The hydraulic pump covers and lapping tools used by Bosch in its German, Turkish,

Brazilian units come from one of Bangalore's small-scale industries. Boeing sources its specialised cables from Tumkur and Mysore in Karnataka. The Indian Railways basket alone has some 70 spares as potential jobs—DRDL, ISRO, Indian Railways, HAL, BEML are just a few public sector buyers looking at indigenisation of their technology imports. According to Goyal, industrial adviser, SSI Ministry, India, globally, Europe and the US are looking at Indian SSIs for sub-contracting their work.

Advances and Emerging Areas of Outsourcing

India's success in providing low-cost, high-quality business process outsourcing services has encouraged many firms to begin offshoring and/or outsourcing many of their high-end knowledge processes as well. Knowledge Process outsourcing (KPO) includes doctors, lawyers, scientists, engineers, educationist, etc. Traditional BPO companies are adding high-end capabilities to their offerings as a way to move up the value chain.

According to Confederation of Indian Industry (CII) study on 'India in the New Knowledge Economy', it is noted that India will emerge as the global hub for KPO. Of late many Indian institutions (like Career Launcher, eLearning, Tutor Vista, Evalueserve) and overseas organisations are focusing on knowledge process outsourcing (KPO), primarily in the area of education and learning for customers from different parts of the globe. According to NASSCOM the estimated market for KPO is around US $15 billion by 2008. According to statistics the current share of Indian BPO is around 36 per cent and is expected to reach 45 per cent by 2010 whereas KPO share is 56 per cent and is expected to reach 71 per cent by 2010. The number of KPO employees is estimated to increase from 25,000 to 250,000 by 2010 (Swami and Sekhar 2005). Financial process outsourcing (FPO) is identified as one of the growth areas for organisations to focus in KPO segment by NASSCOM survey 2005. The global KPO industry is expected to grow to $16 billion by 2010 from $1.2 billion in 2003 (Swami and Sekhar 2005). KPO services include market and business research, data mining and analysis, patent litigation and legal/paralegal research, biotechnology, banking, insurance and financial services, pharmaceutical research and development, graphics and animation, engineering design etc. India has a great potential to become the hub for KPO industry and there are five major factors in favour of India.

(a) The success of offshore outsourcing strategy and the positive experience of Western firms led to offshore more knowledge intensive processes.

(b) India is natural to take on KPO work because it can offer domain expertise in a number of industry verticals like healthcare and pharmaceutical to biotechnology and legal research.

(c) India has wealth of science, engineering and technical institutes that guarantee steady supply of qualified graduates.

(d) India is a low cost and high quality centre for many BPO activities.

(e) KPO has caught the imagination of smaller players, expanding the market and offering a range of services at different price points.

As India widens the spectrum from BPO to KPO, the opportunities are tremendous. However, there are challenges like highly specialised nature of KPO requires higher quality standards, better risk management and superior investments in infrastructure, training and retaining of experts. In the next few years, the KPO industry in India expected to grow around 60–70 per cent and lead to faster economic development. On the other side, retail industry is growing through the concept of malls. According to a study by Images multimedia, in India there are about 96 malls (as on August 2005) and is expected to grow at 60 per cent and is estimated to reach around 360 by the end of 2007 covering second tier cities and major towns. The US and UK companies expected to increase their budget by 20–50 per cent in 2006 ('Outsourcing Budgets of companies to increase by 20% in, 06: Survey', *Financial Express*, 4 March 2006).

Outsourcing now crosses over into many business environments, including engineering and technology, accounting, call centres, word processing, database management, publishing and printing, and legal and administration. Labour-intensive administration, bookkeeping, legal transcription, proofreading, and system design jobs are likely candidates for overseas workers. The Internet has provided a global link between end consumer and retailers continents apart. Advances in digital network transmission and telecommunications have allowed network and telephone calls to be easily routed to other countries. India is the leader for call centre operations, but the Philippines and South Africa are other emerging areas where highly skilled English- speaking workers are available at a fraction of the cost. Spanish-speaking labour is available in Mexico and South America for companies with Spanish-speaking clients.

One of the hottest topics is the foreign outsourcing of tax preparation services. Many charted accountants were caught off guard by the emergence and rapid adoption of foreign outsourcing over the past few years. Five years ago, the CPA Vision Project warned of traditional CPA services becoming commoditised, and urged CPAs to develop new core competencies to enable them to deliver more value added services and retain their relevance in a changing marketplace. Foreign outsourcing of tax preparation is here to stay and is growing exponentially at firms of all sizes. Up to 200,000 US tax returns are prepared by Indian chartered accountants in the year 2004, up from 20,000 a year ago. The foreign outsourcing trend is enabled by technology and motivated by staff shortages and fee pressure. US return prepares scan source documents and send them to the Indian accountants via encrypted e-mail or private networks. The Indian accountants retrieve the scanned images, prepare the returns using the popular US professional tax prep packages, and transmit the completed returns back to the US firm.

According to recent studies by many practitioners and researchers, the following have been identified as potential areas for outsourcing:
- agriculture products;
- banking and investment;
- bio technology;
- detective services;
- health services;
- higher education and training;
- hotel/hospitality/tourism/catering, etc.;
- HR and payroll processing;
- information technology (IT) and it enabled services (ITES);
- IT hardware and manufacturing and IT standardisation;
- infrastructure, etc.;
- logistics and supply chain;
- maintenance and repair operations (MRO) in airline industry;
- medical and pharma products;
- product design;
- publishing, legal, cyber crimes;
- real estate and construction;
- retail supply and supply chain;
- satellite services;
- security and manpower supply;
- services design and delivery;
- telecom equipment manufacturing and telecom services; and
- textile and paper industry, etc.

Global Standards

General Motors developing standards for information technology business. Often viewed as the poster child for outsourcing IT work, the automaker has teamed up with the Carnegie Mellon Software Engineering Institute to develop standards for IT *outsourcing*. According to Fred Killeen, CTO of GM, by dealing with all IT vendors in a common way, GM hopes to reduce waste and see faster and better results. General Motors wants to develop standard contracts, a standard way to manage an IT programme or project, and a standard way to measure whether vendors are doing the job. General Motors says standards will improve the way it does business with its IT suppliers. General Motors also plans to encourage other automakers, auto suppliers and any other company that does business with IT vendors to adopt these standard practices. The idea is to reduce the cost of *outsourcing* IT business because GM subcontracts nearly all of its $3 billion in annual

IT spending. It deals frequently with many companies that have their own processes.

GM has been working with its key IT suppliers—EDS, IBM Corp., Microsoft Corp., Hewlett-Packard Co. and others—for the last 20 months to develop standard practices with GM. There exists savings due to standardisation. However, it believes that there will be both the acquirer and the provider of IT services will realise savings and efficiencies. The cost savings comes from improving the processes and then implementing them globally. Further, it allows the organisation to standardise the way the organisation implements systems and how it operates the outsourced environment and that takes cost down, reduces complexity and improves the probability of success.

Dubai Outsourcing Zone (DOZ) is organising a World Outsourcing Forum to discuss implementation of regional and international standards in the outsourcing industry. Dubai Outsourcing Zone is encouraging local and international outsourcing players to adopt certifications and standards like ISO 9000, COPC, Six Sigma, BS 7799 and ISO 17799 for business community as a yardstick to compare different outsourcing facilitators. DOZ is also urging outsourcing companies to address the need to comply with key regulations in client countries to raise the credibility of the outsourcing industry as a whole. Leading the way, DOZ will ensure compliance with the proposed standards in the outsourcing industry cluster that it is currently building within Dubai. As part of this effort, DOZ is in talks with prominent outsourcing industry bodies such as the International Association of Outsourcing Professionals (IAOP) and NASSCOM. DOZ also seeks to pioneer a 'Centre of Excellence'; a resource centre of 40 to 50 of the world's best outsourcing professionals. This centre of excellence will have some of the cream of global outsourcing professional talent in various fields like IT, business process management, transition management, Customer Service, HR, Finance, etc.

Conclusion

Firms must continually manage outsourcing. Once the business activity has been passed to a third party it becomes part of the firm's external spend and should receive the necessary attention. This chapter has provided a brief overview of the range of operational tools, techniques and advice available in the public domain. It has shown that firms can easily develop an operational toolkit to manage the outsourcing process and ensure that the suppliers meet the agreed objectives. Those who proceed without such a toolkit, and the consequent ability to control suppliers, will find that even 'strategic partners' are willing to take advantage of them.

The important message of the chapter is that firms must understand which operational tools and techniques are appropriate to the individual circumstances they face. Writers such as Quinn and Hilmer, Probert, Williamson and Lacity and Hirschheim, to name a few, understand this and provide flexible advice which can be applied as required.

The cases and models described in this chapter would help while taking decision with regard to vendor selection and evaluation under different circumstances. Various advances and emerging areas for outsourcing were also highlighted.

References

Akinc, U. 1993. 'Selecting a Set of Vendors in a Manufacturing Environment', *Journal of Operations Management*, vol. 11 pp: 107-22.

Alefeld, G. and J. Harzberger. 1983. *Introduction to Interval Computations*, NY: Academic.

Anthony, T.F. and F.P. Buffa. 1977. 'Strategic Purchase Scheduling', *Journal of Purchasing and Materials Management*, Fall, pp: 27–31.

Baily, P. and D. Farmer. 1990. *Purchasing Principles and Management*, London: Pitman.

Bendor, P.S., R.W. Brown, M.H. Issac and J.F. Shapiro. 1985. 'Improving Purchasing Productivity at IBM with a Normative Decision Support System', *Interfaces*, vol.15, pp: 106–15.

Benton, W.C. 1991. Quantity Discount Decisions under Conditions of Multiple Items' Multiple Suppliers and Resource Limitations, *International Journal of Production Research*, vol. 29, pp: 1953-61.

Bitran, G. R. 1980. 'Linear Multiple Objective Problems with Interval Coefficients', *Management Science*, vol. 26, pp: 694–706.

Buffa, F.P., and W.M. Jackson. 1983. 'A Goal Programming Model for Purchase Planning', *Journal of Purchasing and Materials Management*. pp 27-34.

Burt, D. and M. Doyle. 1993. *The American Keiretsu: A Strategic Weapon for Global Competitiveness*, Homewood, Business One Irwin, pp: 185–86.

Chaudhry, S.S., F.G. Forst and J.L. Zydiak. 1993. 'Vendor Selection with Price Breaks', *European Journal of Operational Research*, vol. 70, pp: 52–66.

DeWispelare, A.R. and A.P. Sage. 1981. 'On Combined Multiple Objective Optimisation Theory and Multiple Attribute Utility Theory for Evaluation and Choice Making, *Large Scale Systems*, vol. 2, pp: 1– 19.

Dickson, G.W. 1966. 'An Analysis of Vendor Selection Systems and Decisions', *Journal of Purchasing*, vol. 2, pp: 5–17.

http://www.financialexpress.com/fearchive-frame.php

Ghodsypour, S.H. and C. O'Brien. 1998. 'A Decision Support System for Supplier Selection Using an Integrated Analytic Hierarchy Process and Linear Programming', *International Journal of Production Economics*, vol. 56–57, pp: 199–212.

Goffin, K., M. Szwejczewski and C. New. 1997. 'Managing Suppliers: When Fewer Can Mean More', *International Journal of Physical Distribution and Logistics Management*, vol. 27, pp: 422–35.

Hahn, C., C. Watts and K. Kim, 1990. 'The Supplier Development Programme: a Conceptual Model', *Journal of Purchasing and Materials Management*, Spring, p.6.

Handfield, R., S.V. Walton, R. Sroufe and S.A. Melnyk. 2002. 'Applying Environmental Criteria to Supplier Assessment: A Study in the Application of the Analytical Hierarchy Process', *European Journal of Operational Research*, vol.141, pp: 70–87.

Hong, J.D. and J.C. Hayya, 1992. 'Just-in-Time Purchasing: Single or Multiple Sourcing?', *International Journal of Production Economics*, vol.27, pp: 175–81.

Ishibuchi, H. and H. Tanka. 1989. 'Formulation and Analysis of Linear Programming Problem with Interval Coefficients', *Journal of Japan Industrial Management Association*, vol.40, pp: 320–29.

_____. 1990. 'Multi-Objective Programming in Optimisation of Interval Objective Function', *European Journal of Operations Research*, vol.48, pp: 219–25.

Kaplan, R. 1990. 'Contribution Margin Analysis: No Longer Relevant', *Journal of Management Accounting Research*, pp: 2–15.

Kaplan, R. and D. Norton. 1992. 'The Balanced Scorecard: Measures that Drive Performance', *Harvard Business Review*, January–February, pp: 71–79.

Ketler, K. and J. Walstrom. 1993. 'The Outsourcing Decision: Vendor and Contract Characteristics', *International Journal of Information Management*, vol. 13, pp: 449–59.

Kingsman, B. G. 1986. 'Purchasing Raw Materials with Uncertain Fluctuating Prices', *European Journal of Operations Research*, vol. 25, pp: 358–72.

Krajewski, L. J. and L. P. Ritzman. 1999. *Operations Management–Strategy and Analysis*, New York: Addison Wesley,

Kumar, M. 2006. 'A Hybrid Approach for Vendor Selection Problem', *Udyog Pragati*, vol. 30, January–March, pp: 20–29.

Lacity, M. and R. Hirschheim. 1993. 'The Information Systems Outsourcing Bandwagon', *Sloan Management Review*, Fall, pp: 73–86.

Lamming, R., P. Cousins and D. Notman. 1996. 'Beyond Vendor Assessment: Relationship Assessment Programmes', *Conference Proceedings, International Purchasing and Supply Education and Research Association*, Eindhoven, pp: 615–20.

Mohanty, R. P. 1990. 'How Developed is Materials Management in India? A Survey', *Malaysian Productivity Journal*, vol. 12, pp: 5–12.

Monozka, R.M. and S.J. Trecha. 1988. 'Cost-Based Supplier Performance Evaluation', *Journal of Purchasing and Materials Management*, Spring, pp: 2–7.

Moore, D. L. and H.E. Fearon. 1973. 'Computer-Assisted Decision Making in Purchasing', *Journal of Purchasing*, vol. 9, pp: 5–25.

Mummalaneni, V., K.M. Dubas and Ch. Chao. 1996. 'Chinese Purchasing Managers' Preferences and Trade-offs in Supplier Selection and Performance Evaluation', *Industrial Marketing Management*, vol. 25, IS 24.

Nakahara, Y., M. Sasaki and M. Gen. 1992. 'On the Linear Programming with Interval Coefficients', *International Journal of Computer Engineering*, vol. 23, pp: 301–304.

Narasimhan, R. 1983. 'An Analytical Approach to Supplier Selection', *Journal of Purchasing and Materials Management*, Winter, pp: 27–32.

Narasimhan, R. and K. Stoynoff. 1986. 'Optimising Aggregate Procurement Allocation Decisions', *Journal of Purchasing and Materials Management*, Spring, pp: 23–30.

Pan, A.C. 1989. 'Allocation of Order Quantity Among Suppliers', *Journal of Purchasing and Materials Management*, Fall, pp: 36–39.

Probert, D. 1997, Developing a Make or Buy Stragegy for Manufacturing Business, Stevenage Institution of Electrical Engineers, p. 29.

Quinn, J. B., and F. Hilmer. 1994. 'Strategic Outsourcing', *Sloan Management Review*, Summer, vol. 35, pp: 43–55.

Richards Peidl, N. 2003. 'Seven Pitfalls that Ruin Vendor Relationships', *Credit Union Magazine*, September, vol. 69, ABI/INFORM Global, pp: 96–101.

Roodhooft, F. and J. Koning. 1996. 'Vendor Selection and Evaluation: An Activity Based Costing Approach', *European Journal of Operational Research*, vol. 96, pp: 97–102.

Rosenthal, E.C., J.L. Zydiak and S.S. Chaudhry. 1995. 'Vendor Selection with Bundling', *Decisions Science*, vol. 26, pp: 35–48.

Saunders. C, M. Gebelt and Q. Hu. 1997. 'Achieving Success in Information Systems Outsourcing', *California Management Review*, vol. 39, pp: 63–79.

Sharma, D., W.C. Benton and R. Srivastava. 1989. 'Competitive Strategy and Purchasing Decisions', Proceedings of the Annual Conference of the Decision Sciences Institute, pp: 1088–90.

Swami, P and M. Sekhar. 2005. 'From BPO to KPO', *Business India*, August–September, pp: 46–52.

Treasury, H. M. 1995. *Setting New Standards: A Strategy for Government Procurement*, London: HMSO.

Turner, I. 1988. 'An Independent System for the Evaluation of Contract Tenders', *Operational Research Society*, vol. 39, pp: 551–61.

Watts, C. and C. Hahn. 1993. 'Supplier Development Programmes: an Empirical Analysis', *International Journal of Purchasing and Materials Management*, April, pp: 14–20.

Weber, C.A., J.R. Current and W.C. Benton. 1991. 'Vendor Selection Criteria and Methods', *European Journal of Operational Research*, vol. 50, pp: 2–18.

Webber, C. A., J.R. Current and A. Desai. 2000. 'An Optimisation Approach to Determining the Number of Vendors to Employ', *Supply Chain Management: An International Journal*, vol. 2, pp: 90–98.

Williamson, O. E. 1985. *The Economic Institutions of Capitalism*, New York: Free Press.

Wind, Y. and P.J. Robinson. 1968. 'The Determinants of Vendor Selection: The Evaluation Function Approach', *Journal of Purchasing and Materials Management*, Fall, pp: 29–41.

Annexures

Annexure 1

Using the Technology (Theory)

As more companies focus on improving communication, better customer relationships and cost savings, it is becoming increasingly important to get value for money from your website.

Websites

Rationale

Ask yourself who uses your site, why and how they get there? Before you go after new customers, make sure you are looking after your current ones. Use your website to offer troubleshooting advice or account information. You could also cut time spent dealing with press or recruitment enquiries by making information packs available for download. Finally, register your site with search engines, ask relevant industry sites to include a link to it, and make sure your current customers know you have it.

Quick Fixes

If your website has not delivered the results you expected, you may not need to spend a huge amount on improving it. You simply need to follow the steps detailed below:

- Contact details should be easily accessible.
- Information must be current and error free.
- Make navigation, page titles and writing simple and clear.
- Give an incentive if you want people to register.
- Animation or large graphics take time to download—make sure they are actually useful—they need to inform or sell, not just impress.
- Check internal links work and that links to external sites are helpful, not simply sending your customers away.
- If you sell online, explain the length and complexity of the purchasing process.
- Benchmark your site against your competitors for speed, functionality and ease of use.
- Give people a reason to return—update your content regularly.

Selling Online

If you think your business model lends itself to selling over the Internet, you could invest in e-commerce functionality. For less than £1,000, this technology lets you process credit card transactions securely online. As people become more used to buying online, fraud worries are receding. A professional-looking site redesigned with clear information about your security precautions can help customers overcome any worries about credibility.

Promoting your Website

There is no point in spending time and money on your website if no one knows it's there. There are many ways in which you can promote your website, and most are quite simple. Make sure your web address is included on all printed material, such as business cards, letters and flyers, as well as on all outgoing e-mails. You may also want to consider reciprocal marketing (linking to your trade association and other sites with complementary content), e-mail marketing and online advertising.

Search engines are also a useful way of attracting customers, particularly if your company operates in a price-sensitive or niche market. If you want your website to generate significant revenue, consider enlisting the help of a professional search engine placement agency.

Broadband

This is only the beginning of the Internet revolution.

Many small businesses and home offices connect to the Internet using modems. These narrowband connections have a slow data transfer rate, which means web pages and files can take a long time to download. Broadband connections transfer data up to ten times faster and are permanently connected. This means you can send and receive large files quickly, you don't have to dial up each time you want to connect, and you only pay a flat rate fee.

What can it do for you? Broadband will let your business:

- receive e-mail, surf the web and take telephone calls—all at the same time, all using the same connection;
- cut down on paperwork and time spent on administration and data transfer;
- make more use of the Internet to access research, and up-to-the-minute data, and keep an eye on competitors;
- use facilities like videostreaming to save on time and money spent travelling to meetings;
- set up a virtual private network, so staff can connect to your server wherever they are.

What Are Your Options?

You can get broadband in four ways:
- ADSL—using telephone lines;
- Cable—using cable TV lines;
- Wireless—using a fixed antenna and modem;
- Satellite—using an antenna and a two-cable connection to your computer.

In UK the cost, availability and data transfer rates of these services vary. If you are a very small operation, the cost of broadband could be as low as £40 a month, but you may have to pay an installation charge of between £50 and £200. In India it is comparatively less and is just Rs 150 to Rs 500 depending upon the speed and infrastructure requirement. In India it is comparatively less and is just Rs 150 to Rs 500 depending upon the speed and infrastructure requirement. However, these prices are only a guide. Broadband costs vary considerably, depending on which solution you decide is best for your business.

E-mail

E-mail is now a widespread feature in business.

Around 90 per cent of UK businesses use it, and one-fifth claims their company could not survive more than one day without e-mail access. In India will take up to two more years when e-mail working will become a part of business success. As e-mail is becoming more and more popular, make sure your business gets the most out of electronic communication, and that staff do not feel they are at the mercy of their inbox.

Setting up E-mail

It is fairly easy to get e-mail if your business has a computer less than five years old. All you need is Internet access, an account with an Internet Service Provider (ISP), an e-mail server and e-mail software. It is a good idea to compare various packages as features and prices vary considerably. For example, it costs approximately between £9–£60 per person, and there may be additional charges for licenses.

Getting the Most Out of E-mail

Although e-mail is an exceptionally useful tool, it should be viewed as just one part of your communications toolkit. If you have a number of staff, you could benefit from an e-mail policy that covers what you would consider offensive or obscene material if it were sent and discourages excessive personal use. It can also urge people not to clog up your system with unnecessary e-mails - not everyone needs copying in on everything and many matters are better handled face to face. Though e-mail is less formal than letters, it should still be professional; so ensure e-mails are spell-checked before they are sent out.

Marketing

E-mail can provide an extremely cost-effective way of marketing to your customers. Whether this is with regular newsletter updates or special offers, it gives you the ability to target customers cheaply and instantly, without the time lag and costs associated with printing. Be careful not to overuse this option though. What makes it so effective — the personal, time-sensitive interaction — is also what makes people react to irrelevant or unwanted e-mail. Even if you don't run an e-mail campaign, you can use the automatic signature feature to include your company's contact details and a brief description of your offer on all outgoing e-mails.

Customer Service

While it can be an excellent way of reducing the costs of customer support, the instant nature of e-mail has made customers more demanding. They do not expect to wait for days to receive responses by e-mail. The best practice here is to manage expectations by setting up an automatic e-mail response. This will send an instant acknowledgement to the customer in which you can thank them for getting in touch and let them know how long it will take you to respond.

Communicating with Staff

The immediacy and lower cost of e-mail makes it easier to keep your staff informed.

A regular e-mail newsletter can help staff to understand other areas of the business, share marketing intelligence and foster a sense of belongingness and involvement in the company.

Mobile Communications

You can make better use of your time—from managing e-mails to accessing company information on the move. Mobile staff can be more productive and remain in contact with the office, while warehouse workers can use portable barcode scanners to check stocks more easily.

A Mobile Office

With a Personal Digital Assistant (PDA) or laptop and a mobile phone, you can have your own 'virtual office'. You can access e-mail on the move, send and receive documents and digital photographs or tap into your company's database or customer information. As well as being enormously useful for mobile sales staff or home workers, this is a relatively cheap option and applicable to firms of any size. Costs range from £70 to £500 in UK and Rs 15,000 to 20,000 approximately in India.

3G Phones

Like Wireless Application Protocol (Wap), 3G allows you to connect to the web using your mobile phone. Unlike Wap, 3G is permanently connected and also has a higher data transfer rate. Some 3G phones are faster than a home broadband connection. They have other useful features including video messaging, digital cameras, and the ability to play music and video files. The staff can use them to instantly show colleagues images and make decisions quicker.

As popularity have increased, the price of 3G phones is beginning to fall. Handsets how start from £50 and a monthly line rental is around £30, with additional charges for calls and services.

A Wireless Office

By setting up a wireless network in your office—a wireless Local Area Network (LAN)—you can dispense with fixed desks and the tangle of cabling. People could work anywhere with a wireless network using radio waves to transfer data at high speed, making 'hot desking' a real possibility.

In UK Wireless packages cost from £120–£500 (including a Wireless-Fidelity [WiFi] router), though you may need a wireless network card (£40–£60) for each computer. Wireless technology is increasingly being built into laptops and PDAs. In India it costs around Rs 30,000 for the same facility.

Bluetooth also connects electronic devices, using low frequency radio waves. It is probably more suitable for creating ad hoc networks for consumer devices, and can connect to another device within a 10 and 100 metre range. More and more electrical devices are Bluetooth-compatible or can be adapted. Compared to Wireless-Fidelity (WiFi), Bluetooth is more of a short-range solution and is not considered robust enough to replace a standard wired network in an office.

The cost of Bluetooth routers start from £120 and adaptors cost around £50.

Video, Tele and Data Conferencing

As the Internet continues to globalise business, companies are likely to find that they have an ever more widely spread network of clients, suppliers and even employees.

Teleconferencing

Though a familiar technology, teleconferencing can still be a very useful alternative to meetings. It is most effective when used with a small number of people and a clearly defined agenda. For other applications like complex discussions or sales pitches, videoconferencing may be a better alternative.

Voice over Internet Protocol (VoIP) allows you to make phone calls using a computer network such as a LAN or the Internet. This means you can integrate your phone system more closely with business data and make cheaper calls. VoIP compresses voice data so it uses 90 per cent less bandwidth than traditional calls. With VoIP, you can also take advantage of cheap long distance and international calls, and free internal calls to anyone on the company network—whether they are on the road or in another office.

Videoconferencing

Videoconferencing allows people to see and speak with trading partners anywhere in the world, present products and discuss new ideas. Although it has been around for over 20 years, recent technological advances have dramatically improved the ease-of-use, and the sound and picture quality.

Videoconferencing isn't just valuable for improving client relationships and cutting costs. It can dramatically improve internal communication in geographically diverse businesses - particularly those with home workers and satellite offices.

Data Conferencing

Data conferencing is an addition to videoconferencing that expands the range of possibilities from discussion and presentation to full interactive and collaborative working. You can transfer and work on a range of files and using electronic white boards, you can illustrate and exchange ideas.

Desktop Videoconferencing

Digital cameras and new software make it possible for you to videoconference using your PC and an Internet connection. Current camera and bandwidth limitations make this more suited to one-to-one discussions rather than important meetings, but in the next few years, the quality is likely to improve substantially.

Many Business Links (and their Scottish, Welsh and Northern Irish equivalents) have videoconferencing facilities available for a small charge.

Electronic Date Interchange (EDI) and Extranets

Electronic Date Interchange (EDI) and extranets help you share information with customers, suppliers and business partners.

What is EDI?

Electronic Data Interchange is the exchange of business documents such as orders and invoices between trading partners. Standardised messaging and business software allows purchasers and suppliers to handle transactions electronically.

Benefits of EDI

Electronic processes are generally easier to audit, faster and less prone to error than manual ones. Electronic Date Interchange takes this logic to its ultimate conclusion and seeks to make the flow of information straightforward, not just within a company, but with its customers and suppliers as well. Benefits include:
- closer trading partnerships and increased customer satisfaction;

- simplified order, invoice and trade documentation;
- reduced postage, paper and administration costs;
- greater control with precision timing and reduced stock holdings; and
- improved accountability and document tracking.

Electronic Date Interchange works best where there is a large volume of transactions, an ongoing management commitment from all parties, and an upfront investment in the system.

Extranet

For companies who want to work more collaboratively with clients, extranets can prove a tremendous asset.

What is an extranet?

Where a website allows you to publish information for public consumption, an extranet lets you share confidential information with a restricted group of clients and suppliers. It can be anything from a password-protected page on a website to an extended network of websites. You can use it to share applications and information, initiate orders and collaborate on product designs— all in real time.

Benefits of an Extranet

Like a website, an extranet is accessed through a web browser. It can be a simple, secure area for exchanging files too large to e-mail, or a place where work can be viewed and approved remotely. Giving clients the opportunity to monitor and test the ongoing progress can reduce the need for travel and create a much greater sense of involvement and collaboration on projects.

Companies who already have a website can set up a simple extranet at very low cost. With greater investment, however, they could create an extranet that allows clients to access account, product and stock information or place orders.

Networking and Intranets

Networking can help your business become a more flexible and efficient organisation.

Networking

A network is simply a set of computers joined together, which lets them communicate and share data, software, storage, printers and other hardware.

A set of computers linked by cable in one location is called a Local Area Network (LAN). This is probably what you have if you have one office and several computers with shared file storage space. A new, and currently quite expensive, alternative to LANs are wireless LANs (also known as WiFis). These are networks based in one location that transfer data by radio waves instead of cabling.

Networks that link different sites are called Wide Area Networks (WANs).

If the cost of linking remote offices is prohibitive, you could consider a Virtual Private Network (VPN). A VPN uses data encryption to allow secure access to a company's network over the Internet. This is cheaper than connecting offices by owned or leased lines.

Benefits

Even a company with just a few computers can benefit from networking. It allows:

- shared hardware;
- shared access to databases and software programmes;
- collaborative working on documents; and
- use of e-mail.

Most of all though, a network helps you organise your business—data can be stored centrally for ease of cataloguing, retrieval and back-up.

Intranets

An intranet is a private network for a company's employees. Like a client extranet, it uses a web browser to access and display information. As with websites, this can be anything from simple pages of news and contact details to complex software applications and databases.

Benefits

From discussion forums, to staff profiles and online training, intranets can be enormously effective for sharing information, improving efficiency and cultivating staff morale.

Some large companies are now using their intranet as a way of moving a whole swathe of administrative functions and workflow tools online.

Successful introduction of any substantial changes to the way people work requires staff. One common tactic is to start small by easing the burden of administrative tasks by putting applications like automated timesheets and expense claims on your internet.

Benchmarking Study 2004

This year's results confirm several of the trends identified in last year's report:

- businesses continue to place greater emphasis on the *value* provided by ICT. This has been characterised by a significant increase in the proportion of businesses measuring the benefits of technology;
- the shift in focus from access per se to the speed and reliability of connection continues. Levels of Internet access appear to have reached a plateau while access speed continued to rise.
- one of the dominant new themes this year is the growing selectivity

of businesses in their deployment of ICT. This is consistent with the increased focus on value and the potential benefits of technology.

The findings also highlight two trends in the UK that have changed:
- encouragingly, there are strong signs that the digital divide between larger and smaller businesses is closing, particularly in the UK;
- less encouragingly, the rapid increases in wireless and mobile technologies appear to have slowed.

Major Trends

There has been a significant increase in the proportion of businesses that are measuring the benefits of ICT. Increases were highest in the UK (up 15 percentage points), Ireland (up 13 percentage points), and the USA (up 10 percentage points). These increases are indicative of businesses becoming more sophisticated in the way they use ICT. The focus on costs adopted by many businesses following the dot.com crash is now being replaced by a more holistic approach to the assessment of ICT investments. Managers responsible for ICT are increasingly being asked to justify their budget requests and are becoming better at assessing potential benefits using metrics such as ROI, IRR, and NPV(1).

More businesses are measuring the benefits of technology.

Businesses Becoming Selective in the Type of Information

The sector analysis has identified significant variations in the level of technology adoption and deployment across sectors. In general, financial services businesses have the highest levels of adoption and connectivity, while businesses in the primary and construction sectors typically have the lowest:
- 96 per cent of UK financial services businesses have a website, versus 80 per cent of UK construction businesses and 74 per cent of UK primary businesses;
- In the 10 other nations surveyed, an average of 88 per cent of financial services businesses have a website, versus 60 per cent and 68 per cent for construction and primary businesses respectively.

Many of the variations between sectors in their ICT profile can be attributed to the inherent differences in general business processes. For example, manufacturing businesses are more likely to benefit from systems that are integrated with suppliers than most services in businesses.

Levels of e-commerce also vary significantly by sector.
- The average proportion of total purchases online (by businesses that order online) is highest among retail businesses (36 per cent in the UK and 38 per cent on average in the 10 other nations) and lowest amongst construction businesses (17 per cent for UK businesses and 21 per cent for the 10 other nations);

Overview

- Similarly, the average proportion of sales made online (by businesses which enable customers to order online) varies in the UK between 28 per cent (transport and communication) and 10 per cent (primary) of businesses;
- In other nations, the proportion varies from 30 per cent in financial services businesses to 13 per cent in government.

Sector variations in the levels of e-commerce reflect differences in product characteristics and the composition of the supply chain. Orders placed by retail businesses are typically well-suited to online procurement: high volume, many standard products and a high percentage of repeat orders from a core supplier base.

Annexure 2

E-marketing Options—Pros and Cons*

Security

It is a common myth that the web and e-mail are insecure. In fact, with the use of encryption technology, virus scanning software and a 'firewall', electronic communication can be much more secure than offline communications. For example, you are more likely to have money stolen from your credit card when using it in a restaurant than you are on the Internet.

Half the battle with online security is creating confidence. By having a professional-looking website, explaining your security precautions and involving suppliers in your plans for any technology changes, your trading partners will respond more positively.

Regulation

Companies using electronic communications are subject to certain legislation. It is important that you familiarise yourself with the following legislations.
- The Data Protection Act—governing how you use and store personal information—www.dataprotection.gov.uk
- The EU's Distance Selling Directive—which applies to sales over the internet—www.europa.eu.int/comm/consumers/cons_int/safe_shop/dist_sell/index_en.htm
- Intellectual property legislation which covers issues about using, infringing and guarding copyright trademarks and domain names.

Training

The future of a company depends on retaining and developing the right skills. It's also important to make sure that your staff have the skills they need to use any new technology you're implementing. This may mean investing in training.

Software can also help by providing a fast, flexible and cost-effective delivery method for training. The result is that employees can learn on-site at their convenience, so saving time, course and travel costs. The quality and range of training available is continually expanding and electronic delivery makes it easier to conduct regular assessments of employees' skills and identify any gaps.

---

* This section looks at (a) some important topics surrounding the use of information and communications technology. (b) glossary.

Knowledge Management

Technology doesn't just help staff work better and more efficiently; it can only change the way a company operates. The ability to share information using intranets and collaborative working has the potential to break down 'silo' mentalities based on departmental and group allegiances. This can unlock people's knowledge and ideas and make them available to the whole company, leading to better ways of working and new products and services. As it generates revenue and cost savings, this can have a big impact on staff morale by fostering an open culture in which people feel valued and listened to.

Getting It Right Marketing Regulations

E-Mail and SMS Marketing: the New Rules

In December 2003 new rules came into force covering marketing e-mails and SMS messages to individuals.

The Privacy and Electronic Communications Regulations introduced an opt-in consent procedure for commercial e-mails which means you can only target people who have agreed to be contacted. This is a change from the previous rules, which only required that customers be given the opportunity to opt out of being marketed to.

To save having to contact all your existing customers to get consent, the rules apply only to new customers. You can continue marketing your current customers provided they can opt out of future messages and the messages cover similar products and services.

The other main point is that you must clearly mark your e-mails with your contact details and include a valid return e-mail address.

Using Cookies

Cookies are small pieces of software which websites store on users computers. They have a very wide variety of uses, but an important one is to track the movements of visitors to websites, counting clicks, establishing how people arrived at the site and how they navigate around it. In short, cookies can be a very useful marketing tool.

Under the new Privacy and Electronic Communications Regulations, businesses have to inform their customers that they use cookies, and provide an opt-out facility for those who do not wish to accept them. In practice this will mean providing the user with a privacy or cookies statement which explains how they are being used and how they can be switched off.

Do Not Overdo It

Done right, e-mail and other forms of e-marketing can be extremely effective. Done wrong, however, and they can be extremely intrusive and annoying almost more so than any form of marketing.

It's essential that you contact customers in a measured, planned and targeted way with offers that they will appreciate. Nothing will turn your customers against you like relentless unsolicited e-mail (known as spam) or SMS messages.

By sending unsolicited commercial communications you may also be breaching the new privacy rules set out in this brochure. It is very important that you take these fully into account when planning campaigns and ensure that you comply with them. Failure to do so could result in fines and a lot of negative publicity.

Appropriateness

Make sure the technology you choose is right not only for the message but for your customers. The set-up and performance of people and computers vary tremendously. Some office computers do not have soundcards, which means music or video files would not be any use. Firewalls, which protect networks, are also common these days. Often they will limit the size or type of file that customers can receive. One solution to these problems is to host large files on your website and simply send an e-mail with a link.

Another important consideration is the connection speed. Do most of your customers access e-mail at work with a fast connection or do they use a modem at home? If it's the latter, then large attachments or images will make the e-mail frustratingly slow to download.

Finally, there is an issue of compatibility. Different programmes will display e-mail differently. An e-mail with images or an HTML component could look messy on a different set-up, or even cause the programme to crash.

The solution is to profile your customers and understand what the best format for them is. Some may like e-marketing with whistles and bells, others might just like a plain text e-mail.

Glossary

ADSL
Asymmetric Digital Subscriber Line—a technology that enables digital material to be sent down existing copper telephone lines and allocates the bulk of the total bandwidth used to downstream transmission from the central server to the consumer.

Bandwidth
Bandwidth (the width of a band of electromagnetic frequencies is used to mean (*a*) how fast data flows on a given transmission path, and (*b*) somewhat more technically, the width of the range of frequencies that an electronic signal occupies on a given transmission medium. Any digital or analogue signal has a bandwidth. It measures the maximum amount of data which can be carried at a given time by an Internet connection. A low bandwidth connection means the Internet connection will be slower. In digital systems, bandwidth is expressed as data speed in bits per second (bps).

Broadband
High-bandwidth Internet access. In general, broadband refers to telecommunication in which a wide band of frequencies is available to transmit information. Because a wide band of frequencies is available information can be multiplexed and sent on many different frequencies or channels within the band concurrently, allowing more information to be transmitted in a given amount of time.

Cable modem
A cable modem is a device that enables you to connect your PC to a local cable TV line and receive data at about 1.5 Mbps. This data rate far exceeds that of the prevalent 28.8 and 56 Kbps telephone modems and the up to 128 Kbps of Integrated Services Digital Network (ISDN) and is about the data rate available to subscribers of Digital Subscriber Line (DSL) telephone service. A cable modem can be added to, or integrated with, a set-top box that provides you TV set with channels for Internet access.

Cookie
Information stored about a visitor to a website in the form of a text file on the visitor's machine.

Database
A means of storing data in an organised manner.

Desktop video
Allows users to communicate with voice and **conferencing** video over the Internet using their desktop computers, which must be equipped with video camera and microphone functionality, as well as the requisite software.

DSL
DSL (Digital Subscriber Line) is a technology for bringing high-bandwidth information to homes and small businesses over ordinary copper telephone lines. XDSL refers to different variations of DSL, such as ADSL, HDSL, and RADSL.

Online virtual markets that enable buyers and **exchanges** sellers to share information and order/pay online. For example, builders, contractors, distributors, wholesalers and manufacturers in the homebuilding industry buy materials and labour online using an e-marketplace.	*E-marketplaces*
Electronic Data Interchange (EDI) is a standard format for exchanging business data. An EDI message contains a string of data **(EDI)** elements, each of which represents a single fact, such as a price, product model number, and so forth, separated by delimiter. The entire string is called a data segment. One or more data segments framed by a header and trailer form a transaction set, which is the EDI unit of transmission (equivalent to a message). A transaction set often consists of what would usually be contained in a typical business document or form. The parties who exchange EDI transmissions are referred to as trading partners.	*Electronic Data Interchange*
Electronic mails (e-mail) is exchange of computer-stored message by tele-communication. E-mail messages are usually encoded in ASCII text. However, you can also send non-text files, such as graphic images and sound files, as attachments sent in binary streams.	*Electronic mails (e-mail)*
An extranet is a private network that uses the Internet protocol and the public telecommunication system to share part of a business's information or operations securely with suppliers, vendors, partners, an organisation's intranet that is extended to users outside the business.	*Extranet*
This is a telephone facility that manages incoming calls and handles them based on the number called and associated handling instructions. Many businesses offering sales and service support use an automated telephone system to validate callers, make outgoing responses or callers, forward calls to the right party, allow callers to record messages, gather usage statistics, balance the use of phone lines, and provide other services.	*Interactive (automated) telephone system*
An intranet is a private network that is contained within an enterprise. It may consist of many interlinked Local Area Networks and also use leased lines in a Wide Area Network. Typically, an intranet includes connections through one or more gateway computers to the outside Internet. The main purpose of an intranet is to share organisation information and computing resources among employees. An intranet can also be used to facilitate working in groups and for teleconferences. An intranet uses Internet protocol.	*Intranet*
ISDN (Integrated Service Digital Network) is digital transmission over ordinary telephone copper wire as well as over other media. ISDN is a tele-communications service that turns a copper phone line into a high speed digital link that can quickly transmit voice, data and video	*ISDN*

images simultaneously. ISDN requires adapters at both ends of the transmission so the access provided also needs an ISDN adapter. ISDN is generally available from the phone organisations in most urban areas in the USA and Europe.

Kbps Kilobites per second. Refers to speed of data transmission.

Leased line A leased line is a telephone line typically supplied by the telephone organisation or transmission authority, that has been leased for private use as a dedicated circuit that permanently connects two or more user locations and is for the sole use of the subscriber. In some contexts, it is called a dedicated line. A leased line is usually contrasted with a switched line or dial-up line. Typically, large businesses rent leased lines to interconnect different geographic locations in their business. The alternative is to buy and maintain their own private lines or, increasingly, to use public switched lines with secure message protocols.

Local Area Network (LAN) A local area network (LAN) is a group of computers and associated devices that share a common communications line and typically share the resources of a single processor or server within a small geographic area (for example, within an office building). Usually, the server has applications and data storage that are shared in common by multiple computer users. A local area network may serve as few as two or three users (for example, in a home network) or as many as thousands of users (for example, in an FDDI [Fibre Distributed Data Interface] network).

Mbps Megabites per second. Refers to speed of data transmission.

Minitel First launched in 1982, the Minitel terminal consists of a small monitor with a keyboard connected to a phone jack. France Telecom distributed this computer-like device free with its normal telephone service. First used as an online yellow pages, Minitel grew at the expense of new alternatives such as the Internet, and at the start of 1999 the number of French Net users was half that of Britain's. In 2000, France had an estimated 18 million Minitel users, compared with fewer than 10 million on the Internet. Now, as the costs associated with Internet access are decreasing and Minitel applications remain limited, the Internet is becoming a much more attractive alternative.

Modem Modulator/Demodulator. The device that takes signals from a computer and translates them into a suitable form for the telephone system. The reverse procedure takes place at a modem on the host computer. It modulates outgoing digital signals from a computer or other digital device to analogue signals for a conventional copper twisted pair telephone line and demodulates the incoming analogue signal and converts it to a digital signal for the digital device.

Online	Online is the condition of being connected to a network of computers or other devices. The term is frequently used to describe someone who is currently connected to the Internet.
ONS	UK Office for National Statistics.
PKI	Public Key Infrastructure. A standardised system of encryption, enabling secure transitions by businesses, governments and individuals at low cost.
PSTN	PSTN (Public switched telephone network) is the world's collection of interconnected voice-oriented public telephone networks, both commercial and government-owned (also referred to as the Plain Old Telephone Service [POTS]). It is the aggregation of circuit-switching telephone networks that has evolved from the days of Alexander Graham Bell. Today, it is almost entirely digital in technology except for the final link from the central (local) telephone office to the user. In Internet's long-distance infrastructure.
Remote access	The ability to gain access to a computer or network from a remote location, usually over the Internet.
Remote (mobile) terminals	Remote terminals or computers use remote access to get access to a computer or a network from a remote distance. In corporations, people at branch offices, telecommuters, and people who are travelling may need access to the corporation's network. Dial-up connection through desktop, notebook, or handheld computer modem over regular telephone lines is a common method of remote access. Integrated Services Digital Network (ISDN) is a common method of remote access from branch offices since it combines dial-up with faster data rates. Wireless, cable mode, and Digital Subscriber Line (DSL) technologies offer other possibilities for remote access.
SatelliteInternet	A satellite Internet connection is an arrangement in which the upstream (outgoing) and the downstream (incoming) data are sent from, and arrive at, a computer through a satellite. Each subscriber's hardware includes a satellite dish antenna and a transceiver (transmitter/receiver) that operates in the microwave portion of the radio spectrum. Uplink speeds are nominally 50 to 150 Kbps for a subscriber using a single computer. The downlink occurs at speeds ranging from about 150 Kbps to more that 1200 Kbps, depending on factors such as Internet traffic, the capacity of the server, and the sizes of downloaded files. Satellite Internet systems are an excellent, although rather pricey, option for people in rural areas where Digital Subscriber Line (DSL) and cable modem connections are not available. The two-way satellite Internet option offers an always-on connection that bypasses the dial-up process. In this respect, the satellite system resembles a cable modem Internet connection. However, this asset can also be a liability,

	unless a firewall is used to protect the computer against hacking. Satellite systems are also prone to rain fade (degradation during heavy precipitation) and occasional brief periods of solar interference when the sun lines up with the satellite for a few minutes each day.
Spyware	Stand-alone programs that can secretly monitor system activity. These may detect passwords or other confidential information and transmit them to another computer.
Trojan Horse	A program that neither replicates nor copies itself, but causes damage or compromises the security of the computer. Often spread by e-mail.
Video conferencing	A video conference is a live connection between people in separate locations for the purpose of communication, usually involving audio and often text as well as video. At its simplest, video conferencing provides transmission of static images and text between two locations. At its most sophisticated, it provides transmission of full-motion video images and high quality audio between multiple locations.
Virus	A program or code that infects another program, boot sector, partition sector, or document that supports macros, by inserting itself or attaching itself to that medium. Most viruses simply replicate themselves, though some also inflict large amount of damage onto infected computers.
Voice over IP	Facility to allow enable voice communication over a data network, by transmitting discrete digitised packets rather than the traditional circuit-committed protocols of the public switched telephone network (PSTN). VoIP calls can be made through an IP enabed switchboard, or through a desktop connected the Internet.
Web, The Worldwide	The (worldwide) Web is a system of pages composed of graphics, sound, ext and user input linked together via the Internet. It is part of, but by no means the only part, of the Internet.
Website	A website is a related collection of worldwide web (www) files that includes an opening file called a home page. A business or an individual can tell you how to get to their website by giving you the address of their home page. From the home page, you can get to all the other pages on their site.
Wide Area Network (WAN)	A Wide Area Network (WAN) is a geographically dispersed telecommunications network. The term distinguishes a broader telecommunication structure from a Local Area Network. A Wide Area Network may be privately owned or rented, but the term usually connotes the inclusion of public (shared user) networks.

Wireless Internet Service Provided (WISP)

A Wireless Internet Service Provided (WISP) is an Internet Service Provided (ISP) that allows subscribers to connect to a server using medium-range wireless links. This type of ISP offers broadband service and allows subscriber computers, called stations, to access the Internet and the Web from anywhere within the zone of coverage provided by the server antenna. This is usually a region with a radius of several kilometers. Assets of WISP technology included flexibility (it is easy to add stations or move them) and broad bandwidth. In remote areas where neither cable nor DSL is available or practical, a WISP can provide good Internet service at reasonable cost, acting as an alternative to satellite Internet connections.

Worm

A program that replicates itself, for example, from one disk drive to another, or by copying itself using e-mail or another transport mechanism. The worm may do damage and compromise the security of the computer. It may arrive in the form of a joke program or a software programme.

INDEX

Achieving best practice in business, 62
  business mix, 62
    design and product development, 62
    file sharing, 63
    meetings with travel, 63
    sharing information, 63
  e-marketing, 67
    after-sales service, 74
    benefits, 68: better conversion rate; global reach; level playing field; lower cost; more interesting campaigns; one-to-one marketing; personalization; shorter lead times; trackable and measurable results; twenty-four-hours marketing
    customer in charge, 74
    customer relationship management, 74
    customer service, 73
    customers spend $ 1 billon a month online, 68
    effective websites, 70
    global shop window, 72
    information your staff need, 74
    make it easier to pay, 72: Farmite animal health
    making sales, 72
    new marketing channels, 70-71: Antec international
    sales, 72
    smoothening path, 72
    targeting prospects, 70
    what is e-marketing
  international business, 74
  reducing costs, 74
  rapid customer contact, 75
  talking to your customers, 75
  complying with law, 75: M/s Europa Bio Products
  benefits of exporting, 76: DGC Distribution Ltd; Frumba Ltd
  introduction to e-business, 62
  operations, 64: chance and hunt
    flexible working, 66
    internal communication, 65
    purchasing alternatives, 66
    purchasing, 66
    relational databases, 65
    sourcing supplies, 66
    storage and retrieval, 65
    streamlining transactions, 66: Clarkes stationers
    workflow, 65
  understanding your customers, 78: The Everyman Theatre
    benefits of good customer service, 81: increased sales; improved efficiency
    hypothesis, 83
    international benchmarking study, 82
    process, 81-82
    think about your business and ask yourself how good is customer service?, 80

Arun Shourie, 57
ASAN, 59
Ashuthosh Pandey, 175
ATM, 59
Azim Premji, 167, 173

Bangalore, 173
Best practices in business 1-2
  Conclusion, 10
    corporate responsibility, 12
    customer service, 12
    hypothesis first, 13; planning in competitive environments; planning in turbulent environment
    innovation, 12
    leadership, 11
    people development, 11
    performance measurement, 12
    prerequisites of successful business, 10
    process improvement, 13
    supply chain management, 11-12
    vision and change, 10-11
  Foreign Direct Investment, 1
  Improving quality, 8
    Boa UK, 9; Brain Alexander
  Innovation and growth, 5
    Fracino, 5-6; Frank Maxwell; Angela Maxwell
  Involving and developing staff, 5
    communication, 4-5
    development, 5
    motivation, 5
    organisational changes, 5
  Learning from customers, 7
    Gecko Headgear, 7-8; Jeff Sacree
    successful business know their customers, 7
  Social responsibility, 3
    BT, 3-4

Index

Vision and leadership, 2
    The Aroma Company, 2; Simon Harrop

Bharat Forge, 49
Bharouka, Stel, 175

Chennai, 138
Canada, 253
China, 1, 46, 253, 254
Cisco, 51
Closing marketing gap, 83
    definition of benchmarking in net, 83
        benchmarking steps, 84-87
    strategic planning, 87-88
        building a brand, 91-93
        developing new products and services, 88-89
        hypothesis, 93
        lower costs and higher sales, 89-90
        market analysis, 90-91

Dan Fineman, 1
Diana Farell, 48

E-commerce, 19-20, 120
    AMAZON.com, 20
    business modals, 26
        B2B— E-commerce modal: aggregators; auction and dynamic pricing markets content; e-distributors; trading hubs
        B2C modal, 26-27
        C2C modal, 28
        P2P modal
    definitions of E-commerce (EC), 21
    electronic commerce versus electronic business, 21
    dimensions of EC, 22
        partial EC, 22
        pure EC, 22
        pure versus partial EC, 22
    traditional commerce, 22
E-Bay.com, 20
EC issues, 29
    commercial issues, 29-30: consumer protection; ensuring market diversity and competition
    security issues, 32: how secure is secure?; institutional aspects of security
EDI (Electronic Data Interchange), 20, 64
EFT (Electronic Fund Transfer), 20
framework of EC
    advantages of EC
    classification of EC applications, 23; electronic market; inter-organisational information systems and e-markets; providing customer service
    disadvantages of EC, 25
    interdisciplinary nature of EC, 24
    status of E-commerce, 25-26
functions of EC, 22
    communication, 22
    process management function, 23
    service management function, 23
    transaction capabilities, 23
future of EC, 45
infrastructure issues, 36
    network access, 37
    network capacity, 36-37
    network development, 37-38
    standards, 38
social and cultural issues, 38-39
    business challenges of CRM, 42
    CRM (customer relationship management), 40-42
    E-CRM architecture, 44
    E-CRM scenario— Indian Perspective, 44-45
    E-CRM, 39-40
    from CRM to E-CRM, 42-43
    need for E-CRM, 43-44
E-mail, 62, 66, 67, 69, 70, 74
Enterprise resource planning, 135
    infrastructure requirements, 160
        manpower, 162
        network, 161-62
        server, 160-61
        softwares, 161
        training, 162-63
        workstations/printers, 162
    introduction, 136
        customers, 138
        introduction to organisation, 137
        mission of metals ltd, 137
        objectives of study, 136-37
        products, 137
        quality, 138
        research methodology used in study, 138
        scope of study, 137
    observations, 139
        industry measurements, 143-44
        performance of metals ltd, 139-143
        projected performance of metals ltd, 145
        swot analysis for metals ltd, 145
        why computerization for metal ltd?, 146
    solution for metals ltd, 156
        e-business components, 158-59
        information security, 159
        intranet components, 158
        Non-ERP components, 157-58
        user interface, 159
    Strategy for metal ltd, 148
        department/section wise observations, 149-54
        IT options for metals ltd, 154-56
        key design issues, 148-49
        objectives of IT strategy, 154
Eastern Europe, 253

France, 137
Fric Daniels, 79

GE, 51
General Motors, 52, 257-58
George Grainger, 63
Germany, 137
Google, 51
Gucharan Das, 48
Gujarat, 54
Government to Citizen Relationships Gyandoot—Tales and Travails, 119
   abstract, 119
   achievements, 121
   complex problems—simple solutions, 129
   conclusion, 130-31
   introduction, 119
      district profile, 119
      present scenario, 120
   Jan Mitra, 123
   progress, 130
   proposed services, 129-30
   road blocks and speed breakers, 130
      human factors, 130
      technological hurdles, 130
   services, 124
      arms licence, 126
      court cases, 125
      fertilizer licence, 127
      GPF sanction, 127
   strengthening of gyandoot, 129
   user charges, 129
   working of Jan Mitra, 123-24
Gyandoot, 119-23, 129

Hero Honda, 49
Hindustan Lever's, 58
Hong Kong, 48
HSBC's, 48
Hyderabad, 137, 138

IBM, 51, 228
ICICI, 54, 59, 97, 110-118
India, 1, 47, 48, 51, 52, 55, 119, 173, 174, 228, 252, 253, 256
Intel, 51
Internet, 53, 66
Ireland, 253
IT (Information technology), 19, 52, 135-63, 167, 172, 179, 224, 253, 257
ITC, 53, 54

Japan, 1
Jim Murphy, 90
John Hagel, 47
John Seely Brown, 47

Kaplan and Norton, 97, 98, 102, 107, 226
Kolkata, 138

Madhya Pradesh, 119
Maharashtra, 54
Mahatma Gandhi, 129
Metals Ltd, 137
Mexico, 253
Moser Baer, 49
Motorola, 51
Mumbai, 138

New Delhi, 138

Operational issues in outsourcing, 210
   activity based costing (ABC) approach for vendor selection and evaluation, 237
      case study, 240-43
   advanced and emerging areas of outsourcing, 255
      global standards, 257-58
   benefits of effective vendor development, 222
      managing vendor relationships, 222-224

   conclusion, 258
   decision support system (DSS) approach for vendor selection and evaluation, 228-29
      application of DSS, 236-37
      database and model base, 231
      model notations, 229
   determining outsourcing contractual relationship, 225
      supplier performance measurement, 225-227
   hybrid approach for vendor selection and evaluation problem, 243
      application of (I_ILPI) model to (SLP_VSP), 247
      application of utility theory to (MIP_VSP), 247
      assumptions, 243
      case illustration of hybrid approach for vendor selection and evaluation, 248-52
      India outsourcing and small players, 254
      IT outsourcing and India, 252-55
      modeling with utility theory, 244-46
   introduction, 210
      vender selection criteria, 213
      vendor selection process, 212
      vendor selection, 210-212
   pitfalls in vendor relationships, 215-17
   quantitative approaches to vendor selection and evaluation, 227
   service level agreements (Slas), 218
      components of effective contractual agreements, 218
   vendor development, 219
      UK Government supplier development guidelines, 219-221
      vendor development programmes, 221

Index

Outsourcing, 167
   advantages of, 180-81
   challenges faced by OEMs, 174-75
      conflict of interests, 176
      outsourcing partners ignorance of supply chain dynamics, 175
      potential danger in outsourcing manufacturing and fulfillment work, 176
      risk of choosing wrong partner, 175
      shortcomings of outsourcing partner, 176
      ultimate onus of responsibility, 175-76
   definition, 169-73
   disadvantages of, 181
   framework, 198-205
   introduction, 167-68
   major challenges faced by organisations, 173
      execution, 174
      growth, 174
      market, 174
      people, 173-74
      visibility, 174
   major reasons for, 176
   practical tips for successful, 182
      compare apple to apple, 183
      don't forget Acts, 184
      don't rush it, 185
      hire a professional, 183
      hold them accountable, 173-74
      keep uncle sam happy, 185-86
      leave yourself out, 185
      pay attention to agreements, 183
      remember your employees, 184
      watch out hidden cost, 184
   risk in, 195-96
   seven sins of, 186-87
      failing to plan an exit strategy, 193-94
      losing control over outsourced activity, 190-91
      outsourcing activities that should not be outsourced, 187
      overlooking hidden costs of outsourcing, 191-93
      overlooking personnel issues, 189-90
      selecting wrong vender, 187-88
      writing poor contract, 188-89

Philippines, 253
Philips, 51
Playing leapfrog: using strengths in ICT to energise manufacturing sector in India, 46
   The Indian Market, 47
      ease in technology usage, 48-49
      conclusion, 59-60
      habit of innovation, 49-50
      ICT in enabling research and development, 50-52: ICT in enabling sourcing and procurement; ICT in enabling manufacturing; ICT in enabling logistics and distribution; ICT in sales and customer management
   ICT in manufacturing value chain, 50
   manufacturing excellence: contribution of ICT sector, 48
   thinking on global scale, 49

Ranbaxy, 47, 48, 49
Ratan Tata, 48
Reserve Bank of India, 111, 112
Robert Waternan, 97

Sona Koyo's foroy, 52
Strategic tool for enhancing performance, 97
   Balanced Scorecard (BSC), 97-98
      shared values, 98-100: principles
      staff, 98
      strategy, 98
      structure, 98
      style/culture, 98
      systems, 98
   balanced scorecard is double-loop feedback, 102-04
      outcome metrics, 104
   case study on ICICI Bank's Universal Banking Strategy, 107-08
      application of BSC in bank, 109-110
      brief history of ICICI and its strategy of 'Universal Bank', 110-112
      facets of BSC approach and ICICI's performance evaluation, 112
      strategy map and BSC framework, 108
   conclusion, 117-118
   creating balanced scorecard for strategic control, 104
      benefits of using BSC in business affairs, 105-07
   introduction, 97
Sundaram Clayton, 49

Tom Peters, 97

US (USA), 1, 48, 49, 50, 76, 107, 142, 171, 255, 256
UK (United Kingdom), 10, 57, 68, 70, 76, 77, 78, 79, 82, 86, 89, 90, 171, 173, 211, 221, 228, 256

Vivek Paul, 254

Wipro Technologies, 173
WTO, 48

About the Contributors

Sandhir Sharma and Gautam Bansal belong to the Faculty, Department of Business Management, Punjab College of Technical Education, Ludhiana.

Komolica Peres is attached with IIM, Indore.

V.K. Gupta is professor at IIM, Indore.

Sanjay Dubey is an IAS officer. He is presently working as District Magistrate and Collector, Jabalpur, Madhya Pradesh and was also the Chairman of Gyandoot Society.

Anand Kr Tiwari is deputy manager at MIDHANI a central government defence public sector at Midhani, Hyderabad.

S. Venkataramanaiah is assistant professor in OM and QT area at IIM, Indore.